Baseball THE
LIVES BEHIND
THE SEAMS

"Baseball" THE LIVES BEHIND THE SEAMS

Maury Allen

MACMILLAN PUBLISHING COMPANY
New York
COLLIER MACMILLAN PUBLISHERS
London

Copyright © 1990 by Maury Allen

Macmillan Publishing Company
866 Third Avenue, New York, NY 10022
Collier Macmillan Canada, Inc.

Library of Congress Cataloging-in-Publication Data
Allen, Maury, 1932–
    Baseball : the lives behind the seams / Maury Allen.
      p. cm.
   ISBN 0-02-501341-6
   1. Baseball—United States—Biography.   I. Title.
GV865.A1A58   1990
796.357'092'2—dc20   89-13111   CIP
[B]

Macmillan books are available at special discounts for bulk
purchases for sales promotions, premiums, fund-raising, or
educational use. For details, contact:

            Special Sales Director
            Macmillan Publishing Company
            866 Third Avenue
            New York, NY 10022

10 9 8 7 6 5 4 3 2 1

Printed in the United States of America

For all those who have loved the game with me from the Ebbets Field kids in Brooklyn at Bedford Avenue and Sullivan Place to the Stadium at 161st, to the Polo Grounds at 155th, to Shea at Roosevelt Avenue, to Dodger Stadium and all the parks in between. You are truly the Good Soldiers of Baseball.

Contents

Acknowledgments

▪▪▪ In more than a quarter of a century of professional baseball watching, it is the heroes and the villains who occupied my professional time. I wrote much about Bucky Dent and Chris Chambliss winning titles for the Yankees and forgot the clubhouse men and traveling secretaries who got them there on time. I spent countless sweat-filled hours saying in as many ways as possible that Mookie Wilson's grounder went through Bill Buckner's glove. I never once mentioned the trainers who tied Buckner's aching parts together with rolls of tape.

No team ever wins a pennant without each and every member of that team contributing to the overall success. The extra swings off a tired pitcher, the extra ground balls hit by a teammate, the small pieces of information slipped to a friend to better play the game.

Those heroes have received their due. Even the villains have been called to account.

It is now time to single out and applaud the foot soldiers of the game, the baseball grunts who march along year by year, enjoying the fringes of the excitement, performing faithfully, listening at the edges, conducting themselves nobly only because they love the game. The rewards are not huge for them. They live with the knowledge of their own private contributions to a championship.

To all those who contributed their time and thoughts, I salute you. For all those who also went along willingly but were left on the cutting room floor, I apologize to you. My thanks go equally to all of you.

I appreciate the efforts of all the concerned teams and their loyal, efficient, dedicated public relations staffs.

This work has its own Good Soldiers from my talented and patient editor, Rick Wolff, to my supportive and trusting agent, Julian Bach. Each hand that touched this work from its inception to its conclusion is entitled to a share of the glory.

Lastly, much applause to my own Good Soldiers, Janet, Jennifer and Ted, for love and support in this effort as in every other.

Baseball THE LIVES BEHIND THE SEAMS

Introduction

None of them are Hall of Famers. Few of them make any serious money. Many of them spend their summers in small hotel rooms, dingy coffee shops and drafty baseball clubhouses.

Oh God, how they love it all.

These are the Good Soldiers of Baseball, men who scout ball players, train them, coach them, nurture them to stardom. They get little glory and their names are often forgotten as the stars of the game become icons on bubble gum cards.

All had these same dreams in their own youth. Injury, illness, circumstance, or most often, lack of big league ability would shunt them aside as others passed them on the way to large stadiums, roaring crowds and huge salaries.

A few tasted the joy of baseball success, the big league locker, the cheering crowds, the adoring fans, the media attention. Then their arms grew tired or their legs gave out or their intensity was lost.

They turned from performance to the fringes of the game, coaching, scouting, minor league managing, umpiring or publicizing.

Hardly ever do they complain now thirty, forty or fifty years after they first took up the game with such huge ambitions. There are no regrets. There is no jealousy. They are pleased with their work and content with their contributions.

They dream of glory as young men. They accept reality as older men. They look back only with pleasure. They look ahead often with satisfaction.

They are in The Game.

It is all that really counts.

Occasionally, they slip into an alternate life, often pressured by family and financial reality.

Most often, they come back and remain until no one will any longer allow them around a locker room or in the hard seats of a dusty, chilled minor league park.

"I was making nine thousand dollars a year as a minor league pitching coach," recalls Montreal's Larry Bearnarth. "I was living in a house I couldn't afford with bills I couldn't handle. I had four kids. I had been offered a job on Wall Street for three times the salary I was making in baseball. I took the job and set out for work one day. It was early and cold. I soon turned the car around and went home."

He took back his resignation from the Expos. He was typical. He couldn't escape the game. He knew he really didn't ever want to leave it.

"Baseball," he says. "That's what I do."

This is what they all do, joyfully, willingly, excitedly, proudly. They are the Good Soldiers of Baseball.

BILL RIGNEY: THE GAME OF HIS LIFE

▰▰ IT MAY HAVE BEEN THE MOST FAMOUS BASEBALL GAME ever played. The New York Giants beat the Brooklyn Dodgers in the third game of the 1951 pennant playoff 5–4 with Bobby Thomson's home run into the lower left field stands off Ralph Branca. Radio broadcaster Russ Hodges bellowed, "The Giants win the pennant, the Giants win the pennant, the Giants win the pennant."

It was Thomson as hero, hitting what became known as the Shot Heard Round the World, and Branca as villain who were most individually identified in that game. But others served. Bill Rigney was one of them.

The chipper, gregarious infielder of the Giants was in the clubhouse deep behind center field when Thomson launched his home run. After more than fifty years in baseball and just past his seventy-first birthday, Rigney, now the assistant to Oakland A's vice-president Sandy Alderson, remembers that blow as his biggest thrill.

"Oh, that had to be the most exciting thing for any guy who had anything to do with that game," he says. "Nobody could ever forget that. Talk about your once in a lifetime experiences."

Don Newcombe was pitching for the Dodgers with a 4–1 lead into the eighth inning. Manager Leo Durocher of the

Giants sent Rigney up to home plate to hit for catcher Wes Westrum. The Giants catcher was nursing a sore hand and just couldn't handle Newcombe's overpowering speed.

"I remember grabbing a bat and hearing Eddie Stanky yell at me that Newk was losing it. 'Just get a good ball, Rig, get a good ball.' I went up there and Newcombe was throwing aspirin tablets. I couldn't see the ball. He struck me out without even a loud foul. I walked back to the bench and muttered, 'He's losing it, all right.' That Stanky would say every pitcher was always losing it."

When the New York half of the eighth inning ended with the Dodgers still ahead 4–1, it didn't look good for Durocher's team. Rigney picked up his glove at the end of the inning and jogged to the clubhouse in center field.

"I stood at the window and watched the Dodgers go out in the top of the ninth. I knew we had come back a lot of times in the bottom of the ninth that year so I still had hope," he says. "We also had our big hitters coming up."

Alvin Dark singled past the outstretched glove of Dodger first baseman Gil Hodges. Don Mueller, the guy the Giants used to call Mandrake the Magician for his ability to hit balls just past the infielders, did just that. With Hodges holding first base to keep Dark close on manager Charlie Dressen's strange orders in a 4–1 game, Mueller hit a bouncing ball between first and second. Hodges lunged but could not catch the ball as Dark raced all the way to third base.

"That's when I started getting excited. I thought we would win it," Rigney says.

Newcombe was laboring now. Monte Irvin, one of the finest clutch hitters in the league and the big RBI man for the Giants, faced Newcombe. The big righthander got him to pop up.

"I only did that so Bobby could become the hero," Irvin kidded years later.

Whitey Lockman then hit a double to left-center field scoring Dark and sending Mueller toward third. When Mueller hit the bag, his spikes caught and he twisted his ankle. He lay on third writhing in pain.

"I was out of the game but I knew this was a serious injury. I ran all the way from the clubhouse to third base as the trainer ran in with a stretcher," says Rigney. "I helped the trainer carry Don to the clubhouse."

Mueller suffered a fractured ankle. Clint Hartung ran for him and Lockman was on second as Thomson walked to the plate.

While all this was going on at third, the Dodgers were making a pitching change. Ralph Branca and Carl Erskine were warming up in the bullpen. Dressen called down to the bullpen where Dodger coach Clyde Sukeforth answered.

"Ralph's throwing hard and Erskine just bounced his curve," Sukeforth told Dressen.

Dressen made the fateful decision. Branca, who had been beaten by a Thomson homer in the first playoff game before Clem Labine pitched a 10–0 shutout for the Dodgers in the second game, was in the game.

He threw a strike to Thomson on the inside part of the plate. The next pitch was a fastball on the outside part of the plate. Branca didn't get it far enough outside. Thomson smashed into baseball history with a line drive home run for three runs and a 5–4 win.

"I just ran back on the field to get to the guys," says Rigney.

The sweet victory for the Giants and bitter defeat for the Brooklyn Dodgers became as memorable a game as was ever played. Almost any resident of New York City over the age of forty can tell you where he was that Monday afternoon in October.

Rigney was little more than a journeyman player in his eight big league seasons. He batted .259 lifetime with four seasons as a regular and four more as a utility player in the Giants organization. All in all, his entire playing career was more than he could have expected when he joined the Giants as a skinny, glasses-wearing, high-strung youngster from Alameda, California, with limited ability but unlimited passion for the game.

"When I was a kid growing up in Alameda I played ball every chance I got. I loved to play but nobody thought I would be big enough to make it. Besides, my father and my grandfather had this very successful tile business and my brothers and I were expected to enter the business when we finished school," he says.

Rigney played semiprofessional baseball around the San Francisco area for a couple of years after high school while he waited for a baseball offer. The Yankees were interested in him after they saw his good athletic ability, his range and his strong throwing arm.

"I didn't think I would get a lot of opportunity with the Yankees. In those days they had so many clubs that you could easily get buried. I figured it would be easier to make the big leagues if I signed with an independent club in the Pacific Coast League and then performed well. They could sell my contract to a big league club," he says.

In 1938, shortly after he turned twenty years old, Rigney signed with the Oakland Oaks of the Pacific Coast League. They farmed him out that first year to Spokane, Washington, where he hit only .083 in his pro debut. Oakland understood the league was too fast for him at that stage and still thought his glove and arm could carry him to the big leagues.

"I think the important thing about me was how much I wanted it. I played with a lot of intensity. Sometimes that can make up for any shortcomings a player might have in natural physical ability," he says.

In his fourth professional year with the Oakland club in 1941, Rigney hit only .208 in 173 games. It didn't look like there was much of a baseball future in the cards for this kid.

"The next season of 1942 I really learned to hit. I cut down on my swing and I went with the pitch. I made contact and used my running speed. I looked for holes in the defense and tried to hit the ball that way. I became a confident hitter that season," he says.

Rigney hit .288 that year. The New York Giants became very interested in the angular shortstop.

"Before spring training started the next year I was in the Navy," Rigney says. "The war was heating up and I didn't want to be drafted into the Army. I enlisted in the naval preflight program in Oakland. They asked me to read the eye chart without my glasses. I couldn't see any of the letters, not even the big E."

Before the Navy actually rejected Rigney, a chief petty officer, a friend of Oakland owner Brick Laws, asked Rigney if he really wanted to get into the naval preflight program.

"I told him I certainly did. He took me back to the room where the eye test was given. He told the officer in charge that if I could see good enough to hit a curveball I should be able to see good enough to join the program. 'Give this guy another test.' I stood at the same line looking at the chart and then he told me to start walking forward until I could see the chart. I must have been almost against the wall before I started reading off all the letters. 'See, this guy's eyes are good enough for the program. He's passed the test.' The officer in charge just picked up my application, looked at the old chief and stamped my form 'accepted.' That's how I got into the Navy," Rigney says.

Rigney spent most of his time in the Navy playing baseball. His eyes really weren't good enough for those Navy airplanes.

Rigney was twenty-eight years old when he reported to spring training with the New York Giants in the spring of 1946. The war was over and every big league club had dozens of young prospects waiting for their opportunity. Rigney made the most of his.

"Ottie [Mel Ott] was the manager and he liked me as soon as he saw me. I could put the bat on the ball, I had pretty decent power and I could field well at three positions. We didn't have a very good ball club but he knew I could contribute in a lot of ways," Rigney says.

Before long, Rigney had won the third base job in an infield with Johnny Mize at first, Buddy Blattner at second and Buddy Kerr at shortstop. He hit .236 as a New York Giants rookie.

"I really enjoyed playing for the New York Giants. I had gotten married during the war and Paula and I settled in Westchester, just north of the city. I had met Paula at Berkeley where she worked as a civilian employee for the Navy. She was the secretary to one of the officers at the St. Mary's preflight school."

Paula and Bill Rigney had three children, a son, Bill, who was a minor league general manager for a while before entering the oil business in Texas; a second son, Tom, who is in the music business; and a daughter, Lynn, who is an accomplished poet, writer and conservationist living with her family in northern Washington State.

"The following season, 1947, was the year we hit all the home runs (221) to set a new record. Mize was my roommate and he hit fifty-one to tie with Ralph Kiner for the league lead. I had seventeen so I think that room had more home runs than any other room in baseball history," he says.

The Giants finished fourth that season despite the home run barrage. Owner Horace Stoneham began getting restless with the inability of the Giants to move up in the standings. He would soon fire Ott, one of his all-time personal favorites, and bring in Leo Durocher from the Dodgers. Durocher had lost favor in Brooklyn after being suspended for the 1947 season by Commissioner A. B. (Happy) Chandler because of his alleged associations with gamblers and other notorious figures. Rigney would never play regularly again but he also was a favorite of Leo's because he played hard when he did play, he was a fighter and he was a good bench jockey, a skill Durocher, the ultimate baseball bench jockey, valued highly.

It was about that time that Rigney's constant chatter and high-pitched voice earned him the nickname of Cricket. Many New York Giants teammates to this day address him as Cricket when they see him at a baseball event.

Eddie Stanky joined the Giants the next season from Boston along with Alvin Dark. They became the second base and shortstop combination that would help the Giants to the 1951 pennant. Sid Gordon was moved in from the outfield to play third base and he soon would be replaced by Bobby Thomson. Rigney relieved all regulars at all three infield positions and became an effective pinch hitter for Durocher.

"It was probably around 1952 or 1953 that I began thinking of managing," Rigney says. "I wanted very badly to stay in the game. I could see my playing career winding down and at the age of thirty-five or thirty-six I knew I was finished. I began picking Durocher's brains about some of his moves. Horace might have been thinking about me as a successor to Leo but it wasn't something I considered at the time."

Rigney's playing career ended after the 1953 season and he was soon appointed the manager of the Minneapolis Millers farm club. He also helped out as a utility infielder and batted .333 as a backup player on his first managerial team.

Rigney finished third in 1954 and won with the Minneapolis club in 1955. He was named the Sporting News Minor League Manager of the Year. That caused other clubs to examine Rigney as a potential skipper. The Giants didn't want to lose him. They also had become disillusioned with Durocher, whose demands became excessive after the World Series sweep over the Cleveland Indians in 1954.

Rigney was named the manager of his old team for the 1956 season. He rebuilt the franchise to respectability and came close to winning in 1960 with a second-place finish to Pittsburgh.

The Giants had moved west to San Francisco by that time and Rigney enjoyed being near his home. There were some other developments that season in baseball that would soon involve the San Francisco skipper. Baseball had decided to expand and the American League added two teams, the Los Angeles Angels and the Washington Senators, as the old Washington club moved to Minnesota. Play would begin in 1961 with ten teams in the league. The National League, adding a club in Houston and another club in New York, would not begin play with ten teams until the season of 1962 when the Houston Colt 45s and the New York Mets made their big league debuts.

Old cowboy movie star Gene Autry was the owner of the Angels. He hired Fred Haney as general manager. Haney had managed in the big leagues at Milwaukee and in the minor leagues in the Pacific Coast. He thought there was only one man who could handle his new Los Angeles team, deal with not-ready-for-prime-time young players and over-the-hill veterans, operate smoothly with the press and be a comfortable area of attention for the fans. That was Bill Rigney. After some delicate negotiations, Rigney was hired as the first manager of the Angels. He did a wondrous job, so good that when he finished third with the expansion Angels in 1962, he was named the Sporting News Major League Manager of the Year.

Characters on that Los Angeles team abounded, with the likes of Bo Belinsky, Dean Chance, Bob Rodgers, Jim Fregosi, Albie Pearson and Ryne Duren. This assortment of ball players was able to spend a good part of the summer in first place and actually hold off the lordly Yankees until late in September. The Angels finished third but Rigney stamped his credentials on the baseball establishment that year as an exceptional skipper.

"That was some bunch to handle," he says. "We had some wild guys. Belinsky and Chance were two of the zaniest I ever saw. That was the year Belinsky hit a sportswriter [Los Angeles *Examiner* writer Braven Dyer], and when I heard about it in the middle of the night I went to his room. He was taking a bath. When I confronted him he admitted he hit Dyer. He said he hit him with an open hand. What he neglected to say was that he had a roll of quarters in his hand when it closed," says Rigney.

The Angels never could do quite as well again in Rigney's time. Their farm system was slow in developing. Many of the 1962 heroes, including Chance and Belinsky, burned out early. A lot of the veteran players weren't much good after that final career year they could offer Rigney in 1962. Even a patient man like Autry grew discouraged with second-division finishes as the Angels finished ninth, fifth, seventh, sixth, fifth, eighth and finally third in an expanded 1969 American League.

On May 27, 1969, the romance between the Angels and Rigney ended. He was fired, hardly a surprising development after so many second-division seasons.

"That 1962 team remained my favorite there. It was a wonderful season. We never thought we could win. I had been in the game long enough by then to know the team would wear out in September. But it was a great run. I enjoyed every minute of that season," Rigney says.

Billy Martin had won a division title with the Minnesota Twins in 1969. As often happens with Martin, success went to his head. He became difficult to handle that year, refused to follow club policy over the winter, wouldn't attend organizational meetings if they didn't coincide with his own outside schedule. He was fired a few weeks after that successful season ended. Martin defended himself.

"Calvin Griffith [team owner] asked me to attend a meeting with him," Martin said at the time. "I drove up to the stadium offices fully expecting Calvin to be ready for a meeting with me. I wanted to go over some things. When I got there his secretary said he was waiting for me in his office and that I should go right in. When I walked in, Calvin was fast asleep on his office couch. I didn't think that was the proper way to have a meeting with the manager so I left. I told his secretary to tell him when he woke up that I was here but he was asleep. Now that he is awake I'm going hunting. The next day I was fired."

What Rigney has understood all the years he has been in baseball is the element of cooperation between the front office and the field personnel.

"You aren't going to go very far if the organization is pulling apart," he says. "You can air your feelings but it isn't a good idea to air too many negative feelings publicly, not if you want to keep working for the people who hired you."

Rigney was appointed the manager of the 1970 Minnesota Twins, the Western Division champion team for 1969. It was probably the best club he ever managed. That team included Hall of Famer Harmon Killebrew, future Hall of Famer Rod Carew, potential Hall of Famer Tony Oliva and a solid pitching staff including Bert Blyleven, Jim Perry, Jim Kaat, Ron Perranoski and Luis Tiant.

"We won the division easily that year. The next season we had a lot of injuries, the pitching staff broke down, guys didn't hit and we finished fifth. I wasn't as smart as I had been the year before," he says.

The following season, 1972, he was replaced by Frank Quilici.

"That's a tough franchise because the operation is small. There isn't a lot of room for error there and when you start losing the fans stop coming. When attendance dropped off I knew I was gone," Rigney says.

Rigney was soon back home in California, back on the golf course, chirping around baseball activities and adding his wit and wisdom to many baseball events.

"Just about that time Charlie Finley starting calling me and asking me questions about ball players in the league. Charlie was always a guy who picked the brains of lots of baseball people. If you were out of work you would soon be a source for Charlie's information network. It could be something about another team's players or about a free agent kid or about a player in another league. I just think Charlie liked the idea of using the telephone as much as he could," Rigney says.

Soon, the owner of the Oakland A's formalized the relationship. He hired Rigney as an assistant for his Oakland team.

"Charlie knows a lot about baseball. I had no trouble working for him. He may be an impulsive guy but he is also a fellow who can take advice," says Rigney.

In 1976 the San Francisco Giants were purchased by San Francisco grocery magnate Robert Lurie. Horace Stoneham, aging and ailing, had finally decided to give up the team and retire to his Arizona home. It was certainly the end of a baseball era for the Giants and Stoneham. Stoneham's father had owned the team before him and young Horace had worked in numerous jobs before he took over the club. He had run the Giants in the Polo Grounds of New York and had agreed, reluctantly, to move west with Walter O'Malley and the Dodgers. The Dodgers went on to fame and fortune in Chavez Ravine. The Giants, under Stoneham, were just one disaster after another in windy Candlestick Park. Threats of bankruptcy and league action for the shaky franchise finally forced Horace's hand. The Giants were sold.

"I knew Bob Lurie as a sportsman from around the San Francisco area. He asked me to come aboard and help him out with his new ball club. I didn't know exactly what he had in mind. I worked with Bob on reorganizing the team and building a farm system. Then he decided to make a managerial change as well," Rigney says.

In one of those commonly delicious baseball ironies, Rigney was asked to step in and replace his old buddy and teammate Wes Westrum as the skipper of the San Francisco Giants.

Rigney had a lackluster season with a lackluster team. The Giants finished fourth in 1976 and Joe Altobelli succeeded Rigney as manager of the team in the following season.

"The operation was going through a lot of changes," Rigney says. "I just didn't have a good team to work with. Maybe I had lost my heart for managing by then."

Rigney would soon shift from the field to the front office of baseball. He was a man who seemed to know everybody else in baseball, a valuable commodity when trying to improve a ball club. His next team was San Diego.

"They hadn't been able to make a move since they began play in 1969. I worked with the front office and I worked with the farm system. I think they were a stronger franchise when I left than when I came," says Rigney.

Rigney had long been a popular person in the San Francisco Bay area. As a native of the neighborhood, he had long been associated with the Giants and had also worked for Finley with the Oakland A's. With free agency beginning to sap the dollars of Finley's operation, he decided to sell the franchise. A deal was completed with Walter Haas, the owner of the highly successful Levi's jeans empire, for the purchase of the A's.

The inexperienced operators were looking around for a baseball man who could supply them with the dos and don'ts of the game. Rigney was their man. He joined the club as an executive front office official with unspecified duties.

"Actually what I do is a little bit of this and a little bit of that. I advise on deals, I offer opinions on young players, I'm consulted on organizational changes, I offer my experience in any area I think can be of use to the team," he says.

It would not be outrageous to say that the smiling presence of Rigney around the team adds an immeasurable asset to the organization. Rigney is on a first-name basis with almost everyone in the game. He will spend hours around hotel lobbies and baseball press rooms. He is always picking up useful information.

"One of the most important things in the game is sizing up talent," he says. "I have a lot of friends in the game. I think that I can often get information about players that a lot of others don't get."

It was general manager Sandy Alderson and manager Tony La Russa who rightfully received most of the credit for the huge success of the Oakland A's in 1988. The team won the division and the pennant before being whipped by the hottest team in baseball in 1988, the Los Angeles Dodgers of Tommy Lasorda and Orel Hershiser.

"It's hard to be disappointed about a team when you win a pennant. It was a great season and it was very exciting seeing some of those kids mature and develop. Jose Canseco is one of the great young players in the game. I think he will be the kind of player who will dominate the league for years to come. I think Willie [Mays] is the best all-around player I ever saw but this kid comes as close to Willie as anybody. I just love to watch him drive a ball," Rigney says.

At the age of seventy-one and in his fifty-first season in the game, Rigney has not lost any of his enthusiasm for baseball. As he sits around the spring training headquarters of the Oakland club in Phoenix, Arizona, he is as bouncy as he was decades ago. He has lost a step or two with some hip problems and he has to wear a huge sun hat to keep his light skin from being irritated by extreme rays and he wears even thicker glasses than he did years ago, but his mind is as sharp as ever. He laughs easily and tells a story about Leo or Willie or Stanky or Dark with as much relish as he did in his days in the Polo Grounds.

"There has never been a single day when I regretted going into baseball and not going into the tile business," he says. "The people I've met, the places I've been, the stories I've told and heard, all of that has just been an incredible pleasure. My family had to deal with some problems because I was on the road so much but they got to go to spring training and take an occasional trip and live in some terrific places. I don't think I would have been able to do that for them in the tile business. The fascinating thing about baseball is that everyone knows it is a business and you have to win and you have to draw fans and you have to be successful. But you still have fun along the line doing all that. I don't think I ever woke up one day in my life that I didn't want to go to the ball park. It was tough on my stomach when I was managing a losing ball club but I've survived."

As he sat in the Arizona sun and talked of his half century in the game, Bill Rigney's joy came rushing through his conversation. This was a man who had clearly made a significant life choice at an early age and knows that he made the correct one.

"I have met more wonderful people and done more wonderful things than I could ever imagine doing in any other way," he says. "There's another aspect to baseball that has been so pleasurable for me. I'm never bored in the game. There is always something new, something exciting, something different. When I was with the Giants and Willie came along we all agreed we'd never see his like again in our lifetime. Then this big kid Canseco comes along and young Mark McGwire and our terrific shortstop, Walt Weiss, and so many other fine youngsters and you know there are more fine youngsters out there. I wouldn't want to miss any of that. As long as they want me, I'll be here."

Then Bill Rigney, who has given so much to the game in half a century, got up from his poolside lounge chair. He leaned against the fence for the next half hour and discussed the Oakland A's with hotel guests. This was clearly a man in love with his life.

2   Herb Stein

BEATING THE BUSHES

■■■ "MY DREAM," SAYS HERB STEIN, A SCOUT FOR THE Minnesota Twins, "is to be sitting up there in Cooperstown when Rodney gains admission to the Hall of Fame. They will be reading off his plaque about the wonderful things he has done, a lifetime average about .330, those seven batting titles, those three thousand hits. Then they will end the presentation of one of the greatest hitters the game has ever seen by saying, 'and he was signed by Herb Stein.' That's what I want to happen."

Herb Stein signed Rod Carew. That is enough glory for any baseball scout.

"We don't get much recognition and we don't make much money but I love what I'm doing. I just love it. I'm seventy-one years old. When I see a kid with a sweet swing in a high school game I still get excited. I still think about finding another star, signing a Rod Carew and watching him make his mark in the game. Sure, things aren't perfect in the game for scouts. But that kind of thrill, signing and seeing a Carew develop, that's almost as good as doing it on the field yourself."

It is a chilly early fall afternoon at Shea Stadium. Stein is there because he loves the game, the smells, the sights, the sounds. He has no particular function there this day but it is a Sunday and where else should a scout be but at the ball park?

They are the unknown soldiers of baseball, these middle-aged men who trudge through old high school fields, sit on rusted metal seats, fence carefully with high school, college and amateur coaches, spend time with other men of their profession, share memories and friends, zealously guard their opinions on sixteen-, seventeen-, eighteen- or twenty-year-old kids.

"It was much more cutthroat in the days before the draft and the scouting bureaus but I still don't share information on a player. That's my job. What I'm most proud of is that the players I've signed who made it weren't number-one draft choices. I had to go deep, very deep to find them. Some scouts won't do that," he says.

He loved the game as a small boy in Manhattan, the son of a moving man.

"My father, Abraham, was a bruiser. He moved pianos. He could put one of those things on his back and walk with it down five flights of stairs in a New York tenement," says Stein. "He had come over from Russia as a small boy. He went to Philadelphia where he had some relatives. That's where he met my mother. Her name was Jennie."

The family had moved to Manhattan by the time Stein was born on December 3, 1917, one of eight children. He was born in Harlem Hospital on 117th Street and Lenox Avenue.

"That was a pretty nice neighborhood in those days. It didn't have the identification as a black community that it does today. It was a middle-class neighborhood, Jews, Italians, Irish, Polish, everything, just a nice area."

He played all the street games—stickball, punchball, softball—on his time off from Public School 57 at 114th Street and Lexington Avenue, Junior High School 184 on 116th Street and Lenox Avenue and George Washington High School. He became a decent second baseman at George Washington.

"I lived near the Polo Grounds and when I graduated from high school in 1936 all I could think of doing was playing baseball with the New York Giants," he says.

The Giants won the pennant in 1936 under manager Bill Terry, the last National Leaguer to hit .400. Stein adored all the Giants but especially Mel Ott, the small right fielder who would lift his right foot in the air before slugging a home run over the right field wall. Other standouts included Dick Bartell, Carl Hubbell, Hal Schumacher and Fred Fitzsimmons.

"I had a good glove and I could make contact. I wasn't very big but I could play and I hustled. I thought I had a chance. Scouting wasn't very sophisticated in those days. Most of the time if you lived in a city with a big league team you attended the open tryouts at the big league park. They were held all the time. Most of their players were signed through open tryouts," he says.

On a sunny June morning, shortly after graduation, Stein carried his new $2.95 glove up to the Polo Grounds, just a couple of subway stops away from his home.

"We collected in center field, near the locker rooms, and were told to walk to the batting cage and wait for instructions. Then a couple of coaches from the Giants, Dolph Luque and Pancho Snyder, began working us out. I was on second base and I looked up and there were a couple of the regular Giants, Dick Bartell and Burgess Whitehead, working out alongside us kids. They were just getting some extra fielding practice before the game. They didn't pay much attention to us but it was thrilling to be on the same infield with two big leaguers. I could hardly breathe."

The coaches would hit hard ground balls at the kids and watch them field and throw. Nobody hit unless he could field or throw impressively enough. They were skilled baseball men. They knew if there were not impressive reflex actions in the field, they could not expect any hitting performances.

"I don't know how many of us there were out there, maybe seventy-five or a hundred, but they started yelling orders to us. 'You, go home. You, come back Tuesday. You, go and hit a few.' I hit some balls hard and then Luque yelled over at me, 'You, go upstairs to the office. See Jack Schwartz. Tell him I sent you up.' I knew Schwartz was an important person in the Giants front office. I was very nervous," says Stein.

The eighteen-year-old climbed the steps to the Giants offices and asked for Mr. Schwartz. He was ushered into a small office.

Schwartz opened a desk drawer and pulled out a contract. He said it called for eighty dollars a month and that I would be reporting next season to the Giants farm team at Frederick, Maryland.

"Now go home and get this signed by your father and when you get it back here, we'll send it on to the National League office to make it official," Schwartz told the stunned youngster.

"I just stuffed that contract in my pocket and raced home. I didn't wait for the subway. I just ran the entire fourteen, fifteen blocks and waited for my father to get home from work. He had to sign it. When he asked me how much I was getting for playing baseball I told him eighty dollars a month. He just looked at me and smiled and signed it. I don't think he believed me. He was making about that for lifting furniture and pianos on his back," says Stein.

Abraham Stein signed the contract. Herb Stein grabbed it and ran back out the door. The Giants were off that day so he could get into the Polo Grounds without much trouble. He raced to the office of Jack Schwartz.

"I didn't mean for you to come back today with the contract," Schwartz said. "We have plenty of time. You're not going to play until next year."

"I want to make sure you had it. I want to play baseball," said Stein.

Schwartz laughed and congratulated the boy for his enthusiasm. It was difficult for Stein to wait for the next spring.

"I would have played for nothing," Stein says. "There was no negotiating about a figure. Whatever he offered that's what I took. I just wanted to be a baseball player. That's all that mattered to me."

Stein reported to the Giants farm club, played that season and the next and then was released.

"There were no explanations. They just decided I wasn't good enough. I was really broken up," he says.

Good fortune was just a phone call away.

"I had this doctor, George Knotts, who knew a man by the name of George Halpern. He was a close friend of Calvin Griffith. That was my big break in life," he says.

Griffith owned the Washington Senators. He had inherited the team from his father, Clark Griffith. Despite having an occasional star on the team, the Washington Senators had already established themselves as one of the worst teams in baseball. It would not be long before most fans would smile at the description of the Senators as "First in War, First in Peace and Last in the American League."

"I didn't care about any of that," says Stein. "It was a chance to be back in baseball."

Stein was offered a contract by the Class B Washington Senators farm team at Greenville, South Carolina. He accepted immediately and reported to manager Bucky Harris of the Senators in their spring training camp in Florida.

Stein played for the Senators organization in 1939, 1940, 1941 and 1942. There were no signs he would ever make the big leagues.

"The closest I came was forty-five feet away in 1942," he says.

Cecil Travis was the star shortstop of the Washington Senators. During that season he was called into the Navy as the start of World War II took more and more players. The Senators reached down and tapped Johnny Sullivan, the

Chattanooga shortstop, for the big leagues. Third baseman Ellis Clary moved over to play short at Chattanooga. A few days later Clary was called to the big leagues. Stein, the second baseman, felt he was getting closer and closer to a big league job.

"I was forty-five feet away from these guys and I knew it had to happen. I was told I would be in the next call-up. They were right. I was called up by my draft board," he says.

Stein went into the Army, trained at Fort Dix, New Jersey, and soon found himself as an Army military policeman in Africa, England and France.

"We arrived in France at Utah Beach on D-2, the day after the invasion. Our job was to secure the towns after the advancing troops had taken them. It was a good deal. Mostly we dealt with the civilian population, which welcomed us warmly," he says.

Stein moved through Normandy, across France and into Belgium with his unit before the war ended. Late in 1945 his unit was in Mons, Belgium. The war in Europe was over. He met a stunning brunette who spoke no English, and he spoke no French. They fell in love and were married before he returned home. Herb and Marie-Jose Stein have three grown children, Danielle, Alan and Jeffrey.

"Our courtship was mostly in sign language with a oui-oui here and there and a no-no along the way until she gave me the final oui-oui about marrying me," says Stein.

Stein returned to baseball at the age of twenty-nine after Army service in 1947. He didn't have much hope for a big league job but thought something in the game might open up for him. He was released late that first summer back.

"I didn't know what I wanted to do. I still thought I would stay in the game. Then I got an offer to manage in Stamford, Connecticut. I went there for the 1949 season and managed in Jesup, Georgia, in 1950. That was it. I had a family to support," he says.

Stein had some odd jobs until he finally landed a solid position as a New York City transit police officer. He remained in that job from 1955 through 1978 before retiring with a half pension.

"One day, about 1952, I got a call from Sherry Robertson of the Washington front office. He said they were looking for a bird dog [a part-time scout] to help out in the New York area. He asked if I was interested. I told him I was and thought I could work it out. By the time I got placed in the transit police I was a full-time scout. I would work in the subways from six o'clock in the morning until two in the afternoon. Then I would go to a ball game," he says.

He would hustle to high school games, talk to coaches, watch amateur ball, sit in freezing rain and never complain.

"What was there to complain about? It was baseball," he says.

In 1961 he had his first score. A husky third baseman named Joe Foy was starring for Evander Childs High School in the Bronx.

"He was a beautiful ball player, strong, fast, a great arm, a quick bat. He could have been a terrific player," Stein says.

Foy was signed by the new Minnesota Twins team (they had moved from Washington) and made it to the big leagues with Boston in 1966 after a trade. He also played for Kansas City, the Mets and Washington. Personal problems and a serious lack of discipline ruined his potential.

"For me it was a start. It proved to the organization I could sign a player who could make it to the majors. That is very important to a new scout," he says.

With Foy's rapid rise toward the big leagues, Stein's status within the new Minnesota Twins organization grew. His territory was expanded to include New York City and other areas of New York State and then into New England.

He would journey as far north as Maine for a promising kid but always felt his first big star, the ticket to fame for a scout, would be found somewhere near his own home in the Riverdale section of the Bronx.

"They don't play a lot of games in New York City high schools. The weather is always bad in the spring. There is a big pull from the other sports. You may only see a kid once or twice before you have to make a decision on a high school boy in New York," says Stein.

On a brisk early spring afternoon, late in March of 1964, Stein received a call at his home from a man named Monroe Katz.

"Katz worked for me in the area. He was a bird dog and was supposed to cover schools I couldn't get to. If he saw a kid he thought was a prospect he would alert me and we would often go watch him together," Stein says.

On this March afternoon, as he prepared to watch a kid he liked at a Bronx school, the phone rang.

"Herb, Monroe Katz."

"What do you got?"

"My son, Steve, tells me there is a kid at George Washington High in Manhattan you ought to take a look at. A skinny second baseman who can hit line drives."

Minnesota had a second baseman named Bernie Allen. He was a football star out of Purdue and the Twins thought they would be set at that position for years. Stein knew that it was harder to sell an organization on a young kid when that kid's position was already well protected on the big league level.

Steve Katz, a student at George Washington, had raved so much about this skinny kid that Stein thought it worth a look. He also liked the idea of returning to his alma mater once in a while.

"This was in the days before the free agent draft. Scouts missed lots of good kids. I thought if this kid was as good as Steve said maybe he was just missed by the others. We could get him for a cheap price," Stein says.

The Minnesota Twins, building toward a 1965 pennant, were a notoriously cheap organization under the Griffth leadership. It often seemed they would rather finish last than spend big bucks to sign a prospect. Griffith's methods seemed close to paying off as the Twins improved to contend in 1964 and eventually win in 1965 with inexpensive talent.

"It was very cold when I got to the George Washington High field. It was late in the afternoon, maybe four o'clock, and the game hadn't started yet. The kids were taking batting practice when I got there. Monroe met me in the small stands behind the field. He seemed excited. 'That's the kid over there, next for batting practice. You won't believe this.' I just sat down and watched," Stein says.

Line drives rocketed off the skinny kid's bat. Most of them went to left field. The boy had incredible bat control. The kid was, Stein remembers, a natural.

"I soon found out his name was Rodney Carew, he was born in Panama and he had come over with his mother only a few years earlier. He had some trouble with English and he was academically ineligible for high school play. The coach, Arthur Flynn, let him work out with the team and sit on the bench during games. He just couldn't use him," Stein says.

Stein moved onto the field to talk with Flynn. He had known him for several years.

"The kid that was just hitting, Carew I think his name is, I'd like to talk to him," Stein said.

"He's a quiet kid, very shy, you might have trouble getting anything out of him," Flynn said.

Stein walked over to Carew just behind the batting cage.

"My name is Herb Stein and I'm with the Minnesota Twins. I like the way you swing the bat," Stein said.

"Thank you, sir," said Carew, as he stared at his shoes.

"Let me have your name and address and phone number. I'd like to see you play in a few games," he said.

Carew provided the information. Stein was concerned about not being able to see Carew play in any games. It's one thing to watch the actions of a kid at bat against a batting practice coach or watch him field ground balls without a streaking runner. It's a different story when the game is on the line.

"I knew this guy, Ozzie Alvarez, who played for the Cavaliers in the Bronx Federation League. I called him and asked him if he could take this kid, Carew, from George Washington High that I wanted to look at," says Stein.

"What position does he play?"

"I think he's a second baseman."

"If he can turn a double play we can use him. We haven't turned a double play all season."

Several days later Carew played for the Cavaliers in a doubleheader. He had ten hits in twelve at-bats. Line drives seemed to leap instinctively from his bat. The sounds of his hits drew attention.

"I decided I wanted to sign him," says Stein. "Now it was a question of making a deal and coming up with a price. I also started worrying about other organizations finding out about him. Somebody told me Flynn worked as a bird dog for the Tigers and if he thought Carew could play he would certainly steer him in that direction."

Stein followed Carew for half a dozen games on sandlot fields in the Bronx and Manhattan.

"The day I remember most was when he played for the Cavaliers in the Bronx Federation in a game across the street from Yankee Stadium in Macombs Dam Park. He was literally a hundred feet from the Stadium and no Yankee scout knew about it. Imagine if he played for the Yankees with that short right field wall all those years," Stein says.

As the weather warmed up in April, Stein called his boss, Hal Keller, in the Twins offices in Bloomington. He told him he thought he had a kid who would be worth looking at. Keller said he would be in New York the following week on other business. He would see Carew the following Thursday afternoon in a game for the Cavaliers.

"We walked into the field and sat on one of the benches behind a fence. I was talking to Hal before the game. All of a sudden, I looked up and here were six scouts from six other organizations. I almost dropped dead. I was certain they had heard of Carew and now the bidding would start. If there was big bidding we would be out of it," he says.

When the bidding began the Twins almost always disappeared. Griffith ran a tight financial ship. That's why scouts such as Stein, who searched the depths for baseball talent, were so valuable.

"Hey, I don't see Harry Greenfield," one of the scouts said.

"Oh, he's not with this club. He's with the Rangers and they are playing in Yonkers today," Stein said.

Stein said he suddenly realized that the six scouts were after another kid, named Harry Greenfield. They knew nothing of Carew.

"The game started and I just sat there as still as could be. The Cavaliers played an inning, Rodney didn't get an at-bat and then the scouts all got up together. They were off to Yonkers to see Greenfield. I just waved as they left and made believe Hal and I just decided to meet here because it was convenient. I tried to give the impression I was looking for no player in particular. I was just looking at a sandlot game. That's what I did often," Stein says.

Carew got four or five hits again that day and Keller turned to Stein and asked, "What is he worth?"

It was the first indication the farm director was interested. Then he registered a complaint. The kid, Carew, a left-handed hitter, only hit balls to left field for his base hits. Stein was ready for that.

"Hal, this kid can hit it anywhere. I asked him about that last week. He said, 'Mr. Stein, I can hit to right field if I want. I just think I'll get more hits going to left. Most of the time they pitch me away. Do you want me to hit to right?' I told him I did and he got four line drive hits to right, including a long home run. Don't worry about him pulling big league pitching."

Now it was time for the Twins to move ahead rapidly if they wanted Carew. It was getting toward graduation time.

Anybody could sign Carew after his class graduated on June 24, 1964. Stein had not yet talked money with the youngster.

Minnesota was playing a scheduled game the next evening at Yankee Stadium. Keller told Stein to bring the kid out. Sam Mele was the Minnesota manager and he knew a lot about hitting. Carew could take a few swings and Mele could offer an opinion on the kid. Stein picked Carew up at his Washington Heights apartment and drove across the Harlem River to 161st and River Avenue in the Bronx. He entered through the players' gate with Carew walking slowly as he studied the Stadium.

Stein introduced Carew to Mele. The manager shook his hand and turned the youngster over to the clubhouse man. He was given a corner locker where a Minnesota uniform with number 54 hung on a hanger.

"By this time I knew he could hit big league pitching. I think he could have hit it then at the age of eighteen. What I didn't know, what nobody could know then, was whether he could field well enough to play in the big leagues. This was before the DH and I hadn't seen him play in the field very much. I was worried about his arm. Keller noticed that right away and said he would have to be a second baseman because he clearly couldn't play short or third," says Stein.

With the late afternoon shadows falling over the Stadium, with the monuments for Babe Ruth, Lou Gehrig, Miller Huggins, Jacob Ruppert and Ed Barrow glistening in the setting sun, Carew walked through the Twins locker room, up the alley to the dugout, and entered that sacred, historic field.

"I'm sure he was nervous but he didn't show it to me," says Stein.

Mele was at the batting cage and he asked one of his pitchers, Jim Perry, to throw strikes to the kid. Perry was scheduled for a start in a few days and he was getting his work in. He threw hard and had excellent control.

"Rodney just rattled everything out there that he threw up to the plate. I don't think he fouled a ball off. He just hit those line drives, whack, whack, whack, all over the place. Suddenly I got scared. I knew the Yankees were watching from their dugout. One of them might tip off their people and they would come rushing down from the office and sign him on the spot," says Stein.

He jumped the rail behind home plate and rushed up to Mele, who was leaning on the batting cage.

"Sam, get him out of there. If the Yankees see him, we're finished."

"This kid can sure as hell hit. What did you say his name was?"

"Carew, Rodney Carew from Manhattan. Please get him out of there."

"OK, kid, that's enough."

Carew hadn't hit more than six or seven balls. Mele had seen enough.

"Sign him. I'll play him tonight."

Nothing works that fast in baseball but Stein was pleased that his opinion of Carew was supported by the team's manager. Now all he had to do was get this youngster's name on a contract at the high school graduation.

Carew undressed quickly in the Twins clubhouse. He said little and just stared at the players on the team, Zoilo Versalles, Tony Oliva, Harmon Killebrew, Bob Allison, Camilo Pascual, players who would figure significantly in the team's pennant the following season.

When he finished dressing, Carew turned to Herb Stein and asked, "Can I keep this cap?"

It is traditional for baseball teams to present team caps to hot prospects. It is one way of gaining their allegiance. Stein figured Carew had earned it with his impressive hitting show.

"I had to ask the clubhouse man because I didn't want him to be short equipment," Stein says. "Then he gave me a hard time over the cap. He said he had lost a few the week before and with a long trip coming up he couldn't afford to give any away. Rodney looked very disappointed. I just kept thinking

the Minnesota Twins would miss out on this kid over a
stupid baseball cap. Just then Calvin Griffith walked into the
clubhouse. I rushed him over to Rodney for a handshake and
then I told him the clubhouse man wouldn't give Rodney a
souvenir cap."

"Is he a prospect?"

"Yes sir. Hal likes him a lot."

"Give him a damn cap."

Three days later Herb Stein picked up Rodney Carew, his
mother, a man he introduced as his father (who later turned
out to be an uncle) and two friends. They all piled into
Stein's Plymouth and drove to George Washington High
School for the graduation.

"I couldn't sign him before the midnight hour of the day
he graduated. I wanted to make sure I was with him. My
own daughter was graduating from the same school that
night. To tell you the truth if she had been graduating from
another school I would have been at Rodney's graduation.
The ceremony went off, Rodney was a high school graduate
and I piled them all back in the car for a ride to Stella
D'Oro's restaurant on 238th Street and Broadway. I had
worked a long time for this," he says.

Stein spelled out the Minnesota offer in the car. The team
would give him a five-thousand-dollar cash bonus for signing, pay him four hundred dollars a month at Melbourne,
Florida, for his first year and give him a progressive bonus of
seventy-five hundred dollars if he made the big leagues with
a thousand for Double A, fifteen hundred if he made Triple A
and the final five thousand for the seventy-five-hundred-
dollar total if he made the big leagues for sixty days. It was
not an extravagant offer but it was fair for a kid who had no
big high school or college reputation.

"I think when we got to the restaurant he was ready to
sign," says Stein. "I was very excited. I had convinced him
the Twins were a wonderful organization, he would get to
the big leagues faster with us than anybody else and he
would love playing for Sam Mele, a real nice man."

The Carew family ate a huge dinner. Rodney seemed pleased at the developments. It was all worked out as Stein studied the clock.

"A few minutes before midnight the owner came over to us and said he was closing up. I told him I was a scout for the Twins, I had to wait until midnight and I was about to sign this boy to a big league contract. He was a baseball fan, he said he understood and he agreed to keep open a little while longer," Stein says.

At about ten minutes after midnight, Stein checked his watch.

"OK, Rodney, we can sign now."

"I'd like to have forty-eight hours to think about it."

"I almost choked on my dinner. I thought it was all wrapped up in the car. I told him I had to close the deal. I knew the Tigers, White Sox and Red Sox had discovered him. I knew the Tigers and Red Sox paid big money for prospects. If they started bidding against us we would lose him," Stein says.

Stein explained to Carew that he knew he was using these other clubs to raise the Minnesota price. He told him that was a very fine, fair offer and he didn't think any other club would match it. Then Stein had a bright idea. He would make a phone call for Carew to the White Sox scout and explain to him the Minnesota offer.

"Let's see if he will match it," Stein said.

Stein did not tell Carew that he knew he would be beaten out if he called the Detroit or Boston scouts. The White Sox also operated on a tight budget and the Twins could get past them in this bidding.

"I also knew it was nearly 2:00 A.M. now and no scout would be too receptive to talking big numbers at that hour. I gave Rodney the phone number for White Sox scout Steve Ray," says Stein.

From the pay phone in Stella D'Oro's, Carew called Ray. He was fast asleep and groggy when Carew explained that he was in Stella D'Oro's with Mr. Stein and had been offered a package worth twelve-fifty and four hundred a month and asked what the White Sox would do about that.

"I'll call my farm director in the morning and then I'll get back to you," said Ray.

With that inaction, Carew was headed to Minnesota.

"I told him I was the scout who had taken him to Yankee Stadium, I was the scout who entertained his family, I was the scout who got him the cap, I was the scout who really wanted him, I was the scout who made him a fair offer," Stein says.

The youngster looked at his mother, who said, "It's up to you, Rodney."

"I'll sign," said one of the greatest hitters the game has ever seen.

Stein pulled a contract from his pocket, filled in the numbers in ink and offered it to Carew. He signed it Rodney Cline Carew and he was bound to the Twins until sold, traded or released. Before the advent of negotiated free agency in 1976, this meant Carew was tied to the Twins at their discretion in perpetuity.

"After that we just shook hands all around, walked out of the restaurant, got my car and drove back to Rodney's apartment at 155th Street and Amsterdam Avenue," says Stein.

Carew was packing the next morning to leave for Melbourne and begin his brilliant career as Stein was phoning the Minnesota office.

"We got him," he told Keller. "I signed him at 2:00 A.M. in Stella D'Oro's."

"Five thousand dollars for a left field hitter," said Keller. "I don't know."

Stein had a few more signings for the Twins before he hit it big again with Frank Viola, a lefthanded pitcher he saw at St. John's University. Viola is considered the best lefthander in baseball. He also signed Gene Larkin out of Columbia in 1984. Larkin may well prove to be a hitter of significant skills.

"Sometimes you screw up," says Stein. "I had this player named Donald Dantoni out of Staten Island way back in the 1950s. He was a beautiful ball player, a shortstop. I thought he could play in the big leagues for twenty years. I couldn't wait to sign him. We finally got him and he was a terrible failure. He had a girl friend who didn't like baseball. That ruined him. There's so much to know about a kid, so much."

Stein never made more than twenty-five thousand dollars scouting for the Twins. A small, balding man with a rapid-fire manner of speech, quick eyes and expressive hands, he will be in those cold high school and college fields as long as he can make it to the parks.

"I love the game, I just love it. I keep chasing after these kids and hoping I can come up with a star. When the Twins won the World Series last year they invited all the scouts and I got a World Series ring. That was a thrill. But you know what the real thrill is? It's signing a kid nobody else knows and watching him make it big."

On some June afternoon this year or next or the year after that, Stein will be sitting on a hard bench in some chilly high school field. He will hear the sound of a baseball bat striking the ball. He will look up and swear he has found the next Rod Carew.

3 Yosh Kawano

CLUBHOUSE
CONFIDENTIAL

▬▬▬ IT HAD BEEN FORTY SEASONS, FROM 1945 TO 1984, before fans of the Chicago Cubs could brag again. The Cubs won the pennant in 1945 and lost the World Series that year to the Detroit Tigers. They labored through the next four decades until they could win anything again. It finally happened with the 1984 Eastern Division title. They lost the National League Championship Series to the San Diego Padres and a chance to return to the World Series after being ahead in the final game. No matter. The shutout streak was over and a division title was a decent enough consolation prize for the Cubs.

Only one man had been inside the Cubs clubhouse on both those memorable occasions. He was Yosh Kawano, the equipment manager of the Cubs, who has been around the team in one capacity or another since he served as a batboy during the 1935 spring session of the Cubs in Los Angeles while he was still a schoolboy.

While the 1984 season had its thrills as the Cubs fought off the memories of so many failures, the season had one other significant moment. For some it was even more memorable than winning.

No greater honor can come to a baseball player than to have his uniform number retired by his team. There are Hall of Famers who have not received that prestigious notice. Yosh Kawano had his number retired in its fashion.

On a windy afternoon at Wrigley Field—there hardly are any other kinds of afternoons there—the Cubs honored the small man with the big heart. They didn't retire his number. They can't do that for equipment managers. They simply named the clubhouse in his honor. From that day on every member of the Chicago Cubs would walk through the Yosh Kawano Clubhouse. It was an honor even fewer personalities of the game would receive.

"Yosh was himself even on that day," says Joe Goddard, the baseball writer of the Chicago *Sun-Times*. "I think he did nothing differently to prepare than he had for all those years. Maybe he changed his hat."

That hat. It is a baseball landmark for many as significant as the ivy growing off the walls at the famed Northside park in Chicago. Yosh wears a floppy fisherman's sun hat every day of his life. Some swear he sleeps with it. Many claim they have been around the club for a dozen years without ever seeing the top of Kawano's head.

The outfit was the same on Yosh Kawano Day at Wrigley Field. The floppy white fisherman's hat. The lived-in slacks. The tattered T-shirt. The soft shoes. It was has uniform back in 1935 and it is his uniform on any summer day in 1989.

"I'm comfortable in these clothes," he says. "I can do my work."

Ball players will often say that the most important person in a team clubhouse is the equipment manager, clubhouse man, aide-de-camp, whatever title these protectors of team property go under.

"Yosh is as much of an institution around here as any person in this organization," says manager Don Zimmer. "He probably knows where more bodies are buried than anybody. He just won't tell."

Kawano is a friendly, small man of bursting energy and organization. He just prefers to keep his own counsel.

"He is probably the most organized man I have ever seen in my life," says Arlene Gill, the secretary to general manager Jim Frey of the Cubs. She has been around Wrigley Field since 1967.

"Whenever he comes up to the office he carries a pile of papers with him. It is his inventory of bats and balls and hats and shirts. He wants the organization to know where everything is if anything ever happens to him. He takes great pride in his organizational skills. He always suggests that anybody could step in and take over his job because he has done such a good job in preparing everything."

Gill has developed a wonderful relationship with Kawano. He confides in her as he does in almost no one else. He protects her when the players get a little too close. He never forgets her birthday or to ask about her health.

"I probably shouldn't be telling you this," she says, in a conspiratorial tone, "but in 1984 when we won the division title and went to San Diego for the playoff he paid my airfare out there and gave me his room. He stayed with friends while I was able to enjoy being around the club hotel. Just don't tell him I told you. Tell him you found out on your own. He hates it when people find out he has done anything kind for anybody. He thinks it damages his image."

The image of clubhouse men in baseball is that they attend to the equipment problems, care for the clubhouse, oversee the operation of the players' living room but never concern themselves with the players themselves. They see too many players come and go and it could be dangerous and emotionally searing if they get too fond of any particular player.

Kawano always gets close to some players.

Ray Floyd, a longtime professional golfer and close friend of Kawano for many years, recalls what it was like in the days before free agency made wealthy men out of .220 hitters.

"A lot of ball players were making five, six, seven thousand dollars a year in those days in the 1950s. It was financially tough for many of them. Yosh would carry ball players from payday to payday. I'm sure he didn't see a lot of that money back. If he had all the money he loaned out returned in one day that would make him a very wealthy man."

Many suggest that Kawano is a very wealthy man anyway. He owns property in Los Angeles and Arizona where the Cubs train. He has invested wisely through the years with help from two of his favorite Chicago managers, Leo Durocher and Herman Franks. He lives frugally, often staying in Los Angeles with a brother or sister. He doesn't spend a great deal of money on clothing.

"What he does do," says Goddard, "is spend a great deal of time in Binions. That's his favorite hangout and guys can always catch him in there."

Binions is one of Chicago's best restaurants and a hangout for the city's sports elite. Kawano has his own table and is often surrounded by some of the biggest names in Chicago sports from athletes to broadcasters. The stories go on well into the night. None ever get printed.

"I don't do interviews with the press," says Kawano. "I want the press to interview the players and not me."

Like most Good Soldiers of Baseball, Kawano loves the game with a passion. He is only concerned with being in it, being around the players, witnessing the thrills and recording none of it. He made a small exception when I told him I wanted to include him in this book because he has devoted his entire life to the game. I thought he would serve as an inspiration to others who cared as much but didn't know how to participate.

"Why do you want to talk to me?" he said, when we chatted one afternoon before a Cubs game at Shea. "Here's Ryne Sandberg. He's the Cubs second baseman. He was the Most Valuable Player in the National League in 1984 when the Cubs won the division title. Talk to him."

Sandberg was dressing a couple of lockers away. He smiled when Yosh tried to steer him to me.

"I've already interviewed Ryne," I said.

"Interview him again," Yosh said.

Finally, after some cat-and-mouse play, he agreed to talk for the fans of baseball. His name was not known very well outside Chicago but he knew that he represented the hopes and dreams of many young men. As millions would dream of playing in the big leagues, millions more would dream of being around the ball players in some capacity or other because it was a dream with more possibility of realization.

Yosh Kawano was born in Los Angeles nearly seventy years ago. He was a little uncertain of dates. His parents had come over from Japan to work the farm fields of California in the early days of the twentieth century, as did many Japanese who left their homeland to seek a better life.

His father had worked as a farmhand with other immigrants. The hours were long and difficult but the life was better than they had known in Japan. He has an older brother, Nobe, who is the clubhouse man for the Los Angeles Dodgers, and a sister who lives in Los Angeles. He has never been married.

"I went to school in Los Angeles but I was never much of a student," he says, "What I really cared about was playing ball. I was pretty good and I thought maybe that would be my career. They used to have some very good professional leagues out there in those days. The Pacific Coast League was probably as good a minor league as there ever was. They played an excellent brand of baseball and some players were probably better than some of the players they had in big league baseball. I guess the difference was there weren't as many of them."

In the spring of 1935 Kawano walked into the clubhouse of the Chicago Cubs in their training camp at Catalina Island near the city of Los Angeles. He asked if they needed anybody to help out around the club and he was offered a job as a batboy. He received no pay but the players did tip him a dime or a quarter when he ran errands for them, getting a hot dog from a vendor, buying a pack of cigarettes or polishing their baseball shoes.

"When the season started I worked part-time for the Cubs team in Los Angeles. They had this very good team in Los Angeles and I loved watching them play all the good teams, especially the San Francisco Seals."

The Seals had a skinny twenty-year-old outfielder by the name of Joseph Paul DiMaggio, brother of the renowned Pacific Coast League star Vince DiMaggio. Kawano got to know the guy who would later be named the Greatest Living Baseball Player at the anniversary centennial in Washington in 1969.

"We became good friends," says Kawano. "I go back a long way with Joe and when you know somebody when they were a kid, you don't get too impressed."

DiMaggio, a basically shy, quiet and sometimes suspicious man, had always gotten along better with the small people of baseball—the batboys, the clubhouse men, the groundskeepers, the stadium attendants—than he had with more important stars or executives in the game. DiMaggio was always concerned that somebody wanted something of him, wanted to use him, wanted somehow to take advantage of him. He never felt that way with these people holding inconsequential jobs.

One of the people DiMaggio was closest to in his time in New York was the Yankee clubhouse attendant Pete Sheehy, who would join the team in 1927 and remain with the clubhouse job until his death some sixty years later. The Yankees would also honor Sheehy as the Cubs honored Kawano, by naming their home clubhouse the Pete Sheehy Clubhouse.

During DiMaggio's famous fifty-six-game hitting streak in 1941, the one record most baseball observers contend will never be broken, DiMaggio developed an ugly red blotch on his backside. He stared at the blotch one day as he walked by a clubhouse mirror. It was in an awkward position on his backside and he could not get a good view of it. He summoned Sheehy over to look at it.

"Pete," the Yankee Clipper said. "Tell me if this thing looks worse than it did yesterday."

"Yeah, Joe, it does," said Sheehy. "It's from all those guys kissing your butt."

DiMaggio, completely deflated by the unpretentious clubhouse man, simply laughed and walked away.

Kawano always had that sort of relationship with stars. It doesn't excite a man when he is throwing a player's dirty laundry into a washing machine. Nor does it excite him when he is around that player at his most vulnerable time, naked and depressed after a bad game.

"I try to treat them all the same all the time, star and rookie, good day or bad," says Kawano. "I do my work and I expect them to do theirs."

Another of Kawano's big pals is Ted Williams, baseball's last .400 hitter (.406 in 1941) and a crusty character.

"I was working for the Cubs in a spring training game in 1936 when this kid pitcher came into the game. He was a skinny lefthander and he threw pretty hard. I think he only pitched an inning or so but I was impressed with how determined he looked out there on the mound. I don't know if we would have heard of him as a pitcher but we sure did hear of him as a hitter," says Kawano.

Williams, another player who developed warm friendships with small people, spent much time in those years with Kawano. That friendship shifted over to big league baseball. They remained close throughout Williams's Hall of Fame career with the Red Sox and remains close to this day.

One spring Williams, a Boston spring training batting coach now, was visiting spring training as the Red Sox prepared to play a training game with the Chicago Cubs. Both teams were struggling at the time and the Cubs needed some sort of excitement to fill the park. Chicago management got the bright idea that if the Red Sox could bring along the great Ted Williams to the game and advertise his presence, more fans would turn out for the game. Chicago owner P. K. Wrigley called Boston owner Tom Yawkey.

"Tom, could you get Ted here for the game?" Wrigley asked.

"I don't think so," said Yawkey. "He's going off on a fishing trip. Ted makes his own schedule."

Thoroughly discouraged by the turn of events, Wrigley mentioned it to Yosh Kawano.

"I'll get him," responded Yosh.

Kawano called Williams at his private apartment and announced that he needed him at the ball park the next afternoon. The Cubs wanted to advertise his presence.

"Will it help you?" Williams asked.

"Yes, it would," said Kawano. "I want to do this for P.K."

"Tell him I'll be there for you," said Williams.

The great slugger showed up, the Cubs filled the ball park that day and a good time was had by all. It was another great triumph for Kawano. He said nothing about the event. The story only surfaced several years ago when Williams told a baseball friend who passed it on to me when I asked about the people Yosh knows.

Modest to a fault, Kawano ducks these stories when asked directly. He loves to tell stories and may drop a name or two here or there but when asked directly about a famous player or a well-known incident he simply says, "I'm the cleanup guy. Talk to the cleanup hitter."

There is one area of his life he rarely talks about. It is far too painful a memory. The reason Yosh Kawano talked about his difficult days during World War II with me was simply his desire to get his unhappiness on the record. The time was right.

In 1987 the United States government, prodded by many officials and numerous citizens of Japanese background, finally came to terms with one of the most horrendous acts in this country's history. Yosh was part of that nightmare.

On December 7, 1941, the Japanese bombed Pearl Harbor in Hawaii in a sneak attack beginning shortly after daybreak. The United States, unprepared for war, was soon engaged in mortal combat with Japan and her two European allies, Germany and Italy. Fear spread through the West Coast of the United States, with daily rumors about possible Japanese landings in California. Hardly a day went by early in December and through January of 1942 that stories did not surface about sightings of Japanese aircraft and ships off the California coast. War fever was everywhere. Air raid drills in schools were a constant distraction. Blackouts were ordered in most West Coast cities and villages. For some strange reason, anger against the Japanese enemy was far deeper than anger against the Germans and Italians. Clearly, there was prejudice against people of a different skin color. Certainly there was heavy propaganda for reasons of national mobilization against the Japanese.

To counter this anti-Japanese attitude, to allay the fears of Californians about an imminent invasion and to theoretically eliminate a possible fifth column of Japanese terrorists in our midst, Japanese were ordered interned.

More than 110,000 Japanese, including some 75,000 American citizens of Japanese ancestry and native-born Americans, such as Yosh Kawano, were rounded up and put in camps, nothing less than prisons for civilians during the war hysteria.

"My father had been here ever since he was a young man," says Kawano. "He worked in various jobs, farmer, laborer, things like that. America was his country. I was born here. I had never been in Japan. One day they just came and knocked on the door and said we had to be packed and ready to move in a few hours. They took our house, they took our car, they took everything."

Kawano and his family were sent to a camp in Nevada. Conditions were difficult. The only thing that kept them from even greater anger than they had was the lack of restrictions. As long as they stayed within the confines of the camps they were free to do as they pleased.

There was, finally, a way for young men of Japanese ancestry to get out. They could join the United States Army.

The second-generation Japanese—called nisei—joined up and fought with distinction in campaigns early in the war through Africa and Italy. They had one of the highest casualty rates in the war and also one of the highest rates of honored medal winners. Several of their number received the Congressional Medal of Honor, the country's highest military award, for heroic action against the enemy.

By 1944, Japanese-American soldiers were being sent not only to Europe, but also to the South Pacific for combat duties against the Japanese. The United States government no longer was concerned with the loyalty of these immigrant Americans. They were no less and no more loyal to the United States than the German-Americans or Italian-Americans who fought alongside them.

Kawano was trained as a military policeman and was soon shipped out with his unit to the South Pacific. He fought in New Guinea and the Philippines with distinction. He earned several combat medals.

He returned to Chicago in time to resume his clubhouse duties for the 1945 World Series. The war had finally ended with the surrender of Germany in May of that year and the surrender of Japan in September after two atomic bombs were dropped on the enemy. He worked as the clubhouse assistant during that memorable World Series and continued those duties through 1952. The following season he was given the title of equipment manager and was put in charge of all the operations in the clubhouse. He did the work all by himself until some ten or fifteen years ago when he began bringing in youngsters to help him sort uniforms.

One of the young men he brought into the clubhouse at Wrigley Field is Greg Nimietz. He has worked with Kawano since 1974. He is a hard worker, loyal, faithful and very fond of Kawano.

"It's very hard to talk about Yosh because he is such a private person. I just have to tell this one story because it says so much about what kind of man he is," says Nimietz.

The clubhouse assistant then related how Yosh paid his way to the 1984 championship series in San Diego and invited him to work and paid his way to spring training in Arizona over the last few years. Ball clubs pay the expenses of one clubhouse man. The other assistants are usually hired locally when the clubhouse man gets to the spring training site.

"He wanted me to work with him and he arranged it," says Nimietz. "How many bosses would do that? All the players love him. He also understands his role is behind the scenes. That's why he is so upset that anyone ever wants to talk to him. He thinks that will take away interview time from the players. He knows they are out there working hard and he wants them to get all the gold and all the glory."

Clubhouse men are also assigned the task of getting new players settled on a team. One of their most important chores is getting a new player his proper uniform number.

"When I was with the Dodgers," says skipper Don Zimmer, "I wore uniform number 23. Players are superstitious about numbers. When you are a star and you join a new ball club you can ask the clubbie for your old uniform number. If it isn't being worn by another star on that team, you will usually get it. I can't remember who was wearing number 23 when I first came to Chicago. All I know is that when I went to the ball park the first day that uniform number 23 was hanging in my locker. Yosh had seen to that. Those are the kinds of things that make you feel at home on a new team."

Zimmer remembers his greeting when he first came to the Cubs in 1960 after six years with the Dodgers in Brooklyn and Los Angeles.

"Hey, Dodger," yelled Kawano.

That was the way the clubhouse man has greeted every other player or coach or manager who has joined the Cubs who played a day for the Dodgers.

"He doesn't do that with other teams. Everybody trades players. It is just that he identifies all the new players as Dodgers if they have been with that organization. Maybe it is because his brother works for the Dodgers and he lives out there," says Zimmer.

Most clubhouse men are rather silent when it comes to dealing with managers and players. They do their jobs and keep quiet. It is why so many of them last so long. Yosh does his job and doesn't keep quiet. He's lasted forever.

"He's a great needler," says Zimmer. "He can really get on you pretty good. The thing that makes him so smart in the way he deals with the guys is that he always knows when to stop. It's one thing to needle a guy after a good day. It's another thing to needle him after a bad day. Yosh always knows the score."

The chores of clubhouse men, or equipment managers in the current terminology, are sometimes hard to define. They have certain rituals. They put clean uniforms out each day. They do the team's laundry. They keep the clubhouse clean and neat. They provide the pregame snacks and the postgame meals.

"See, the thing is," says Zimmer. "They do everything anybody wants done if there is nobody else to do it."

That means they can pick up a smelly, soaked jockstrap from the floor or arrange to have a player's ten-thousand-dollar check cashed.

"One of the things I always liked about Yosh when I was in Chicago," says former Cubs infielder and former San Diego manager Larry Bowa, "was that he did everything that had to be done without embarrassing anybody."

Bowa says that players, especially the volatile types like himself, often lose or destroy equipment in the heat of a game.

"I've been known to burn a cap or tear up a uniform shirt," he says. "The next day I would come to the park and a clean shirt and a clean cap were in my locker. Yosh wouldn't embarrass me by asking about it and he wouldn't embarrass me by discussing it in front of other players. There are a lot of little things that can make a player look like a jerk in the clubhouse. Yosh has this way of shifting the blame from the players to himself if anything goes wrong in the clubhouse. I've seen the managers jump all over him for some small infraction when it was a player who might have caused it."

Through the years with the Cubs, Kawano has been close to almost every player and coach and all managers who were at Wrigley Field. He had a few special people such as Leo Durocher and Herman Franks and coaches Joey Amalfitano and Joe Altobelli.

"I just love him," says Amalfitano unabashedly. "He is a great man and a very important part of the Cubs operation."

Altobelli was a young first baseman with the Cleveland Indians back in 1955 when he first met Yosh Kawano.

"The Indians and the Cubs trained in Arizona and we played a lot of games against the Cubs. I got to know him from those spring training days and I was always very fond of him. He is just one of those guys in baseball you simply take for granted. Things get done, the games go on and nobody knows how come everything worked so efficiently. It is a guy like Yosh who gets it done," says Altobelli.

Jack Brickhouse, the veteran sportscaster who did Chicago Cubs games on the air for many years before retirement two years ago, thinks Kawano is as important on the Cubs scene as anyone around Wrigley Field.

"There is so much tradition in the game," says Brickhouse. "A person like Yosh ties teams together because he knows the history of the club from so many years. That is important to young players. I think it is vital that there is a link with the past and only somebody like Yosh can provide it."

Kawano's most significant trait is probably that he shows a devilish side, especially to young players, but he is very understanding to them as well.

"Yosh probably knows and is closer to more Hall of Famers than anybody in the game. He can kid Ted Williams and Joe

DiMaggio and Ernie Banks as easily as he can kid the lowest rookie who has just joined the club," says Brickhouse.

"Why not?" says Kawano. "Did you ever see Joe dress? One leg at a time, same as everybody else. The suit may be a little more expensive than most others but it is still one leg at a time. I'd like to see one of those Hall of Famers jump into their pants, just once I'd like to see that, two legs at a time."

Kawano spends an average of fifteen hours a day in the ball park in spring training and maybe a little less during the season. On the road he often has to go into the park through the gate reserved for night watchmen.

"I've been around a lot of clubhouses in my time in this game," says Brickhouse. "I can honestly say I have never seen anybody work harder or longer. I know I have never been in the Cubs clubhouse when Yosh wasn't there and I've been around here a lot of years."

Kawano shows no signs of slowing up as he closes in on fifty-five years with the Cubs organization in Los Angeles and in Chicago's Wrigley Field.

"About the only difference now," says sportswriter Joe Goddard, "is that he falls asleep on the plane a little faster than he used to do. A lot of times you will walk past him on a plane and he will be holding a paper or a magazine in front of him and be fast asleep. You can walk by a few minutes later and he will be in the same position. Then something will jolt him and he'll pick up right where he was."

Goddard remembers having dinner with Kawano once in a restaurant in Scottsdale, Arizona, where the Cubs train, called the Pink Pony.

"Everything was fine until the middle of the meal. I could see he was getting drowsy. He put a fork up to his mouth with peas on it and got about an inch away from his mouth and stopped. Then he went right to sleep and stayed asleep maybe four or five minutes while I talked to some other guy. Then all of a sudden he put that fork in his mouth, got those peas without dropping one of them and picked up right where he was."

Those long workdays and short nights would tend to wear out a man half his age. Nobody has noticed any dropoff in his efficiency on the job. He will probably be there as long as Wrigley Field, now modernized with lights, remains on the Northside of Chicago.

"I remember when the Cubs were being sold by the Wrigley family to the Tribune company," says Brickhouse. "They wrote a clause into the deal that Yosh Kawano could never be fired from his job as long as he wanted it. The Wrigleys wanted to protect him. They had been loyal to him after all the years he had been loyal to them."

Kawano laughs when the Wrigley story is repeated to him. He doesn't think working in one job all his life is very unusual.

"This is baseball, you have to remember that," he says. "When I was a little kid I just wanted to be part of baseball. When I realized I probably couldn't play I figured out this was the best way to watch other people play. I have not had one unpleasant day or met one unpleasant person in all the years I've been in baseball."

That can't be true but Yosh Kawano is not the kind of man who will say anything negative about a baseball team or a baseball clubhouse. That would reflect poorly on the game and he works hard to see that nothing like that happens.

"I have made so many friends, met so many wonderful people, had so many thrills in the game that I really consider myself a very lucky man. The Cubs haven't won a lot but that can't be helped. They have always played hard and entertained their fans. I've been happy being around the place."

Baseball without the ivy-covered walls of Wrigley Field wouldn't be the same. The tradition is too important, too warm, too poignant. Wrigley Field without Yosh Kawano wouldn't be the same. This is a guy who has loved the game for more than half a century. It is a good guess the game feels the same way about him.

4 Larry Bearnarth

NO OFFICE ON
WALL STREET

▬▬ IN THE CRUEL WINTER OF 1973, LARRY BEARNARTH struggled out of bed in the early morning darkness. He dressed quietly so as to not disturb his wife, Barbara. This was supposed to be the first day of the rest of his life.

Bearnarth was thirty-three years old. He had been in professional baseball as a pitcher for the New York Mets and Milwaukee Brewers and a minor league pitching coach for the Montreal Expos for eleven years. He had just finished his second season of visiting the small minor league towns where the Expos had farm clubs. The pitching prospects for the organization, which had only begun play in 1969, appeared slim. The frustration level was high.

Bearnarth was making under ten thousand dollars a year in his job. He taught high school in the winter. He had a family that included four growing children and saw no future in baseball.

"A few weeks earlier I had called Mel Didier, the farm director, and Jim Fanning, the general manager of the Expos, and told them I was through. Fanning told me to think about it a little longer. I had thought of nothing else for several months. I was convinced I was finished with the game. I had a good education and I was going to use it. This was the end of the baseball line," he was saying now in the Expos club-house at Shea Stadium.

Bearnarth was born and raised in New York. He had graduated from St. Peter's Academy in Staten Island and won a baseball scholarship to St. John's. He had been an outstanding college pitcher and was signed in 1962 by the fledgling New York Mets. He was assigned to their Syracuse farm club and brought to the Mets in 1963. He had four significant seasons with the Mets before drifting back to the minors and resurfacing with the Brewers.

Montreal hired him at the end of the 1971 season and rehired him again for 1973 as their roving minor league pitching instructor. He did the same thing again that year and was in the process of being rehired for 1974 at almost the same pay when he decided to make a career change.

"I had taught English in high school over the winters and I had also become interested in business. When money started becoming a serious problem as our family grew I decided I had to do something about it. I took a few courses in business and one day I went down to Merrill Lynch and applied for a job in their Wall Street office," he says.

Late in November he was called in for an interview. Handsome, articulate and personable, the husky former pitcher was hired by the giant investment firm.

"I was to begin work that Monday morning," he remembers. "I got dressed, had a cup of coffee and walked to my car. It was still dark. I drove down the street from our home in Dix Hills, Long Island, drove a few more blocks to the Long Island Expressway and headed west to New York City. I got a few more exits closer to the city. The traffic was building up. It was still cold and dark. I kept thinking of spring training only three months away and I kept thinking of the young kids I had worked with and I kept thinking of all the guys I had buddied with in the Montreal organization. I suddenly pulled off on the shoulder of the road, took a deep breath and headed for the next exit," he says.

Bearnarth turned his car around, got back on the Express-way heading east and was back in his home in fifteen min-utes. He pulled off his suit and tie and shoes and socks and got back into the warm bed on that cold morning.

Barbara Bearnarth noticed.

"What are you doing here?" she asked.

"I'm giving it up," he said.

"You haven't started. How could you give it up?"

"Working for Merrill Lynch isn't what I do. Baseball is what I do."

Barbara Bearnarth understood. Larry Bearnarth could roll over again, confident he would never again have to get up early in the morning to drive through the traffic of the Long Island Expressway to a Wall Street office.

"I think if it wasn't cold and dark that day I might have made it all the way into Manhattan," he says. "I just couldn't face that drive."

Bearnarth slept soundly that morning. He knew there was still a chance to remain in the game. He finally moved to the telephone after normal baseball hours began, say ten-thirty or eleven o'clock in the morning. He phoned Jim Fanning in Montreal and told him he would like to take back his resignation.

"We never put it in," said Fanning. "We always like to wait before we do that. You can't imagine how many of our people change their minds about that."

Fanning and Bearnarth had a long discussion about the pitching coach's future. Fanning assured Bearnarth that the organization had high regard for him, respected his skills and saw possibilities for him down the line.

"I guess the most important advice Fanning gave me was to move. He suggested I relocate over the winter near our training site in Florida and use the facilities down there. That way I could work with young pitchers all winter long, work in our winter league program and keep tabs on many of our prospects. He said he would give me a raise, give me moving expenses and help move my career along," Bearnarth says.

Barbara and Larry Bearnarth discussed moving away from family and friends in New York to the new situation presented them in Florida.

"We finally decided to do it," says Bearnarth. "It was a commitment to baseball. I realized that cold morning that I wasn't a Wall Street guy. No matter that I could make five times as much money in Wall Street and that many of my college classmates were making big money and no matter that I was away from home so much. On that morning I learned one important lesson about myself, my family and my life. I was in baseball. That's what I did. That's what I wanted to do. That's where I would always stay. Once I made that decision, Barbara and the kids would be very supportive. They knew that's where I was happiest. They recognized that if I was doing what I enjoyed, if I was happy, the entire family would be happy."

Ever since he was a youngster growing up in Staten Island as a fan of the Brooklyn Dodgers, Bearnarth had wanted to be a baseball player. He participated in other sports in school but baseball was his true passion.

"I rooted for the Dodgers and I imagined myself on the mound at Ebbets Field. I was heartbroken when the Dodgers moved out of Brooklyn. I still got a thrill when I got to the big leagues and faced the Dodgers. They weren't Brooklyn anymore but they still had those uniform shirts that said Dodgers and that still excited me," he says.

Jack Kaiser was the baseball coach at St. John's and he recruited Bearnarth for the school.

"He didn't throw very hard," says Kaiser, "but he knew how to pitch and you could see how competitive he was. It is sometimes more important that a guy has a lot of desire and intensity than it is how talented he is physically. I've seen a lot of youngsters squander talent. You don't see too many use their full abilities as productively as Larry did."

Shortly after graduation from St. John's he reported to the Syracuse Chiefs of the Triple A International League.

"The competition was pretty rough," he remembers. "I might not have quite been ready for that. Maybe my career would have been more productive if I had started in a lower league, learned my trade and moved up more slowly. But the Mets were in a rush for young players and I was pushed along. I also think it was a factor that I was from New York and had pitched at St. John's. I think there was a feeling that I might help them sell a few tickets."

The New York Mets had begun play in the expanded National League in 1962. They had selected Casey Stengel, at the age of seventy, to lead the ball club. Stengel had been fired by the Yankees after the 1960 season when his team lost the World Series in seven games to the Pittsburgh Pirates on Bill Mazeroski's memorable home run off Ralph Terry. Stengel had remained out of baseball in 1961 at his Glendale, California, home. In October, while the Reds were playing the Yankees in the World Series, the Mets held a huge press conference announcing the hiring of Stengel.

When asked why he was fired by the Yankees, Stengel talked about his advanced age.

"I'll never make the mistake of being seventy again," he said, "and I didn't say I'd stay here five years or fifty."

There had been rumors that Stengel had been in declining health during his later years with the Yankees. When that question arose Stengel had the perfect answer for that one too.

"There's nothing wrong with my health," he protested, "from here up."

He was suggesting that even at his advanced age his mind was still as sharp as ever and that was all he needed to do the job. He certainly proved that was an accurate observation. Stengel remained with the Mets through the middle of August 1965 when he fell and fractured a hip at a party at Toots Shor's famed Manhattan restaurant.

The Mets lost 120 games for a baseball record in 1962 but identified themselves as one of the most lovable teams of all time. They not only had the game's greatest character in Stengel, they had players such as Richie Ashburn, Gil Hodges, Frank Thomas, Rod Kanehl, Roger Craig and Alvin Jackson who would prove to be incredible favorites of the fans in the Polo Grounds. Perhaps the most memorable Met of all was Marvelous Marv Throneberry, the Mickey Mantle look-alike reject from the Yankees, who would go on to fame as a beer salesman many years later.

It was this team of inept over-the-hill players that Bearnarth joined in 1963 after a half season at Syracuse. He really wasn't ready for the big leagues.

I had visited the Syracuse team as a young reporter for the New York *Post* in that summer of 1962. My paper wanted me to do a series on the young prospects the Mets had on their Triple A club. It was the first time I had met Bearnarth. He was clearly one of the sharpest players on the team. Kirby Farrell, the Syracuse manager, recommended Bearnarth enthusiastically.

"He's going to be a good one, that kid," he said. "He has a good sinker and he has a lot of guts. I think we'll have him up there before you know it."

All of the Syracuse players had their nicknames over their lockers and over Bearnarth's locker was the nickname Bear, a play on his last name and a description of his toughness as a pitcher. When he joined the Mets the following season, Stengel heard players call him Bear. Never one to get names correct, he always referred to Bearnarth as Big Ben.

"He would call down to the bullpen for a relief pitcher and I would hear him tell the pitching coach, 'Get Big Ben ready.' At first it bothered me but once I realized that was the way Casey was with everybody it no longer bothered me."

Stengel depended on Bearnarth in tough game situations. It was still unusual back in the early 1960s to use a young pitcher as a relief specialist. Most relief pitchers were veterans. Bearnarth made fifty-eight appearances for the 1963 Mets, won three games and had four saves, accounting for a little less than one fifth of all of their victories.

"We weren't very good but we were always in the game. We really were a very exciting team," he says. "We had a chance to win or lose every game with a strange play. The Polo Grounds accounted for a good part of that because of the shape of the park. There were short fences in both left field and right field so that almost every hitter, regardless of his batting average or what he was doing in another park, was considered a home run threat. The big guys might hit one over the roof but the little guys might slice one in the stands for a home run. You could never let up in a game in the Polo Grounds."

Bearnarth was a very effective pitcher with a 3.42 ERA in his first season, a very impressive mark on a team that was as bumbling as the Mets were. He had a good sinker, threw a slider and a curve and had excellent control. He walked only forty-seven hitters in 126 innings.

"Any time a pitcher got out of an inning without being scored on it was considered a triumph," Bearnarth says. "After all, we had a lot of guys on that team who couldn't field very well. This was Marvelous Marv's Mets years, you have to remember."

As the team moved to Shea Stadium in 1964, Bearnarth got into forty-four games and had a 5–5 record, clearly the best mark of any pitcher on a club that lost 109 games and won only 53. Bearnarth, however, lost his job as the number-one reliever on the club to a rookie named Bill Wakefield, who got into sixty-two games, won three, saved two more and pitched 119 innings. Wakefield came up with a sore arm over the winter in South America and never pitched another inning in the big leagues.

Bearnarth also went to winter ball that year with disastrous results.

He decided that he needed another pitch and decided to work on a screwball. He got a winter baseball job pitching for a team in Caracas, Venezuela. Before he left for winter baseball, I told Bearnarth to drop me a line and let me know how he was doing down there. He was always interested in journalism and I said if he wrote some details about what life was like pitching in South America for the kid from New York, the *Post* would publish it. Bearnarth would gain some writing credits. He had often mentioned that he was interested in journalism and thought someday he might pursue a career in the field.

Several weeks after the regular season ended I received a letter from Bearnarth. It was wonderfully detailed, humorous, very intelligently written, a perfect description of the life and times of an American in Venezuela during the baseball season.

With some slight clarifications and a change in tenses, the letter was printed in full in the New York *Post*. It received a warm response from fans. They understood that Bearnarth was being as honest as possible about the life down there. He was expressing in an interesting form the problems faced by all American players in those foreign lands. He clearly was not making any derogatory remarks about the South Americans, their lifestyle or their customs. He was simply stating in a colorful way that American players had a difficult time in that environment.

The letter was picked up by the Associated Press and printed across the country. It was also picked up by the local reporter for a Spanish-language paper based in New York. He translated the letter into Spanish and when it was read to me by a Spanish-speaking friend, it sounded harsher, more cruel and more sarcastic about life in general in South America. I could clearly see the fans in South America would not take kindly to some of Bearnarth's remarks. I heard nothing further from Bearnarth for several days.

Then I received a call from my office.

"Larry Bearnarth has been arrested in Venezuela," said Ike Gellis, the *Post* sports editor. "Your name is mentioned in the story about the article. Do you know anything more about it?"

"No, Ike, this is the first I heard about it. Can we bail him out?"

"We're checking with the AP now," he said.

The next day a full wire service report came to the *Post*. Bearnarth had gone to the mound the night after the article had been printed. He fell behind a hitter and the fans began booing. Soon, they were screaming obscenities at him. Garbage was being thrown at him from the stands. The ball park was in an uproar. Several fans jumped on the field headed for Bearnarth. Before they could get there, security guards hired by the club for this purpose surrounded him and got him out of there.

"Just before I walked off the field I threw the ball into the stands," Bearnarth remembers. "It was a very hot time."

Officials would give Bearnarth no time for a plea. He meant no harm, was not being nasty to the locals and was only in South America to find another pitch.

"I really didn't know what the fuss was all about. All I knew was that I was sitting in a jail cell with my uniform still on," he says.

The owner of the team soon arrived at the scene. After some very long negotiations, a fine was paid by the club and Bearnarth was freed on one condition. He would leave the country within the next forty-eight hours.

"I was out in twenty-four," he says.

Bearnarth returned to his Long Island home without his new pitch. He also made one more vow when we talked on the phone after he returned.

"No more letters," he said. "If you want any information from me, call me on the telephone."

He had another strong season out of the bullpen in 1965 with a 3–5 mark and another save, giving him a total of eight in his first three Mets seasons, better than any other Mets relief pitcher. Stengel would soon be gone after he fell and fractured his hip at the old-timers party at Toots Shor's. It would end a beautiful relationship.

"I really loved Casey. He was a great man. He gave me a chance to pitch and he helped me in every way he could. I just didn't have good enough stuff or throw hard enough to really be a great major league relief pitcher. He got the most out of me that anyone could," he says.

More important, Bearnarth says, he learned more baseball sitting in the dugout, the clubhouse, planes and buses listening to Stengel than at any other time in his career.

"A good part of the success I have had teaching pitching comes from Stengel," he says. "He really understood the game."

Bearnarth admits he laughs every time he hears Stengel's name and remembers many stories about the old professor.

"I loved the game and I always wanted to be part of it," Bearnarth says. "I was pitching for the Mets that first season and one day Stengel came up to me in the clubhouse after one of those crazy games that we used to lose. He said, 'Ben, you're going to be a great coach.' I thought that was pretty strange. I was twenty-three years old."

When he thinks about it now, he realizes that Stengel, in his wisdom, was telling him that he probably didn't have the stuff or the physical equipment to be a great big league pitcher. If Bearnarth wanted to stay in the game, he had to stay in as a coach or manager.

"It was good advice," says Bearnarth.

Wes Westrum was the manager of the Mets for the 1966 season. He had less patience than Stengel for the errors of young pitchers and he wanted desperately to move out of last place, a goal he would finally achieve that season when he beat out his old boss and mentor, Leo Durocher, for ninth place. Durocher finished in tenth place with his Chicago Cubs.

Bearnarth was in the minor leagues in 1967 and remained there until 1971. Another break came along when the Milwaukee Brewers, under manager Dave Bristol, came up short of pitching. They selected Bearnarth in the minor league draft and he made the club in spring training. He was thirty years old.

"I didn't get a lot of opportunity to pitch in Milwaukee," Bearnarth says. "The weather was bad, the pitching got backed up and by the time the weather cleared, Bristol wanted work for his starters. He used a lot of them in relief."

Bearnarth was soon released and his big league pitching career was over. He had gotten into a total of 173 games in five seasons and had learned an awful lot about pitching even if he couldn't perform too many wondrous chores on the mound himself.

"I went home to Long Island and began thinking about what I might be doing. Before too many days I got a call from Jim Fanning. He wanted to know if I would take a job with the Montreal organization as their roving pitching coach. I jumped at the opportunity," he says.

Bearnarth traveled across the country looking at Montreal's young pitchers. He would stay a week or ten days in one city before moving on to the next one. He was rarely home and the salary was poor. There were four children at home now to feed and conditions grew worse.

"After that 1973 season I just decided that it wasn't fair to my family. I enjoyed the job even though I was away a lot but I had to make more money," says Bearnarth. "I decided to get out."

It was with a heavy heart that Bearnarth accepted the position with Merrill Lynch.

"I really didn't want to leave baseball. That was clear. But on the other hand the Expos gave me no indication that I had much of a future in the organization. I couldn't stay a minor league pitching coach forever. Nobody does that. It is a job that every man hopes will lead to a big league job," he says.

He made the move to high finance that cold day in 1973, got onto the Expressway, saw the traffic, turned around and went back to baseball.

"Hell, that was my life," says Bearnarth. "That's what I do."

Several days after he had made the commitment with Fanning to move to Florida, take the increased salary and work with some of the Montreal pitchers down there, the phone rang. It was Del Crandall, the manager of the Milwaukee Brewers.

"I want you to come back to Milwaukee with me as my pitching coach," the former catcher of the Milwaukee Braves said.

"I can't," said Bearnarth. "I just told Jim Fanning I was moving to Florida to work with the kid pitchers."

"This is a big league job," insisted Crandall.

Bearnarth had given his word. Even though it is a common practice for baseball people to move from one organization to another, Bearnarth had decided to see the job through. He wanted to see some of his young pitchers make the big leagues and he wanted to see them pitch in the World Series for the Expos. He told Crandall he could not accept his offer.

"I've never had any regrets," he says. "I am still hopeful the Expos will make it to the World Series while I am here."

Bearnarth remained the minor league pitching coach of the Expos from 1971 through 1975. When things became discouraging again, he finally made it to the big leagues. The Expos hired Karl Kuehl to replace the ousted Gene Mauch in 1976. Bearnarth became his pitching coach. Pitching coaches last as long as the manager wants them. Kuehl was short-lived in Montreal. He was fired before the season was out and replaced by Charlie Fox. Dick Williams took over in 1977.

Bearnarth went back to the minor league pitching job in 1977 and managed the Montreal farm club in West Palm Beach in 1978 and 1979. He then managed in Memphis in

1980 and 1981. He returned to his roving pitching coach job again in 1982 and remained there through 1984.

There had been several changes in the Montreal setup, with Jim Fanning succeeding Williams in 1981 and bringing the Expos to within a Rick Monday home run of a National League pennant. Bill Virdon was the next manager and Fanning returned again to finish out the 1984 season while the Expos searched for a new field skipper.

There was a young man at their Indianapolis farm club who had much appeal. His name was Robert Leroy Rodgers but the baseball world knew him as Buck Rodgers. He had been a fine big league catcher with the California Angels, coached in Minnesota, San Francisco and Milwaukee and managed the Milwaukee Brewers to the 1981 title in the split strike season, only to lose to the Yankees in the playoff. The Yankees went on to defeat Oakland in the American League Championship Series before losing to the Los Angeles Dodgers in the World Series.

Rodgers was fired early in 1982 after a rebellious Milwaukee club refused to hustle for him and stayed out of baseball in 1983. He then accepted a position as the manager of the Montreal farm club in Indianapolis for 1984. He won the pennant and was named the manager of the Expos after the 1984 big league season ended. He was in Caracas, managing in winter ball, when Montreal hired him. He flew back for the press conference announcing his position and soon returned to Venezuela to finish out his season there.

Larry Bearnarth received a call from Venezuela at his Florida home. He wasn't so sure he wanted to accept it considering his previous problems in Venezuela.

"This is Buck Rodgers," the voice said.

"Hi, Buck. Congratulations on your Montreal job."

"I want you to become my pitching coach at Montreal."

Bearnarth says that he was very surprised when Rodgers called him and offered him the job he had held some ten years earlier. He barely knew Buck.

"When I was the roving pitching coach for the Expos our club was playing in Indianapolis and Buck was the manager. I went there several times that year to see the pitchers. Buck knew a lot about pitching since he had been a catcher in his playing days. We worked well together. He was a very smart baseball man and I knew they wanted him back in Montreal," says Bearnarth.

Bearnarth admits he made one more smart move while he was in Indianapolis. Maybe that move was what got him back into the big leagues.

"I invited Buck to lunch," he says, "and I paid."

The free lunch may have impressed Rodgers but the knowledge Bearnarth showed about pitching clearly impressed him even more.

"Larry is very dedicated, very knowledgeable about pitching," says Rodgers. "He has an awful lot of patience, especially with young pitchers, and he can get a lot out of them. I consider him an outstanding pitching coach, outstanding."

Bearnarth returned to the big leagues as the pitching coach for Rodgers and has been there ever since.

"There are still problems with the family as a big league pitching coach. Montreal is too cold for Barbara and the kids are in school so she doesn't come up there except for an occasional trip. She likes to call me the Duke of Windsor of baseball. She says I give up the family I love for the game I love. We have had to make some compromises. Every baseball family does. The kids have accepted our life with ease now. My best athlete is my daughter Kristin. She is a breast stroker at the University of Indiana and she has hopes for the 1992 Olympics. I'll take off to see that," he says.

Bearnarth has done very well with the Montreal pitching staff. The team was hit hard by pitching injuries in 1987 and 1988 but was effective when they were healthy. The relief pitching was especially good in 1987 with a 29–14 mark and fifty saves. He has educated his relievers to challenge the hitters and hates to see his pitchers behind in the count or walking anybody.

"My philosophy is that you challenge the hitters when you come in as a relief pitcher. You can't give in to the batter or pitch around batters. You have to go right after them if you want to win the ball game," he says.

Bearnarth has made a long study of the mechanics of pitching. He watches films and he studies pitchers as they warm up and as they perform in games. He can spot a flaw in a delivery and has helped all of his Montreal pitchers to be more effective.

"I think my great strengths lie in the mechanics of the art of pitching and in the attitudes of the pitcher. I think I do a real good job in maximizing a pitcher's skills by working with him on his mechanics. A hard thrower can gain a foot on his fastball with proper mechanics. The idea is to make the ball move and that is sometimes a very small mechanical problem. I have learned to deal with that," he says.

Bearnarth is also very good with the subtle relationships necessary for a successful pitching coach. He is a pleasant man with a marvelous sense of humor and pitchers find him easy to talk to.

"I think the big thing is to convince pitchers you are on their side. You are not correcting them to embarrass them, you are correcting them to improve them," he says. "I think all our pitchers understand that."

As he approaches his twenty-seventh year in professional baseball in 1989, Bearnarth feels he is ready to manage a big league club if the opportunity presents itself.

"I'm very happy working with Buck and the Expos. I wouldn't go to another organization in the same job but I would have to consider a managerial job. Baseball has been my professional life and after a while, you just would like to see how you could handle the top spot. I think I could do a real good job. I know there would be a lot of Casey Stengel in me, especially when I was talking to the sportswriters. Handling the press is an important part of handling the managerial position. Nobody was better at that than Casey."

Larry Bearnarth has come a long way from those horrendous days with the horrible Mets of Marv Throneberry and Rod Kanehl and Frank Thomas and Casey Stengel and all the rest of the Amazing Mets of more than a quarter of a century ago. He relishes the memories but he would rather win with Montreal than reminisce about losing in New York.

"We have a good ball club in Montreal and I think we are very close to having a winner. We have some good young pitchers in our system and I think in a year or two they could become big winners. I would like to be part of that. I think it would be wonderful to see a pennant in Canada for this team. The fans have been very supportive and they deserve it," he says.

It is a long time since Bearnarth put on his suit and tie on that freezing morning in Long Island and headed for his new life on Wall Street. He is still glad that he turned back just in time.

"Sure, I would be richer today and probably living in a bigger house and probably driving a fancier car," he says. "But there is no way of getting the joys and satisfactions and fraternalism of baseball in an office on Wall Street. I have no regrets. I love what I'm doing. Besides that, it is inhuman to get out of bed in the cold and dark of a winter morning. Do a lot of people really do that?"

5 Vada Pinson

THE OTHER HALF
OF THAT TEAM

██████ IN THE EARLY DAYS OF MARCH AT THE 1958 SPRING
training headquarters of the Cincinnati Reds in Tampa, Florida, a nineteen-year-old youngster named Vada Pinson was
rattling line drives all over the park.

The thin outfielder had batted .367 the previous season in
Visalia, California, in his first full season of professional baseball in the California State League. He had been invited to the
big camp as a result of that fine season in his first full pro year.

"Birdie Tebbetts was the manager of the Reds," recalls
Pinson, now a coach with the Detroit Tigers. "He would
watch me day in and day out. One afternoon he came up to
me and said if I kept hitting line drives like that he would
have to keep me. He didn't want to keep me. I was too
young. Besides, I didn't show any power. I was just spraying
line drives all over the park. That game I decided I would
show him some power so I pulled a couple of balls off the
wall and one ball over the wall. He seemed very confused.
He just walked by and shook his head. He kept repeating, 'I
don't want to keep him. He's making me keep him. I don't
want to keep him.' This went on for a few days. Finally he
turned to one of his coaches, Jimmy Dykes, and told him to
watch me for a while."

Dykes had been in baseball as a player, coach and manager well over forty years at that time. This was barely a decade after Jackie Robinson had broken the color line with the Brooklyn Dodgers. Like most old-time baseball players, Dykes had not been terribly comfortable with the change in the game as represented by the addition of blacks in baseball.

"I was a very quiet kid in those days," says Pinson. "I'm still quiet. Anyway he watched me hit for a while and I guess he wanted to make some suggestions. He just grabbed the bat out of my hand and acted out the changes. I tried to do what he suggested. He took the bat again and exaggerated the changes. I took the bat back from him and he seemed happy as I made the adjustment."

Dykes continued to address Pinson in pantomime for several days.

"Every so often he would say something in fractured English. I guess he was trying to imitate the Spanish language," says Pinson.

Finally, Pinson couldn't take this act any longer.

"Mr. Dykes, if there is something you want me to do with my stance, why don't you just tell me," Pinson said.

Dykes almost fell over. He had never heard Pinson utter a word and he certainly didn't expect the youngster to be as accomplished in English as he was.

"He had looked at me, saw the color of my skin and decided I was Cuban. I guess he had never seen a light-skinned black before who was an American. When I told him I was born in Memphis, Tennessee, I thought he would fall over in a dead faint. He was really shocked," says Pinson.

Dykes was never quite comfortable with black players. He would actually become the manager of the Reds after Tebbetts was fired later that season. He couldn't keep the talented Pinson off the team but he did little to encourage him.

"Birdie Tebbetts was supportive. He just thought I was young. I made the ball club that spring when we played an exhibition game against an Army team at Fort Knox, Kentucky," says Pinson.

The game began with the youngster in center field. Before he went to bat Tebbetts called him aside.

"We're going to be cutting the squad in a few days. I have to convince my coaches you have enough power to stay up here. See if you can hit a home run," Tebbetts said.

That was a tall order for the wiry 160-pounder. He was a lefthanded hitter who was facing a lefthanded pitcher that day.

"I figured I just had to adjust my swing and see if I could hit a long ball. Birdie wanted me to make the ball club but he didn't want to push me on that veteran team. I had to convince the coaches and convince the other players that I could do enough to help that team win. I just concentrated on getting a good pitch on the inside part of the plate. I pulled it over the wall. I could see Birdie in the dugout talking to Dykes as I rounded third base. I guess that was the moment I really started my career with the Cincinnati Reds," says Pinson.

What a brilliant career it was. Pinson would play eighteen seasons in the big leagues with Cincinnati, St. Louis, Cleveland, California and Kansas City, collect 2,757 hits, bat .286, perform nobly in the field and on the bases and finish as a strong contender for Hall of Fame honors for many years.

If there was one aspect of Pinson's career that probably contributed to keeping him out of the Hall of Fame, it was his link to Frank Robinson. They have been friends for more than forty years.

"He is my best friend," says Pinson. "There's nothing I won't do for Frank and I don't think there is anything he won't do for me."

Robinson was born in Beaumont, Texas, and moved with his family to Oakland, California, when he was seven. Pinson had moved there from Memphis with his parents when he was five. The Pinsons and the Robinsons lived in the blue-collar area of Oakland near the waterfront.

"My father was a longshoreman on the docks. The work was steady. We didn't have a lot of money but there was always food on the table. My dad's name was Vada Pinson, Sr. My mother's name was Vivian. She also did some domestic work to help out the family. I was an only child. I guess they could only afford one. Most of the time when my parents were at work my grandmother took care of me. Her name was Lilly Perkins and she is still in pretty good shape at the age of ninety-one," he says. "She just recovered from an appendicitis operation."

Pinson knew Robinson from the neighborhood but they became much closer in high school. Frank, three years older, already was a star athlete at McClymond's High when Pinson entered the school.

"That may be the high school that turned out more successful professional players than any other school in the country. Besides Frank and myself there was a pretty good basketball player there by the name of Bill Russell and a football player by the name of John Brodie. There were many, many more who made it from that school. It was quite a place for sports," he says.

Actually the young Vada Pinson, a thin, shy, soft-spoken young man, was not considered much of an athlete in his early days in the school. He was considered an important member of the school orchestra.

"I was a pretty good trumpet player and I was working hard to become the lead trumpet player in the school band. I would go home every day, practice on the trumpet and then come back to school for some baseball practice late in the afternoon. I played in all the baseball games but I spent most of my free time with the trumpet. Then came an important change in my life," he says.

The baseball coach at McClymond's was a man named George Powles. He could spot talent a mile away and he saw much potential in the lithe youngster. It came down to the trumpet or the baseball bat. One day Powles approached Pinson.

"Now Vada," he began, "I know how much you enjoy playing the trumpet. I wouldn't ask you to give it up. I also know you like playing baseball and if you are thinking seriously about a career in the game you have to devote more time to it. I think you ought to stay around school after classes and work on your baseball. When that's finished you can go home and practice your trumpet. What do you think about that?"

"I'll have to talk it over with my mother," he said. "She wants me to concentrate on my trumpet."

Powles impressed upon the youngster that he probably had more of a chance for a career in baseball than he did as a trumpet player. After all, there was only one Louis (Satchmo) Armstrong, while Jackie Robinson had opened up the game for many more like himself.

"I decided to concentrate on baseball. I never regretted it. I still like the trumpet. I listen to music all the time now and I often wonder just how far I might have gone if I had stuck with that instrument," Pinson says.

Robinson graduated into professional baseball and in a couple of years the scouts would start coming around looking at Pinson. By 1956 he had grown to his full maturity. His speed and defensive abilities were outstanding and he could hit good pitching consistently.

Robinson had signed with the Cincinnati organization in 1953. He was their rookie sensation in 1956. That June, Pinson graduated from high school and received a twenty-five-hundred-dollar bonus to sign with the Reds.

"I was assigned to Wausau, Wisconsin, in the Northern League. I drove my new car—the one I bought with the bonus money—across the country from California to Wausau. It wasn't a very pleasant trip. There were a lot of places along the way where I couldn't get gas and I couldn't get any food because I was black. Route 66 was not a very hospitable highway. It's a lot of years later and times are different now and the laws have changed, but you can't go through those experiences and completely forget them. I never was a fighter about that stuff. I took it quietly but it hurt, it hurt very badly and I won't ever forget them," he says.

Pinson says that sometimes he has to remind black players today when they complain about big league conditions what times were like for their brothers thirty years ago. He has often shocked his young charges with stories about rough treatment along the baseball trail.

"When I got to spring training I stayed in a rooming house with Frank. The rest of the Cincinnati players were kept in a beautiful downtown hotel. We had to live and eat away from the rest of the team. It was only 1956 when Frank joined the Reds and 1958 when I got there. Jackie Robinson had just retired and there were quite a few blacks in the game. Still, there was a quota system and everybody knew it. If I was going to make the Cincinnati Reds ball club I was going to be better than anybody else. I always felt the pressure. I went along but I felt the pressure," he says.

By 1959 Pinson was established as the regular center fielder of the Cincinnati Reds. He had grown quite close to his senior playing partner, Robinson, but he also got a lot of advice and help from several white players on the Reds.

"I was especially close to Gus Bell. He was very helpful to me in getting adjusted to the big leagues and helping me learn the pitchers and the defense. I think he was also the first white player to ever ask to have dinner with me on the road. He was a fine man and if it wasn't for people like Gus it would have been even rougher than it was. And it was plenty rough," he says.

Pinson hit .316 and .287 in his first two full seasons with the Reds. He was quickly gaining status among his peers. The next season would clearly identify Pinson as one of the finest young players in the game.

The 1961 season was one of the most exciting in baseball history. The Yankees dominated the sports pages with one of the most thrilling individual races when Roger Maris and teammate Mickey Mantle challenged the Babe Ruth home run record of sixty set in 1927. Mantle finished that year with fifty-four home runs after missing the last couple of weeks with an infection. Maris, despite incredible pressures in what may well be the most difficult season any baseball player ever experienced, hit sixty-one home runs to break Ruth's record.

The commissioner of baseball, Ford Frick, had ruled that Maris must break the Ruth mark in 154 games or the record would be marked by an asterisk in the book. Maris did not get his final home run until the last game of the Yankee season. It was game number 161 for Maris and game number 163 for the Yankees. Controversy destroyed the Maris experience. The Yankee right fielder, for his part, always maintained that he had nothing to do with the schedule and hit his record number of home runs during the regular season.

"A season's a season," said the Yankee slugger.

While that was going on in the American League the Cincinnati Reds were winning in the National League. Frank Robinson had a brilliant season with a .323 average, 37 home runs and 124 runs batted in, which earned him the National League Most Valuable Player trophy. Pinson, for his part, batted .343 with 16 homers and 87 RBIs. Roberto Clemente won the batting title with a .351 mark for the Pittsburgh Pirates.

"Frank was always the key guy on our Cincinnati club," says Pinson. "When he was hot he could carry the club for weeks. He was hot all year that season and really carried the team into the World Series."

Robinson had a poor World Series with a .200 average, Pinson had an even worse one with two hits in 22 at-bats for an .091 mark and the Yankees, even with Mantle injured and Maris physically drained from the home run race, won the Series in five games.

Pinson and Robinson teamed for several more years in Cincinnati before a shocking trade in 1965 sent Robinson to Baltimore in a deal involving pitcher Milt Pappas. Cincinnati general manager Bill DeWitt explained the deal to the press by saying, "Robinson was thirty but he was an old thirty."

There was a hint of racism, a definite feeling among many observers that the Reds felt Robinson was getting bigger than the team. DeWitt simply wanted to break up the team of Robinson and Pinson. Many felt these two players were going their own way as the rest of the Cincinnati players went theirs. That was tolerated while the Reds were winning but when they started losing, restless Cincinnati fans began calling for their heads. DeWitt was simply responding to the cry of some of his fans.

Before Robinson left the Reds to continue his Hall of Fame career and become the first player to win the prestigious Most Valuable Player award in both leagues when he led Baltimore to a 1966 pennant, there was a major incident.

Earl Lawson was the outspoken sportswriter for the Cincinnati *Enquirer*. He thought nothing of telling players how they should approach the game and in small towns such as Cincinnati, sportswriters had an inordinate amount of power and prestige.

"I was having a good year and had an outside chance for the batting title," says Pinson. "The club was struggling but I was hitting the ball. Lawson wrote that if I wanted to win the batting title I should concentrate more on my bunting. I ran well and could get some bunt hits. What Lawson didn't know was that Frank was hurting and wasn't swinging the bat well. He had missed some games and I was the only guy in the lineup with some home run power. I finally blew my cool when Lawson confronted me in the clubhouse about not bunting. I hit him. It was the only time I had ever done anything like that. He sued and it was settled out of court. It was very embarrassing."

When the incident occurred, Pinson could only think back to an earlier episode in school in Oakland. It was the closest he came to losing his temper.

"I had some words with this kid in school. I can't even remember what it was over," he says. "All of a sudden he pulled a knife on me. I decided I couldn't let him get away with that. I moved toward him. Fortunately, coach Powles was there and he stepped in. He got me out of the way and took me home. It cooled me down. He taught me that no good can ever come from fighting. Except for the incident with Earl Lawson I can't ever remember losing my head in all the years I've been in baseball."

Pinson hit .271 for the Reds in 1968. He was traded the following season to the St. Louis Cardinals. He moved on after one year in St. Louis to Cleveland, California and Kansas City. He ended his career after the 1975 season with a .286 lifetime average.

"I didn't know what I wanted to do," he says. "I wanted to stay in the game but nothing came along. I decided to rest and see what developed. I just went home and played a lot of golf."

There was friction in his marriage and he and his wife, Jacqueline, were soon divorced. He remains close to his four children.

"After you have played baseball for a living for twenty years it is difficult to step away from it. It was part of me, part of my daily routine. I couldn't imagine what it would be like not being in the game. I had a painful year in 1976. I didn't do much of anything and I had difficulty watching the game or coming out to the ball park as a fan. I recognized then that I needed baseball in some way or other. The game had been good to me and I wanted to return some of the things I had gotten. I never thought much about coaching or managing while I played, but I suddenly realized I could help young people in the game. That became very important to me. I wanted to pass on some of the knowledge I had acquired in a lot of difficult seasons," he says.

Pinson is a good-looking man with a resonant voice. He thought about a career in broadcasting. He didn't quite know how to go about it.

"It seems some guys just walk off the field and a big job is waiting for them. It didn't work that way with me. Nothing was waiting for me. I had started in the game making $6,500 a year. I had ended it making $70,000. It was a good salary but it wasn't like the salaries being paid to players today. I couldn't live the rest of my life without working the way ball players can do today if they.choose. I'm not jealous of them. They have earned the big money. I can't help but wish we had those kinds of salaries in my day," he says.

In the fall of 1976 he got a call from the new Seattle Mariners team. They wanted some experienced coaches. Darrell Johnson was the new Seattle manager after having won a pennant in Boston in 1975 and then having been fired after the following season.

"I knew Darrell from playing against his Boston clubs and we had been together a short while as players when he spent some time with the Reds. We weren't close friends, but I guess he knew of my interest in getting back in the game," he says.

"I always respected Vada as a player and as a man," says Johnson. "I knew we would have a young, inexperienced club in Seattle and I thought he could be a big help to us."

The following spring, 1977, Vada Pinson was back in uniform with the new Seattle team.

"It was hard to explain my emotions when I took my first coaching job. I knew I would miss playing but I also knew that I would be part of baseball again. I loved being around the clubhouse and talking with the players and sitting in the dugout and walking on the field and hitting fungoes. I loved every part of it. It was a tough adjustment in those early days because I wanted to hit again but I dealt with it. The important thing was that I was going into a big league clubhouse again. I was doing what I always wanted to do, being part of the game I loved so much," he says.

Pinson recognized that a good part of the transition from player to coach was a question of attitude.

"I still thought I could play a little longer when they let me go. I'm sure I was unhappy about that. The year off was probably the best thing for me. You can't stay away from the game at the age of thirty-seven and then walk onto a field and think you can play. I knew I couldn't play. I also knew down deep in my heart I could really help others play better," he says.

Pinson rapidly took to coaching. While the Seattle club was not a very competitive team, there were small signs of progress all around the club.

"When I worked with a young player and I saw him do better it was the same thrill I had as a player when I improved. I really began to understand how much a coach can contribute to a ball club, not only in helping a player improve his skills but in helping a player, especially a young player, understand the game. Sometimes that means dealing with defeat or dealing with a bad day or even handling some criticism from the manager or the front office. There are so many different things that go into being a big league player. Not all of them are in a box score. I have always been a guy who believed in a positive approach. If I had a tough day, say I went oh for four, I was always confident the next day would be better. I tried to instill that kind of approach to the game in all our players. Your skills can only carry you so far. The rest of it is a discipline, a mental toughness that you learn to harness as you become more experienced. It's the old line about a glass of water. For some guys it is half empty and for other guys it is half full. For me it was always half full. I could always see better things coming and I could always deal with some of the disappointments of the game. I think that attitude helped me survive as long as I did."

Pinson was comfortable in the Northwest. Seattle was a pretty city to be in and he found much less pressure there than he had experienced in Cincinnati.

"There seems to be very little attention paid to race in that part of the country," he says. "It was something I enjoyed very much about Seattle."

Johnson was let go by Seattle in August of 1980. His successor was Maury Wills, the third black to ever manage a big league team. Pinson's pal, Frank Robinson, became the first with the Cleveland Indians in 1975. The second was Larry Doby, Bill Veeck's old Cleveland pal, hired to finish out the 1978 season with the White Sox. Doby, who was the American League's first black player in 1947 and the second black in baseball only three months after Robinson broke the color line in Brooklyn, was simply not up to the job. He was quickly let go the following season.

Wills, the spark plug of the wonderful Los Angeles Dodgers teams in the early 1960s, had clamored publicly for a chance to manage. He finally got that opportunity when Johnson was fired. That didn't work, either. The pressures were enormous and Wills, a combative, opinionated sort as a player, had immediate confrontations with his charges. He lost control of the club and had endless problems in his first spring training, in 1981. By the first two weeks of the season the local press began suggesting that Wills would not make it as the team's manager. He was fired less than six weeks into the season.

Wills would later reveal that a good deal of his conduct was affected by controlled substances. He admitted to a drug problem and would have serious battles with addiction for many years. The Los Angeles Dodgers would pay for his medical treatment and he would surface again several years later as a respected member of the Dodgers organization. He knew his chances for managing again were slim.

After the 1980 season, all of the Seattle coaches were fired. Pinson moved from Seattle to the Chicago White Sox. Bill Veeck had hired a bright young man from Tampa, Florida, with a law school degree to handle his team. Manager Tony La Russa hired Pinson as his hitting coach after the Mariners let him go.

Rene Lachemann was the new Seattle manager after Wills was let go and he quickly brought Pinson back to Seattle in 1982.

"I was very happy going back. I had really become very fond of the area. People were very nice to me and it was a beautiful setting. I enjoyed getting up in the morning and looking out of my apartment balcony at the mountains. I think everybody should spend some time in Seattle," he says.

Pinson remained there for three more seasons. In 1985 new manager Chuck Cottier was allowed to pick his own coaches and Pinson was on the move again. This time he struck pay dirt. He was called by the successful, wordy, flamboyant manager of the Detroit Tigers, Sparky Anderson.

"I want you to come with me," said Anderson.

"That would be an honor and a thrill," said Pinson.

The Tigers had won the pennant in 1984 and defeated San Diego four games to one in the World Series. Pinson was joining a solid club after some tough baseball years with the expansion club in Seattle.

"The wonderful thing about going with Sparky was that I knew I would be with a contending club," he says. "Sparky's record was so good that it was clear you had the talent to win or Sparky would find a way to compete if you didn't win. That's always the best part of baseball, winning or having a chance to win late in the year. With a team like Seattle, it always got a little dull in September. Some of the players were just going through the motions."

Pinson became the batting coach of the Tigers and was a big help to one of the best-hitting teams in the game. He was patient with young players and encouraging with veteran players.

"The best thing about being with Sparky's team is that the environment is so comfortable. Sparky is in complete control of the team and everybody understands that. He sets the rules and you follow them. The players know that if they do their jobs and follow those rules they will get along fine," he says.

Anderson is one of the few veteran managers who believes in old-fashioned discipline. There are no bearded players on the Tigers (though Kirk Gibson came awfully close several times), there are no players out of uniform on the field, there are no players doing their own thing on Sparky's time.

"Baseball is too tough a game to allow everybody going off in their own direction," says Sparky. "There happens to be room for only one captain on this ship. That's me. As long as I am the manager the players will do what I ask. Either that, or this team will get a new manager," he says.

Anderson's triumphs in Cincinnati and Detroit indicate that his methods work, especially if you have a solid pitching staff led by a great pitcher named Jack Morris. Pinson has studied Sparky closely. He knows if the opportunity presents itself he will incorporate much of what he learned at the master's knee in his own managerial style.

"I would like to manage, certainly," says Pinson. "I also recognize that there is a quota system for blacks in managing the way there was when I was playing. The quota right now seems to be one, Frank. He has the Baltimore job but you don't see too many other blacks in baseball's leadership jobs. I don't doubt for a minute that I could be as successful a manager as any of the managers around. I have been in this game a long time and I am certainly as qualified as any other man."

Pinson was sitting in front of his locker in the visitors' clubhouse in Yankee Stadium. He didn't seem much different from when we first met nearly thirty years ago when he was the whippet center fielder of the Cincinnati Reds.

"Sometimes I have to pinch myself to remember that I have been in the game over thirty years," he was saying now. "There have been some rough experiences along the way but I try to push them out of my head. I try to remember the good times, the wonderful friends I made in the game, the clutch base hits I got, the elation I felt at winning."

As he pulls his Tiger uniform shirt on over his head, it is clear time has been very kind to Vada Pinson.

"I was fifty years old a couple of months ago. It's hard for me to believe it. My life is as good as it can be. I have a wonderful new lady I may marry in the future, my kids are all doing fine and my life in the game is very satisfying. I don't know what the future holds. I may stay here with Sparky. I may get a chance to manage. I may move on someplace else. I may decide the wear and tear of the season, the travel, the absences from home are too heavy. I may decide that what I want to do now at this stage of my life is to go into broadcasting."

Pinson paused for a moment and seemed to be remembering games in the distant past, the solid performances he revealed almost every day of his career, the wonderful tandem he was part of with Frank Robinson.

"When the season is over and we are both home in California and I'm visiting at Frank's house we sit there and talk and laugh about the old days and it is all so wonderful. Frank's wife, Barbara, just looks at us and she laughs. 'You two are like a couple of kids,' she once said. I guess that's what makes us all stay in the game. You pull that uniform on, you go out in that fresh air, you hit a fungo or you see a kid you've worked with do well and you feel young again. The game has a hypnotic effect on you. I really can't explain the emotion I feel sometimes when I get to the park. It's just that in some ways this has been my entire life. This is where I feel the most satisfaction, the most joy, the most freedom."

It was time for Vada Pinson to go to work. He had to help some young hitters, build the confidence of some aging ones, carry out some of the chores assigned to him by Sparky Anderson.

"When the game is over," he was saying as he moved to the clubhouse door, "we'll talk some more. You know me a long time. You know how quiet I am. Somehow when it is about baseball, I find my tongue. I never get tired talking about it. I loved playing the game. I love being in the game. I just can't think of a happier way to spend my years. I've forgotten those difficult days. I just like to keep my glass half full."

6 Bill Buhler

RIGHTHAND MAN FOR SANDY AND OREL

■■■■ IT WAS A QUIET SUNDAY AFTERNOON IN THE FAREWELL 1963 Polo Grounds season of the New York Mets. The Los Angeles Dodgers of Sandy Koufax, Maury Wills, Don Drysdale, Tommy Davis, Frank Howard and the rest of the team destined to sweep the Yankees in the World Series were in town for three games against Casey Stengel's struggling team.

Just a few people were in the Dodger clubhouse some three hours before the game. A few of the early risers were playing cards, coach Leo Durocher was fiddling with a lineup card he would later offer manager Walter Alston and trainer Bill Buhler was straightening out his adhesive tapes and headache medicines. After all, this was a Sunday morning in New York and the Dodgers, a team that knew how to play, also knew how to party.

Durocher had been complaining of a heavy cold in these chilly September nights in the East. He had finally decided to do something about it. Shortly after he arrived at the park he received a penicillin shot from Mets team physician Dr. Peter LaMotte. Sometime later he walked to the Dodger clubhouse.

"I heard this gasp and turned around to see Durocher slumping to the floor and losing color," recalls Buhler, as he sits now in the sparkling trainer's room of the visiting Dodgers at Shea Stadium. "I knew I'd better act fast."

While Buhler asked a young batboy to call Dr. LaMotte on the clubhouse phone, Durocher was writhing and flailing his arms.

"I remember him saying over and over again 'I'm going, I'm going,' but he never actually lost consciousness," says Buhler.

The thirty-five-year-old trainer, in his fourth Los Angeles season as head man, pulled on Durocher's tongue so he wouldn't swallow it. He reached for an oxygen mask the club carried on the road for such emergencies and pulled it over Durocher's nose and mouth. He reached into his medical bag and pulled out a syringe. He turned Durocher over on the training table and injected adrenaline into the backside of the fifty-seven-year-old Los Angeles coach.

Durocher's breathing was soon normal, if slightly labored. Dr. LaMotte arrived in the clubhouse. He administered more adrenaline directly into Durocher's veins. The crisis passed.

"If the trainer hadn't acted as swiftly and correctly as he did," LaMotte told the press, "we would have lost Leo."

The allergic reaction Durocher suffered from the penicillin shot was not unusual among the variety of emergencies trainers of baseball teams see. Most of them carry the nickname "Doc." All of them, at one time or another, act in that capacity, especially in clubhouse emergencies, sudden violent accidents or late-night hotel ailments or injuries.

"Our work is mostly routine, taping, a rubdown, bandaging a minor cut," says Buhler. "Every once in a while you get something real serious like Leo's problem. You just have to act fast."

The feisty Durocher, now in his early eighties, never fails to hug Buhler with a hearty "How ya doin', Buddy" when they meet at some old-timers event at Dodger Stadium.

William John Buhler was born in South Bend, Indiana, the home of Notre Dame University, sixty years ago. His father, Dan, was a tool-and-die maker. Buhler was a good student and an outstanding athlete in football and baseball at South Bend High before winning a scholarship to Valparaiso University in Valparaiso, Indiana.

"I was one of the greatest football ends in high school. Notre Dame recruited me but I wanted to go to school away from home," says Buhler. "I was thinking of medicine but I couldn't really consider it seriously. There were no scholarships to medical school. I decided to become an athletic trainer."

Early in 1952 he wrote a letter to several baseball teams. Buzzie Bavasi, the general manager of the Brooklyn Dodgers, responded quickly.

"Buzzie had gone to DePauw University in Greencastle, Indiana, and he knew of the reputation of our school. He invited me to Brooklyn for an interview," says Buhler.

The Dodgers soon hired the tall, handsome, athletic-looking young man from Indiana as their assistant trainer for spring training and the regular trainer for their minor league teams. Buhler was told to report to Vero Beach, Florida, the spring training camp of the Dodgers, on January 26, 1952.

The team he would soon meet was one of the most famous in baseball history. Writer Roger Kahn has immortalized the Brooklyn Dodgers of the early 1950s in his book *The Boys of Summer*. The boys included Jackie Robinson, Duke Snider, Roy Campanella, Pee Wee Reese, all Hall of Famers, Gil Hodges, Carl Erskine, Don Newcombe, Carl Furillo, Billy Cox and Ralph Branca.

It was Branca who, a little more than three months earlier, had been stigmatized forever with an oh-and-one pitch that Bobby Thomson hit into the lower deck of the Polo Grounds for a pennant-winning home run. It became known as the Shot Heard Round the World. While broadcaster Russ Hodges was screaming on radio, "The Giants win the pennant, the

Giants win the pennant, the Giants win the pennant," Thomson was circling the bases saying to himself, "I just beat Brooklyn."

"So heated was the rivalry between us," Thomson once said, "that the only thing my mind could record at that moment was that the home run had helped the Giants beat Brooklyn. Beating Brooklyn was all we ever cared about."

"Gil was from Indiana and he was very friendly to me right off the bat. All the guys were. I became close to Gil and Clem Labine and Sal Maglie and Don Drysdale in later years. I got along with everybody. I got along with Jackie as well as anybody did," Buhler says.

Robinson had come to Brooklyn after an exceptional minor league year with the Montreal Royals in 1946. When he joined the team in 1947 the Brooklyn trainer, Harold "Doc" Wendler, stayed away from him as much as he could. Wendler told friends he was concerned Robinson's black skin might rub off on him.

"Doc was from Ohio and had been an outstanding football player. He studied osteopathic medicine and had a degree. He took a lot of pride in his work. He had moved to Louisiana and I guess he had picked up some different attitudes down there. He was really a fine man. We stayed in touch all the years after his retirement. He just passed away a couple of years ago. The Dodgers always invited him back for old-timers events connected with those Brooklyn teams," Buhler says.

In 1955, the year the Brooklyn Dodgers would win their only World Series ever, Buhler set eyes for the first time on a gregarious, chatty lefthanded pitcher by the name of Tommy Lasorda. Lasorda had been a very successful minor league pitcher at Montreal. He just didn't throw hard enough to impress in his few big league chances. He barely made the ball club that spring and when cutdown day came, the Dodgers just chose to keep a wild first-year lefthander from Brooklyn named Sandy Koufax instead of Lasorda.

"Who the hell would have ever heard of him if it wasn't for me?" Lasorda bellows.

The Dodger manager is sitting in his Shea Stadium office after a game against the Mets. He is dining magnificently on linguine and clam sauce ordered in from his favorite New York Italian restaurant. He is wearing a gray T-shirt reading PLEASE DON'T FEED THE MANAGER and much of the sauce is spilling over onto his ample stomach. The shirt is a gift from Buhler, who is constantly agitating Lasorda about his excess poundage. "I work hard, I eat," says Lasorda. "I don't work hard, I don't eat. So I work hard.

"You ask how the trainers have changed in those years since I broke in," he shouts. "I'll tell you how they changed. When I broke in all they had was a jar of rubbing alcohol to use on you. They would rub the pitchers' arms with half of the jar and drink the other half. Now the trainers have computers with files like the CIA. They know every disease, every injury any player ever had when he comes to this ball club. It used to be nobody ever knew the trainer. Now he's the most important guy on the team with the press. The trainers have more meetings than the United Nations. Buhler gives more press conferences than I do on everything from a hangnail to brain surgery."

Lasorda is off and running now and he is talking about his early days in Brooklyn.

"Jobs were hard to come by and guys didn't get out of the lineup unless they were dead. Especially me. I wanted to pitch in the big leagues. I'd been at Montreal too damn long. I love Montreal but I wanted to pitch in Brooklyn. One day I'm in a game against the Cardinals and Wally Moon is on third base and I throw a wild pitch. I get to the plate and the ball is about to get there from the catcher and I know there is no way this guy is going to score. I got him beat with the throw and I'm going to tag him in the head and that will be the end of that play. Now here comes Moon. He could run and he was a tough guy. We later had him with us in Los

Angeles. I love the guy. I didn't love him then. He comes in to me, I tag him hard and he cuts the hell out of my knee."

Lasorda takes a deep breath and he is whirling again.

"That's the third out and I hobble to the bench and everybody sees the blood oozing out from my uniform. I'm sitting there with my hand over my knee and Pee Wee and Jackie come over and Pee Wee pushes my hand away and the blood is just gushing out of there. Pee Wee says, 'Show that to the trainer inside.' Jackie just looked down and turned right away. He didn't like the sight of blood. I thought he was going to get sick right then and there. Now Doc Wendler is checking it out and everybody on the bench is telling me to go inside and Walter Alston [the Brooklyn manager] is down at the other end of the bench. He doesn't know what the hell is going on. I just told Pee Wee the manager can take me out if he wants, that's his prerogative, but I ain't coming out on my own. If he wants me out of there, he'll have to get me out off the mound. The inning finally ends for the Dodgers and I'm getting up to go out and pitch again. Pee Wee nodded to the other guys on the bench and Newcombe and Russ Meyer grab me and hold my arms. By the time I swing free another pitcher is on his way to the mound and I'm out of there anyway."

Doc Wendler finally got to examine Lasorda in the clubhouse. His uniform was soaked from the knee down with his own blood.

"They bring the team doctor in there and he says the tendons have been completely exposed and if I don't get it treated I might never walk again. By now I'm out of the game," says Lasorda, "so I don't much care. They took me over to some hospital near Ebbets Field, put in a couple of thousand stitches and that was it. I limped for a long time. You didn't expect me to get out of the game on my own. I was trying to make that ball club so I could get a pay raise to seventy-five hundred."

Lasorda is a runaway train when he is on a subject he likes. He likes talking about the role of trainers.

"I'll tell you about trainers. Now Bill here, he's in the big leagues with all this fancy equipment and guys to help him and kids to carry his bag and computers to find out what pills to give a guy if he has a disease. I was managing in Ogden, Utah, in 1966 and I was the trainer, the clubhouse guy, the road secretary, the public relations man, the general manager, every damn thing. My ball players were eighteen, nineteen years old, babies, and I had to diaper them. This one kid comes into the clubhouse and tells me he hurt his leg. I tell him, 'So what.' He says in college when he hurt his leg the trainers always put it in the whirlpool for half an hour. Now I'm really upset because he's giving me that college ball crap. I don't want to hear that. I want him to run into a wall for me to catch a ball. So I tell him we don't have a whirlpool. When he gets to the big leagues maybe we'll have a whirlpool for him. I told him to go in the back of the clubhouse, stick his leg in the toilet and flush it. That's our whirlpool."

Lasorda was asked if he could think of any other differences in the methods of trainers in his playing days and today.

"Yeah," he bellows. "When I played they would only rub the arms of the stars. I never had my arm rubbed. Maybe that's why I wasn't a great big league pitcher. That might have turned my entire career. No, they couldn't rub my arm, they had to waste time on guys named Koufax and Drysdale."

Buhler is listening to Lasorda's act while he prepares to treat the Dodgers of today. He says that pitchers' arms are cared for much the same today as they were when he broke into the big leagues in the 1950s.

"Koufax was probably the first to use ice to reduce swelling in his arm. Most pitchers just get a good rubdown before a game, a little liniment and some rest in the trainer's room," Buhler says.

In all the years he has been in the game, he says, he has seen only two pitchers have their careers ended prematurely by serious arm injuries.

"Carl Spooner came up, pitched a couple of shutouts and then had a serious arm injury. It was probably a rotator cuff injury but the doctors didn't know about those things in those days. No matter what the injury was, if the pitcher couldn't pitch he had a sore arm. That was all there was to it," he says.

A strong, hard thrower by the name of Jack Banta also had his career cut short by an arm problem.

"His was a little different. He tore something in his elbow. Today he might have surgery and be pitching again. In those days they just released you if you couldn't pitch," he says.

Buhler says that in all his years with the Dodgers he can remember only two injuries that he considered so serious that he thought the player could not possibly recover and continue his career. Both did.

"I remember when Tommy Davis fractured his ankle against the Giants in 1965. He was sliding into second base. When he hit the bag his spikes caught and his ankle twisted and you could hear that loud crack all over the ball park. He was in terrible pain when we carried him off the field," Buhler says.

Davis, the 1962 and 1963 batting champion, was out of the lineup until late September. He recovered well enough to play eleven more seasons in the big leagues but he never again had the devastating speed he once possessed.

The other accident that Buhler recalls vividly was the injury to pitcher Tommy John's left elbow in 1974. It forced him to miss the rest of that season and all of the 1975 season before he could return in 1976 with a reconstructed elbow. John became known as baseball's "bionic man," since the elbow was completely reconstructed with some of the tissue taken from his hip and placed on his elbow.

John was still pitching effectively for the Yankees in 1988 at the age of forty-five.

"Most of my body is that age but my arm is only thirteen years old. Maybe I should have a bar mitzvah for my elbow," he laughs.

"I was sitting on the bench and just saw Tommy howl in pain," Buhler says. "Red Adams [Dodger coach] claimed that he actually saw the elbow snap and bounce back and forth like it was held on by a rubber band. I don't know if that actually happened but it was a very severe fracture. I wouldn't have imagined that Tommy could ever pitch again, let alone pitch as long as he has."

Most of what transpires in a big league trainer's room is routine. There are the headache pills to dispense after a long Saturday night or the routine tapings or the rubbing of sore muscles or the healing of slight wounds. More important, players enjoy the fraternity of the trainer's room, free of the press, free of the snooping eyes and ears of the manager and coaches, and knowing the trainer is an adherent of the much-abused baseball motto, "What you hear here, stays here."

The Dodgers, in particular, have long had a tradition of openness in their locker room. They are generally more candid and trusting of the press than other teams, especially teams such as the Yankees with a long tradition of clubhouse secrecy and intrigue.

Captains of each team seem to have set the tone generations ago. Old sportswriters claim Lou Gehrig, a very laconic personality, often spent quiet time in the trainer's room at Yankee Stadium in the 1930s. It immediately became off limits to the press, very few of whom actually ventured into the team locker room anyway. That refuge was later used by Joe DiMaggio, Mickey Mantle and Roger Maris before present-generation Yankees escaped media hordes by hiding there whether or not any treatment was needed. Most of the treatment was for their psyches.

The Dodgers, in contrast, had small trainer quarters in Ebbets Field. With Pee Wee Reese as their gregarious captain, sportswriters could watch the trainers work and could interview and argue with players in that private area. It became one of the favorite courts of law for Jackie Robinson in his talkative Dodger days.

Only in recent years, when the mass media overflowed in baseball clubhouses, did the Dodgers finally impose the same rules on the press. The trainer's room was off limits to a l but players. Lots of good stories were lost and lots of com nunication between players and press was ended.

The Dodger clubhouse that Buhler first walked into in spring training was open, friendly and filled with talented players and incredible personalities. One of the reasons that the Dodgers of the 1950s have lasted in baseball lore has to be the chemistry of those personalities.

"They were a very exceptional group of men. I got along with all of them. I see most of them regularly when they return for old-timer games and it is as if we had never parted," Buhler says.

The tall, handsome Hoosier, his hair turned white now at the age of sixty but still standing straight and trim, recalls with much affection the days in Brooklyn. He even has an extra-special reason.

"I used to be in the office often at 215 Montague Street with reports on our players. I would join the Dodgers late in the season each year to help Doc Wendler out and then return the following season to the minor leagues. My direct boss was Fresco Thompson, who had the responsibility for the Dodger minor league teams. He had a very pretty secretary. I met Barbara in Fresco's office. We were married about a year later," he says.

Bill and Barbara Buhler have raised four children and now make their home in the Long Beach, California, area about twenty-eight miles from Dodger Stadium.

"Don Drysdale lived out that way when he was playing and we used to drive in together. Now I drive in with Mark Cresse, the bullpen coach. Sometimes he takes his own car because I usually have to stay a lot later than the coaches and players do," he says.

Cresse, a husky former minor league catcher, has been in the Dodger organization for fourteen years. He pitches batting practice, catches batting practice, works in the bullpen during games and serves as the butt of many of Lasorda's jokes. He has known Buhler ever since he joined the team under manager Walter Alston.

"Everybody calls him Doctor Bill and everybody on this team really respects him," says Cresse. "You never hear any of the players ever kid him about getting older or being around the Dodgers in those old days with Jackie and Pee Wee and Sandy and those guys. He is a very modern, up-to-date guy. I think the players can't kid him because they wish they looked like him. He is probably in the best shape of anybody around here. I wish I looked like him. I used to ride with him more than I do now. I drive him from the airport when we get in on long trips. It's a little too much for his wife to come out for him at those late hours."

The Dodger coach said that he has learned little from Buhler about the old Dodger days, about Ebbets Field, about Jackie or Pee Wee or any of the other legendary Dodger names of summers past.

"Doctor Bill is a very modern man. He talks about today's games and today's players. I can't really remember him ever talking about those old guys. Maybe once he mentioned Carl Erskine, who was one of his favorites," Cresse says.

Former Dodger shortstop Bill Russell, now a coach on the team, says that one of Buhler's strengths is that he has clearly adjusted to the new times and new attitudes of players.

"He goes with the flow," says Russell. "If times were different when he broke in and players had different needs in the trainer's room and different attitudes, Buhler doesn't fight them on it. The trainer's room is a place for guys to relax and get ready for the game. Bill makes it as easy as possible in there."

Buhler says he hardly ever thinks about how long he has been around the Dodger organization. Each day is an adventure. Each player who arrives is somebody new to help and each change in the organization is just another example of the never-ending progress in baseball.

"I'll tell you one situation that did bring home how long I was around," he says. "When I first reported to Vero Beach we had this guy who used to drive the bus all over Florida with us. He had this little son who came with us on most of the trips. He probably was no more than five or six years old when he started out with us. He was everybody's favorite kid. Gil Hodges took a special liking to him and really spent time with him, talking to him on the bus, having a catch with him in the ball park, really paying attention to him. Then the years go by and he shows up as one of our best players. It was Steve Garvey."

Garvey first joined the Dodgers in 1969. Many of the players he had been with as a small boy were still around.

"Steve was a fine young man. He was very respectful. He was a pleasure to know," says Buhler.

Buhler put in only one full year in Brooklyn with the Dodgers. It was in 1957, the final season at Ebbets Field before the team moved west to Los Angeles and the eventual gold mine at Chavez Ravine, home of Dodger Stadium.

"We had an apartment in the Prospect Park area near Ebbets Field. They were almost all day games in those days and I would be in the ball park at ten o'clock in the morning and I would usually be home for dinner by six. It was a very nice life. I would ride the subway a couple of stops and then I would walk a block or two to Ebbets Field. The Dodger fans were all very friendly and there was a wonderful feeling around the ball park. The Dodgers were really important in Brooklyn. It seemed as if there wasn't much else of interest there except the Dodgers. It was a wonderful family atmosphere and all the players were very close," he says.

The move to California at the end of the 1957 season was very traumatic for most of the players.

"No matter where they came from, and some of them were from California, it was very upsetting. They had established homes in Brooklyn, loved Ebbets Field, felt comfortable there and really hated to move. That's why 1958 was such a difficult year," he says.

By 1959 the Dodgers had made the adjustment to California and had another contending ball club. They were in another terrific pennant race with the Milwaukee Braves. That was the team of Hank Aaron, Eddie Mathews, Warren Spahn, all Hall of Famers, and Bob Buhl, Johnny Logan, Lew Burdette and Joe Adcock.

The Dodgers and Braves tied for the pennant. Then came the playoff. The Dodgers won the first game 3–2. They fell behind in the second game, rallying to win the pennant in a 6–5 victory when the Braves failed to turn a double play.

"That was the most exciting victory I can ever remember," Buhler says.

After the 1959 season Doc Wendler retired and Buhler was named the head trainer of the Dodgers.

"When I got that job I was thrilled. There was nothing else I wanted to do with my life. That was the best job I could have and I wanted to keep it as long as possible," he says.

The Dodgers tied again for the pennant in 1962. This time they blew a lead and lost the pennant to the Giants when relief pitcher Stan Williams walked the winning run home.

After that game the Dodgers were a very unhappy team. The clubhouse door was closed to the press. While reporters, on deadline, banged on the door, the Dodgers remained hidden inside. Finally, Duke Snider, the only player still remaining from the 1951 playoff loss to the Giants, emerged in the runway.

"I remember after we lost in 1951 and I went home and my wife, Bev, was trying to console me and finally she said, 'Well, at least you'll never have to go through this again.' I wonder what she will say now," Snider said.

When the clubhouse door finally opened and smashed champagne bottles were spotted on the floor, the only quiet place seemed to be the trainer's room. Buhler was at his accustomed spot ministering to the sore arms and broken hearts of the Dodgers.

There were many joyful years after that. The Dodgers won in 1963, 1965 and 1966 and won again in 1974, 1977, 1978, and 1981 before their last title in 1988.

"I must admit that I certainly did look forward to those championships. I think I got to counting on my World Series shares as a big part of my salary," says Buhler.

The Dodgers have traditionally been a generous organization. While Buhler's salary range is comparable to that of most other experienced big league trainers (somewhere near fifty thousand dollars), he picks up extra money by lecturing at clinics and at schools and by addressing organizations devoted to sports medicine and physical training methods for athletes. Few trainers have the standing Buhler does with his peers.

Perhaps the most challenging aspect of Buhler's career came after a serious injury to catcher Steve Yeager in 1977. Yeager was on deck as the next hitter while shortstop Bill Russell was at bat. Russell fouled off a pitch and cracked his bat. One half of the bat stayed in his hands and the other half went spinning madly toward Yeager. In a shocking accident that silenced observers at Dodger Stadium, the jagged end of the splintered bat stuck in Yeager's throat, just above the Adam's apple.

Buhler reacted immediately. He was able to remove the bat and covered Yeager's neck with clean towels. The huge gash had to be surgically repaired later before the catcher could return to action several weeks later.

"There were several problems. The neck was still tender and we had to protect it if he was to play," Buhler says. "We tried a few different devices and finally I decided to cut a piece of leather from an old shin guard and hang it from the bottom of the catcher's mask. This gave Steve protection but it didn't hamper his breathing or his vision, something that was certainly vital to a catcher during the game."

Many catchers later adopted similar devices in various shapes to protect themselves from the foul balls that come back violently under their masks. Some catchers wear a mask with a device—of hard leather or plastic, or in some cases a steel rim covered by a softer surface—actually built onto the edge of the mask.

"The most important thing for us was that it helped get Yeager back in the lineup and he helped us win another pennant," says Buhler.

Lasorda is fond of saying that he bleeds Dodger blue. He has been with the Brooklyn or Los Angeles Dodgers organization since he joined the team in 1948 after he was drafted by the Dodger organization from the Phillies. Lasorda was still training with the Dodger farm club in Montreal in 1952 when Buhler first reported to spring training.

"I like to think I've been bleeding Dodger blue even before Tommy," says Buhler.

There are few individuals more respected, more admired, more trusted around the Dodgers than Doctor Bill. From the bombastic Lasorda to the quietest rookie, only kind words express the feelings Dodger people have for Buhler.

"This organization really is family," he says. "I couldn't imagine ever doing anything else. I'll keep this job as long as they let me. I don't see any reason to leave."

The hours are long, the travel is difficult, the pay is certainly not what Buhler could have earned had he had the finances for medical school.

"I have absolutely no regrets. I have loved every second of it. I love baseball and I feel as if I have contributed to the game and our team in some small ways. If I have helped our players that is satisfaction enough," he says.

After working every single day from the middle of January when the Dodgers assemble voluntarily for a little jump on spring training through the final day of the World Series, if the Dodgers make it, Buhler works only three days a week in the off-season.

"That gives me more time to read, to walk, to play a little tennis, to visit more with my family. Then after Christmas I start thinking about preparing the weight charts and working on the spring schedules. It just energizes me every season and keeps me young. I love the game and I love all the people in it," he says.

William John Buhler is no less enthusiastic, no less excited about coming to work, no less dedicated to his players than he was as a kid out of Indiana almost four decades ago.

"If I could have afforded it and had gone to medical school I probably would have enjoyed being a doctor back in Indiana," he says. "I don't think I would have had as much fun, met as many interesting people and enjoyed my life as much as I do in baseball."

At an age when many people are planning their retirement years and imagining that home in the sun, Buhler is preparing for another season as the trainer of the Los Angeles Dodgers.

"I couldn't imagine this team without him," says Lasorda.

The Los Angeles Dodger trainer couldn't imagine that, either.

7 Bob Sheppard

BASEBALL'S
SWEETEST SOUND

▬▬ IT IS CLEARLY THE MOST IMITATED VOICE IN BASEBALL. Hardly a day goes by in a baseball season that some fan does not cup his hands around his mouth, clear his throat and bellow in his best voice, "Good afternoon, ladies and gentlemen, and welcome to Yankee Stadium." Baltimore broadcaster Jon Miller has made an art form of doing the resonant sounds of the Yankee public address announcer at banquets and dinners for a good many years. "I can do a pretty good imitation," says Miller, "but only Bob Sheppard does Bob Sheppard."

For thirty-eight years that voice has introduced Mickey Mantle and Reggie Jackson, Don Mattingly and Dave Winfield, Joe DiMaggio and Joe Pepitone, Whitey Ford and Ron Guidry. It has been heard by millions of people attending games in the House That Ruth Built in the Bronx and by many millions more over national television.

"Without Bob Sheppard it wouldn't be Yankee Stadium," says Yankee owner George Steinbrenner.

Sheppard remembers one day it wasn't Yankee Stadium. He made it sound as if it were.

"I'm still hoping Sonny Werblin forgives me," says Sheppard.

It all began with the opening of the new sports complex in the Meadowlands of New Jersey. The football Giants—Sheppard does their public address announcing also—had wandered from the old Polo Grounds in Manhattan to Yankee Stadium, on to the Yale Bowl in New Haven and finally to their own sparkling football stadium across the Hudson River in New Jersey. The memorable date was October 10, 1976, and the huge letters GIANTS greeted fans as they drove into the Meadowlands parking lot.

"The Yankees were in their first playoff that year against the Kansas City Royals," remembers Sheppard. "They were playing in Kansas City and I watched part of the game on television before driving over to the Meadowlands for the late afternoon game."

Werblin, the dynamo promoter who brought Joe Namath to New York with the football Jets, had pulled off an almost impossible dream. He had chaired a public authority that pushed through a massive bond issue to fund the building of the magnificent facilities in the Meadowlands. The land once used as pig farms in the New Jersey swamps was now the home of the Giants and one of the most marvelous sports centers in the country.

A former agent and representative of famous singers and actors, Werblin bought the struggling American Football League club from former broadcaster Harry Wismer. The Titans of the AFL were gone and a sparkling new team, soon to occupy Shea Stadium with the Mets, was created in its stead. Werblin's New York Jets team won the third Super Bowl behind the brazen leadership of Namath, the drawling Pennsylvanian who had been educated in football and life by Bear Bryant at the University of Alabama. The Jets broke the hold of the established NFL and a merger soon followed.

When Werblin became engaged in a dispute with his partners on the Jets, he sold out his shares. He was soon knee deep in the task of bringing big league sports to New Jersey.

The opening of the Meadowlands Complex on that October 10, 1976, was the culmination of a glorious dream.

Sheppard was at the microphone for the first time in the Meadowlands. The capacity crowd on hand for the game against the Dallas Cowboys was roaring with anticipation as the teams waited in the tunnel off the field for their introductions.

"Good afternoon, ladies and gentlemen," intoned Sheppard with the ever-so-popular melodious sound that had become so much a part of the New York sports scene, "and welcome to Yankee Stadium."

The murmur began in the section nearest the press box and ran quickly through the stadium. The unthinkable had happened. Bob Sheppard had made a mistake. It was clearly an imperfect world.

"Once it was out of my mouth," says Sheppard, "I knew there wasn't much I could do about it. I corrected myself quickly and began with the lineups. Every time I see Sonny Werblin now I continue to ask him if he will ever forgive me."

Werblin, a promoter at heart, understood that the slip was the best thing that could have happened to his new sports complex.

"There were a lot of people who might not have heard of the Meadowlands who did because Bob Sheppard made a mistake that day. I know it wasn't intentional but it turned out to be a very successful event for us," he says.

The slip of the master's tongue may have been just the promotable gimmick Werblin would have called for had he thought of it.

"It was like signing Joe Namath for $400,000, real big money in those days," he says. "A lot of players were getting $300,000 and $350,000. For a little more money you get about a million bucks worth of publicity."

"I wasn't embarrassed about it," says Sheppard. "It sort of became a joke between Sonny and myself over the years."

Even though Sheppard has done Giants games almost as long as he has done Yankee games, his national identification is with the baseball team.

"When I hear people imitating me it is almost always announcing the starting lineup at a baseball game," he says.

What makes Sheppard the best at his profession is part nature and part hard work. His deep, melodious, resonant voice is a gift of nature. His use of language and especially his pronunciation of names is the result of very hard work.

"I never go into a game without knowing exactly how the player wants his name pronounced," he says. "If I have any doubt at all, I ask. I might start with the team broadcasters and the public relations man. Sometimes they have their own pronunciation. They often admit they aren't sure how the player wants it. In that case I go up to the player and ask."

There was a young shortstop on the Baltimore Orioles breaking in with Hank Bauer's team in 1965. He would last almost two decades and be regarded as the finest-fielding shortstop of his time. Sheppard wanted to get the name correct.

"I saw the name and knew it could have several variables," he says. "I went up to him and asked how he wanted me to pronounce it. He said, 'I don't care. Any way you like is fine with me.' I pressed him to say it aloud and he still said there were so many different ways he got used to all of them."

Sheppard went back to the public address announcer's booth and soon was introducing the rookie shortstop to the Yankee Stadium crowd.

"Batting eighth for Baltimore," he said, "number 1, Mark Belanger."

"I have heard it pronounced Bell-an-jay, the French way, and Bell-an-jare and a lot of other combinations," Sheppard says. "In Yankee Stadium it has always been the simplest way, Be-langer, accent on the second syllable."

Public address announcers go back in baseball almost as far as the game does. Before there were printed scorecards there were representatives of the team advising the fans as to the names of the players. They used large cone-shaped megaphones to call attention to the game. The early public address announcers became vital links between the team and the town. Their pronunciation was gospel. Players would often change the pronunciation of their own names to fit the sounds of the announcer. Once he called their names a certain way, they were identified that way.

Two of the more famous public address announcers were Tex Rickerd in Brooklyn's Ebbets Field for more than four decades and Chicago Cubs public address announcer Pat Piper, who lasted more than fifty years at Wrigley Field.

Each had his own style. Rickerd gained attention with his brusque manner of delivering the lineup. He also had some trouble with his grammar as evidenced by one of his most famous faux pas. A fan had placed his suit jacket over the railing of the center field bleachers in Ebbets Field. The umpires had spotted the jacket and motioned to Rickerd in the press box area to make an announcement. "Will the fan in center field take his clothes off." The Brooklyn crowd laughed at the call. Rickerd, unsure of what they were laughing at, immediately added, "Do it now."

In Chicago Pat Piper was as much an institution around the ball park as the ivy on the walls. He would begin his work each afternoon by bellowing, ". . . 'tention, . . . 'tention please, get your pencil ready, here are the lineups." Piper, a waiter in a local Northside restaurant in Chicago, would walk over to the ball park from his job. He would take off his tuxedo jacket, put on a Cubs sweater and baseball cap and go to work.

Sheppard, a tall, graceful, eloquent and elegant man with trimmed white hair and a military bearing, delivers his announcements with the same flavor Sinatra delivers the best lyrics. Each word rings carefully through the sound system. No name is slurred. No announcement is more important than any other. Sheppard's voice is one of the most lyrical musical instruments of baseball.

"I came from an educated family and the sound of words was always important in my house," he says. "My father, Charles, and my mother, Eileen, each enjoyed poetry and music and public speaking. They were very precise in how they spoke. They measured words, pronounced everything carefully and instilled a love of language in me by how they respected proper pronunciation."

Born in the Richmond Hill section of Queens, Sheppard was an exceptional athlete in high school at Richmond Hill, starring on the baseball and football teams all four years. He entered St. John's University and majored in language and speech.

"I was playing a little semiprofessional football in Long Island while I was at St. John's. One day there was a charity game in Freeport, Long Island, between the New York Yankees and the Chicago Rockets of the old All America Football Conference. That was a pro team that lasted a few years after World War II, and I was asked to help out on the sidelines. Their star was a triple threat back named Spec Sanders. He could do everything. Actually they didn't have much more than Sanders so they never won many games," he says.

One of the executives of the Yankees knew Sheppard and came up to him before the game began. He said they needed somebody to do the public address announcing for the game.

"I had never done anything like that but I agreed to try. I was always interested in language and speech and actually was aiming at a career as a speech teacher," he says.

Sheppard hiked up to the top of the stands, was given the lineups for the two teams and improvised the rest.

"Nobody told me what to do. I just had the lineups and I welcomed the crowd, such as it was, and began reading out the lineups. I found that I could make myself clearly understood and I enjoyed my contribution to the game. I was very careful about all the names," he says.

Sheppard got through his first game without incident. A few days later he received a call from an executive with the rival Brooklyn Dodgers team in the same league.

"I had been an athlete and a sports fan so I knew all about the Brooklyn Dodgers baseball team and even a little about the football team. They had some famous players, Ace Parker, Pug Manders, a few other names I recognized. I took the subway the next day out to their offices at 215 Montague Street in Brooklyn. We discussed the job for a while and finally this official said he would like to hire me. He asked me how much I wanted. I can't remember what I said but in those days I doubt if I got more than ten or fifteen dollars a game. It was just fun to be part of the game," he says.

After Sheppard had worked for the Dodgers for a couple of seasons, the job ended as the club folded. Before he could concern himself with the end of his short-lived career, Sheppard was back with the football Yankees.

"The league was reorganizing and the Yankees were in the new setup. One day I got a call and I was asked to come to the Stadium. I traveled up there and there wasn't much of a discussion," he says. "They had heard me in that charity game and they had heard me over in Brooklyn. They knew I could do the job and I was hired by the football team."

Sheppard did Yankee football for two more seasons before he was hired by Yankee general manager George Weiss to handle the microphone at Yankee Stadium. It was the spring of 1951.

"That was a rather significant season in Yankee history," he says. "Joe DiMaggio was going out and Mickey Mantle was coming in. Mickey and I were rookies together in that season. I always loved calling Joe's name. It had such a wonderful sound. I still enjoy it even now when he comes back for old-timers day and I get to call his name again for the crowd. It has to be one of the famous names in baseball history."

As a man of great pride and accuracy, Sheppard strives hard to get his names pronounced correctly with just the proper flavor. He is especially careful about Latin names, especially since New York has a large Latin population and any mispronunciation of a Latin name could cause a fuss.

"The Chicago White Sox had a pitcher by the name of Francisco Barrios a few years back. I just loved the sound of his name. It seemed so musical, so lilting. I just wanted to make sure of its proper sound. There was an old radio broadcaster and newspaperman in New York named Buck Canel. He's gone now but he was my resident expert on the proper pronunciation of Latin names," says Sheppard.

Canel was a man of part Latin, part French and part American heritage. He was a fine sportswriter and broadcaster and was a major figure in Latin American sports circles.

"Fidel Castro stopped a speech one time to call out my name in a crowd and say, 'Hello, Buck,' " Canel once said.

Castro had played college baseball in Havana. Canel knew the young revolutionary when he was pitching for his college team.

"No curveball," said Canel.

While the careers of Canel and Castro took divergent paths, they would meet occasionally at some major Latin American sports event. Canel would soon become the most prominent voice in Latin sports broadcasting. Castro was a faithful listener. Canel became famous in Latin America for broadcasting the American World Series to most countries south of the border. He once estimated that he had in excess of two hundred million listeners for World Series games.

"He was certainly a reputable source and I leaned on him often. He was a good friend," says Sheppard.

Sheppard was always confident of his calls. Few names, even foreign ones, actually threw him. He did have one name that caused him some concern.

"There was an infielder back in the 1950s named Wayne Terwilliger. For some reason that name concerned me. It seemed like a name that would be easy to swallow if I didn't pronounce it carefully. I always did it extra slowly to be right. He is now a coach with Minnesota and when I announce the coaches I am still extra careful on Wayne Terwilliger," he says.

As he approaches his fifth decade as a Yankee broad-caster, Sheppard's routine has changed little. He spends the mornings during the college year at his teaching position at St. John's University where he is an adjunct professor of speech. Then he drives to Yankee Stadium for the night baseball game. He arranges his college schedule in such a way that his absences through the years have been negligible.

"I'm sure the students are aware of what I do in the evenings," Sheppard says, "but in all the years I have been with the Yankees nobody has ever mentioned it. I don't discuss anything in class but the schoolwork and I don't discuss the St. John's curriculum at Yankee Stadium."

He arrives early at the Yankee Stadium press room, checks the printed lineup on the board, confirms difficult pronunciations of visiting players' names with other broadcasters or club officials and dines quietly with sportswriters and team executives. He is a learned man of a variety of tastes and may often be discussing the latest book, a fine piece of music, an article he read in a scholarly journal or a sports event with dinner companions. He almost always eats with organist Eddie Layton and is joined by various members of the press. Bus Saidt of the Trenton *Times* finds Sheppard one of the most interesting of dining companions.

"Both Bob and I are very interested in music," Saidt says. "We often discuss the latest performance of some group we have enjoyed, especially jazz groups."

Sheppard will ride the elevator to his mezzanine-level booth next to the press box about an hour before the game. He will go over the lineups again, check that he has all the uniform numbers up to date and prepare for the game. He will almost always be carrying a new book with him. He spends most of the time before the game and in between innings with his head buried in a book.

He is out of the ball park with the final out and on his way to his Queens home. He and his lovely wife, Mary, have four grown children. One of his daughters is a Catholic nun who works with retarded children.

"The best part of the job is the time off it allows me. Mary and I love to travel and when the team is on the road we often take long, relaxing trips to various spots," he says.

In the late 1970s he was taking a driving trip through New England. The Yankees happened to be playing in Boston and he had never seen Fenway Park. Bob and Mary Sheppard decided to drive to Fenway and catch a game in the historic ball park. They were sitting in the stands when the publicity man of the Boston Red Sox, Dick Bresciani, spotted him along the aisle. Bresciani asked Sheppard if he was traveling with the Yankees.

"No, we are just here on a vacation. We wanted to see Fenway Park," he said.

Bresciani insisted that Bob and Mary join him in the private dining room upstairs on the press level for a visit with Boston executives and a chance to visit with the local press. Sheppard agreed after much coaxing.

"After we got upstairs and the game began, Bresciani asked me if I would do him a huge favor and come into the press box and say hello to Sherm Feller, their public address announcer. I didn't want to bother him but Dick insisted it would be exciting for Sherm. I agreed," he says.

Sheppard walked through the press box as the Yankees came to bat. Feller shook hands warmly with Sheppard and then announced the next Yankee hitter.

"Suddenly he turned to me and said he would really like it if I would do a half inning for the fans in Fenway. I didn't want to do it but Dick and Sherm were very persuasive. I moved to the microphone," he says.

As fate would have it the next Yankee hitter was Reggie Jackson. The Yankee slugger was aware of everything and everybody in a ball park. There were suspicions he was on a first-name basis with every fan in every park in America. He certainly was on a first-name basis with every public address announcer in America. There were few things Jackson enjoyed at a ball park more than the sound of his own name.

No one had ever rolled it on the tongue as smoothly as Sheppard had.

"I went to the microphone as Reggie stepped toward the plate. I gave it my regular Yankee Stadium announcement. 'Number 44, right fielder Reggie Jackson, number 44.' The fans began looking up toward the press level. Jackson stepped out of the box, put the bat down and began searching the park for that familiar voice. I think he was very shocked," says Sheppard.

"That's about as familiar a voice as there is in baseball," says Jackson. "I was really surprised when I heard it. It threw me off. You get used to all the public address announcers in all the parks after a while. When I heard Bob's voice and looked out at Fenway Park it just didn't fit. I finally was able to look up there and see that familiar white hair so I knew Bob was visiting at Fenway. I could go back into the batter's box and concentrate on hitting."

Sheppard's voice is so distinctive that it is shocking on those rare occasions when he is absent at the Stadium or even more shocking when it appears over the microphones in a strange ball park.

"The only other time I ever did any announcing in baseball outside the Stadium was some years back in Anaheim. It was similar to the Fenway situation. Mary and I had gone on a trip west and took in a game in Anaheim Stadium. Red Paterson was the California Angels publicity director and we knew him from his days with the Yankees. We went over to say hello and he asked if we could announce the lineups of both teams before the game. I didn't really want to do it but he thought it would be a pleasant surprise for his fans. We agreed to do it. I was calling out the names and got to Roy White, who was always one of my favorite players. He heard the difference immediately and waved to the press box," Sheppard says.

After all these years on the job, Sheppard's presence is a significant part of the aura around the Stadium. He takes his job seriously and he also appreciates his small place in Yankee history.

"It has been thrilling to be a part of the World Series games and the pennant races and all the dramatic events at the Stadium. I especially enjoy the old-timers game and calling out the names of the former greats. I just enjoy baseball so much and I enjoy being around the ball park," he says.

This tall, distinguished gentleman represents the Yankees in his own way. He is the Joe DiMaggio of public address announcers, a classy, stylish man who seems a throwback to an era when baseball around the Stadium had a more sophisticated tone.

"If I have any complaint about baseball today," he says, "it is simply that so many teams seem to have given in to the coarseness around the park. Even the public address announcers seem to be catering to that fashion with outrageous conduct. There is an entirely new generation of people in the public address booths. I believe many of them are screamers and shouters and tend to agitate the crowds rather than inform them. My idea has always been to supply the information about the next hitter, the next pitcher, the pinch runner in the most careful, controlled way one can offer. Now it all seems to be done with the most noise and least appreciation of language and pronunciation that can be mustered."

If a day at the ball park is a complete experience that includes the game, the hot dogs, the parking, the weather, the comfort of the seats and the random choice of fans next to you and their conduct, the sound of Bob Sheppard's voice calling out the starting lineups for both teams clearly adds a measure of satisfaction.

"I don't look at what I do as a job. It is a joy. It gets me out to the ball park every day. It gives me a chance to associate with people in baseball, swap stories, share experiences, enjoy the fraternalism. I was blessed with a good voice and I have worked hard to perfect it. I am very happy that I have been able to put these talents to such good use," he says.

Sheppard is clearly a distinguished gentleman who appreciates his contributions to baseball. Like DiMaggio and other great players, he knows that each day he must give his best.

"It is very important that I get the names correct and announce them in such a way as to give the fans a chance to get them down and keep the game in order," he says. "I feel that it is a responsibility that I take very seriously."

If Joseph Paul DiMaggio, Jr., was born to play center field for the New York Yankees, Robert Leo Sheppard was born to be the public address announcer for the team. The Yankees have been the most successful, the most famous, the most admired team in baseball history. Sheppard is clearly the class act of bringing the names of those players to the fans in the stands. It could hardly be a real baseball game at Yankee Stadium if it didn't become official with the rich sounds of Bob Sheppard's voice calling out clearly, "Good evening, ladies and gentlemen, and welcome to Yankee Stadium. Here are the lineups."

Even if once in a while the Meadowlands becomes the Stadium, it is worth it. Bob Sheppard is a pleasureful earful.

8 Eddie Lopat

THE YANKEE FROM MANHATTAN

■ ONLY A DOZEN OF THEM WEAR THE MAGNIFICENT DIA-
mond ring with the huge number 5 in the center. Their
names are Yogi Berra, Joe Collins, Johnny Mize, Phil Rizzuto,
Gene Woodling, Hank Bauer, Charlie Silvera, Bobby Brown,
Jerry Coleman and Reynolds-Raschi-Lopat.

The names of the last three—Allie Reynolds, a burly
hard-throwing part Indian righthanded pitcher; Vic Raschi,
known as the Springfield Rifle; and Ed Lopat, nicknamed
Steady Eddie and the Junk Man, a crafty lefthander from the
West Side of Manhattan—are linked in baseball lore almost
as one pitcher, certainly the heart of one staff.

It was these three pitchers and the nine others who alone
played on all five of Casey Stengel's World Championship
teams from 1949 through 1953, the most successful winning
teams in baseball history. The Yankees of 1936 through 1939
won four titles in a row and the Oakland A's of Charles O.
Finley won three in a row from 1972 through 1974, but only
Stengel's Yankees could record five straight world titles.

These three pitchers, known as The Big Three to sports
fans in that era, accounted for 167 victories and lost only 80
games in the first three seasons of that span. They were clearly
the dominant pitchers on baseball's most dominant team.

They were led by Stengel, who died in 1975 at the age of eighty-five, and Jim Turner, the pitching coach, who turned eighty-five in August of 1988. He lives in Nashville, Tennessee.

"I got a call from Jim a few weeks ago," Eddie Lopat, now a Yankee special assignment scout, was saying in the press room at Shea Stadium. "He said that he wanted to have one last reunion with us. He said he would pick up all the expenses and we should come down and party with him. He told me he has all the money he needs now and he just wants us all to be together, probably for the last time."

Turner recognized his mortality at the age of eighty-five. Lopat is spry at seventy. Reynolds was seventy-three early in 1988 and has been diminished by age and illness. Raschi, the youngest of the three pitchers, turned sixty-nine early in 1988.

"A week or so later I got a letter from Jim. He said we had made him rich, did so much for him, made him famous, changed his life. He was so looking forward to having us all together," Lopat says.

On October 14, 1988, two weeks before the scheduled reunion, Vic Raschi died of a heart attack at his home in Groveland, New York, in a rural area near Lake Conesus. He was the first of the members of that five straight titles team to pass away.

"Vic had been sick for quite some time. The last time I saw him I could see that he was slowing down. It was very sad for all of us but I felt especially bad for Jim. He wanted us together that one last time," Lopat says.

But now even the death of Raschi could not end the link. Yankee history will forever record the efficiency, courage, toughness and success of those three pitchers in dozens of games through those years.

"There was an incredible bond between us," says Lopat. "We were competitive, for sure, but we each pulled very hard for the others. I don't think we had the greatest talent ever assembled on any baseball team. I do think we used our talent and played together better than anybody else. Winning five in a row is an overwhelming accomplishment. I can't see that ever happening again."

When Lopat says anything about baseball, people tend to listen. The man has been in the game over fifty years as a pitcher, minor league manager, big league manager, general manager, scout, pitching coach and now special assignment scout for the Yankees.

"I grew up as a kid in Manhattan rooting for Babe Ruth and Lou Gehrig and all the other Yankees. Playing baseball, being in the game, being part of it is all I ever wanted," he says. "I never did anything else in my life. I never wanted to do anything else. If somebody is fortunate enough to play baseball and then make a living at it afterward, I couldn't imagine him going anywhere else. You hear of guys being fired. You don't often hear of a guy quitting the game."

Born Edmund Walter Lopatynski, the future Yankee left-hander was the son of a shoemaker who had his small repair shop near Ninety-eighth Street and Madison Avenue in Manhattan. He was one of seven children.

"I was always crazy about baseball and followed the Yankees in the late 1920s and early 1930s," says Lopat. "I was a first baseman and a pitcher at De Witt Clinton High School and began thinking seriously about a professional career when some scouts asked me to attend a tryout."

Lopat boarded the subway train one day late in the summer of 1936 from his Manhattan home to the Ebbets Field home of the Brooklyn Dodgers.

"Brooklyn wasn't a very good baseball team then, so it seemed a lot easier to make it with the Dodgers than it might have been to make it with the Yankees," says Lopat.

"I was seventeen years old and I was still in high school. I got a job as an usher at Radio City Music Hall that summer and went to the Dodger tryouts. It was quite a long haul from my home and the first day I got there to Ebbets Field there were more than four hundred kids trying out. That must have been every kid who was playing baseball in New York. I was a first baseman and that's what I wanted to do. When they called for the first basemen I went over to that group and saw a lot of big kids," he says.

The Dodgers coaches and scouts cut that huge group in half the next day and Lopat was asked to return. He was asked to return every day for the next ten days as the group kept getting smaller and smaller.

"I think the subway was only a nickel then but it was still a small fortune for me. If I didn't have that Radio City job I never could have made it to those tryouts. I have always had a soft spot in my heart for Radio City ever since because of that," he says.

Lopat was now in a small group of under fifty youngsters and after the final drill, he was asked to stay behind. The Dodgers said they could not sign him but they thought he could play professional baseball. He was offered a contract by an independent club in Greensburg, Pennsylvania. It was there that he began his professional baseball career in 1937. He was a weak-hitting first baseman with a good glove and not much realistic hope for a big league career.

"It was just that I loved the game so much I would do whatever I had to do to play," he says. "I thought I could improve enough as a hitter to make the big leagues. I knew I wasn't any Lou Gehrig but not many guys were."

Independent minor league teams would pay their bills and even make a few bucks in those days by selling the contracts of players to clubs in higher classifications or, if they really had a gem of a player and got lucky, to a wealthy big league club. No less a baseball personage than Babe Ruth made it to the big leagues this way when the independent Baltimore Orioles sold his contract to the Boston Red Sox in 1914. The Red Sox sent him to their Providence, Rhode Island, farm before bringing him up to the big leagues as a pitcher late that year. Boston would make $125,000, an enormous sum in those days, when they, in turn, sold Ruth's contract on January 3, 1920, to the New York Yankees. By then, Ruth was doing more hitting than pitching. He would continue that way with the Yankees except for an occasional appearance on the mound.

Lopat would learn a lot of geography over the next seven years by moving from Greensburg to Jeanerette, Louisiana, to Kilgore, Texas, to Longview, Texas, to Shreveport, Louisiana, to Marshall, Texas, to Salina, Kansas, to Oklahoma City and Little Rock before making it to the big leagues in 1944 with the Chicago White Sox. He was twenty-six years old that summer.

"I had been playing first base and doing some occasional pitching in Jeanerette in 1937 and 1938. I had been working on the sidelines a lot as a pitcher but mostly I was still a first baseman. One day my manager, Carlos Moore, came to the mound and took out our pitcher. He had been hit hard and Moore was disgusted with him because he couldn't throw strikes. He came over to me at first base and told me to get rid of my first baseman's glove and get a finger mitt. He said, 'From now on, you're a pitcher. At least you can get the ball over the plate.' I pitched seven innings and won the game 4–3. After the game he told me he would only pitch me from that time on. 'If you don't make it as a pitcher, I'll sell you as a first baseman. There is always some club looking for a guy who can play first.' It wasn't the greatest endorsement in the world of my ability but it did make me a pitcher," says Lopat.

In 1939 Lopat was pitching with Longview. He won sixteen games, lost only nine and had an earned run average of 2.11 to lead the league. He felt certain he was on his way to the big leagues as a pitcher.

"That next season I got ill early in the year with an ulcerated stomach. It really set me back and drained me of all my strength. I couldn't throw very hard to begin with in professional ball. Now I was throwing even worse than before. That was really the low point of my minor league career and the first time I had serious doubts about my future," he says.

After an 0–3 start at Shreveport in the Double A Texas League, Lopat was dropped to the Marshall club in the East Texas League in B ball. His future was not very promising.

"That was the time I realized I would have to come up with another pitch if I was to make it. My fastball just wasn't good enough," he says.

Lopat had sacrificed a few years of his professional training as a first baseman. Now he was slipping further behind because he tried to make it as a two-pitch pitcher—a not-so-fast fastball and a not-so-sharp curve—and that wasn't working.

Two men came into Lopat's life in 1943. Both would have an enormous impact on his career. Each would remain friends with the young lefthander for life. The first man was a veteran pitcher named George Willis (Ace) Hudlin and the second was a young, ambitious newspaperman by the name of Ben Epstein.

"I joined the Little Rock club in 1943," says Lopat. "Willis Hudlin was on that club. He took a liking to me, we roomed together and he talked pitching all the time."

Hudlin was born in Wagoner, Oklahoma, in 1906. A husky six footer who could throw hard, he joined the Cleveland Indians in 1926. He would remain as a pitching mainstay of the Indians until 1940 when he was traded to the Washington Senators. He would later play for the St. Louis Browns and the New York Giants for a short while. He pitched minor league ball at Little Rock in 1943 and pitched again for the St. Louis Browns in the war year of 1944.

"He was getting hitters out at the age of thirty-seven with that screwball he had picked up along the way. I asked him to show it to me shortly after I saw him throw it. That pitch turned my career around," Lopat says.

For many years, Hudlin watched Carl Hubbell, the Hall of Fame pitcher for the New York Giants, during their spring training exhibition games against his Cleveland team. When Hudlin got to New York to finish out the 1940 season with the Giants, he asked Hubbell to help him with the pitch. The pitcher, known by Giants fans as the Meal Ticket, worked with the veteran on the sidelines before a few games. Hudlin had it mastered by the time the year ended. He used it extensively in the minors in 1941, 1942 and 1943 and the screwball helped him get back to the Browns for a final big league season in 1944 at the age of thirty-eight.

"The more I threw the pitch the better I got with it," says Lopat. "It isn't all that tough a pitch to throw but it is tough to control."

From a struggling pitcher with six wins and four losses in 1942, Lopat exploded on the Southern Association with nineteen wins against ten losses, a league-leading 3.05 ERA and only sixty-two walks in 245 innings in 1943. Ben Epstein noticed.

"He was a sportswriter for the Little Rock paper and one day he saw me pitch. I threw that screwball and I threw curves and I threw an occasional changeup and I threw a fastball that I spotted. One day he came up to me after a game and asked me how I could be winning with that garbage I was throwing. I told him the hitters were all off stride and I thought I could win in the big leagues now if I got the chance. He asked me if it was all right if he wrote about my stuff in the paper and called me a Junk Man. I laughed and told him that would be all right because I could probably surprise some of the hitters with my hard stuff. That's the way it worked out. I probably struck out more hitters with my fastball than any other pitch because they weren't ready for it. I wasn't ashamed of my pitches. I was getting people out, wasn't I?"

Shortly after Lopat moved to the big leagues, Epstein followed as a sportswriter for the old New York *Daily Mirror*. He covered the Yankees for his paper and was there when Lopat came to New York in 1948. Epstein soon popularized the nickname Junk Man and also was the creator of a more dignified nickname, Steady Eddie. Yankee fans loved that nickname because it came to symbolize a guaranteed strong effort by the Yankees any day Lopat took the mound.

"Benny and I remained very close in New York all those years. He was still a young man when he died but he had become a very popular New York sportswriter," says Lopat.

A year after his death, the New York chapter of the Baseball Writers of America created an award named in his honor. It was called the Ben Epstein Good Guy award and was given to a player or baseball personality who, like Epstein, was highly regarded by the press as a good guy.

After the marvelous 1943 season at Little Rock, Lopat expected a big league chance. It came late that year when the Chicago White Sox, a team with a working agreement with the Little Rock club, purchased Lopat's contract. He was signed to a 1944 contract for thirty-five hundred dollars a year.

The 1944 Chicago White Sox, typical of most teams in the depths of World War II, were a ragtag outfit of players who could easily have personalized a popular song of the war days called "They're Either Too Young or Too Old." Jimmy Dykes was the veteran skipper, Bill Dietrich was the best pitcher and a couple of veterans named Hal Trosky and Wally Moses were key hitters. Mike Tresh, a journeyman catcher, was also on the team. Lopat would later manage Tresh's son, Tommy, in the Yankees minor league organization.

"I was put into the rotation right away and got a chance to pitch regularly against big league hitters. I thought I had a pretty good rookie year. I convinced myself I could pitch in the big leagues," he says.

Lopat won eleven games and lost ten with the seventh-place White Sox. He had an ERA of 3.26 and impressed most of the clubs he faced. He would win ten games the next year and then jump to thirteen and sixteen in his final two seasons with Chicago.

The Yankees had won the American League pennant in 1947 and beat the Brooklyn Dodgers in one of the most exciting World Series ever played. One of their veteran pitchers, Bill Bevens, who had just missed a World Series no-hitter with two out in the bottom of the ninth at Ebbets Field, was forced to retire with a bad arm. The Yankees needed a starting pitcher. Manager Bucky Harris and general manager George Weiss began talking about a deal with the White Sox.

On February 24, 1948, Lopat, four months short of his thirtieth birthday, was traded by the White Sox to the Yankees for slugging catcher Aaron Robinson and pitchers Fred Bradley and Bill Wight.

"We wanted a guy who could pitch regularly for us and could give us a lot of innings," Harris told the press. "It's also an advantage that he is a lefthander."

"That has to be one of the happiest days of my life," recalls Lopat. "I was coming back to New York where I had grown up and I was going to the great Yankees. They had just won the pennant. I thought I could contribute to a lot more wins. The other good thing was I didn't have to face DiMaggio anymore."

Joe DiMaggio, back from service in World War II, still commanded much respect as he moved into the later stages of his career. He had joined the Yankees as a rookie in 1936 and now, a dozen years later, was still looked on as one of the best in the game. Ted Williams was his opposite number in the American League while a young lefthanded slugger in St. Louis named Stan Musial was beginning to record big batting averages steadily for the Cardinals.

"I really didn't have all that much trouble with DiMaggio when I faced him," says Lopat. "You knew that you had to make good pitches all the time. Joe never relaxed at bat. If you made a mistake he was ready. Ted was tough, too, of course, but he was lefthanded and so I could do some things with him that bothered him. I think I threw that screwball at him most of the time and he had trouble pulling it. Ted liked to pull everything. If you put a pitch on the outside part of the plate he would still pull it. DiMaggio was different. If you threw a pitch up and away to Joe D he would slap it to right field for a double or a triple. I always tried to keep the ball down and in on DiMag. One thing I'll tell you for sure about DiMag. In my book he was the greatest all-around player of my time. He could do everything and do it with grace and style. There's only one DiMag."

Vic Raschi made the Yankee ball club in 1946. Allie Reynolds was traded from Cleveland to the Yankees in a big deal involving Joe Gordon in 1946. Lopat started with the Bronx Bombers in 1948. These three pitchers would be the significant starters for those five championship years starting in 1949, with a little help from a lefthanded youngster named Whitey Ford. He joined the Yankees in June of 1950, won nine games and lost only one and then was away in service in 1951 and 1952. In 1953 Ford won eighteen ball games, Lopat won sixteen, Reynolds, troubled by a bad back, won thirteen, Raschi won thirteen and Johnny Sain, used out of the bullpen a good part of the time, won fourteen ball games.

"Reynolds was my first roommate on the Yankees. He was a tough guy, the Chief, and he was all baseball. He was a tremendous competitor and he thought that he could handle any batter in the game. I guess the best proof of that was when he pitched one of his no-hitters and got Ted Williams for the last out. Williams had hit a foul pop with two out in the ninth and Yogi dropped it. It didn't faze the Chief at all. He came right back and got Ted on another foul ball to Yogi. I think Yogi was happier than the Chief after that last out," Lopat says.

Bucky Harris inserted Lopat into the rotation behind the two hard-throwing righthanders, Raschi and Reynolds. Things didn't go as smoothly as Lopat had hoped.

"I wanted to do so well for the Yankees that I started out pressing. I was squeezing the ball and I was making pitches I didn't usually make. I made some mistakes in the early going. I looked up in the first six weeks and I was two and five. I wasn't worried about my career and I didn't doubt my ability. I knew I had proven all that in Chicago. It was just that I wanted to do well and was very disappointed that I wasn't," he says.

The newspapers were all over Lopat. They began suggesting that he had won a lot of games with the second-division White Sox. Many pitchers could do well with bad teams but when it came to successful teams they weren't quite as tough. Ben Epstein was sympathetic in print but the other reporters knew that Epstein and Lopat went back a long way together. Harris sized up the situation. He called Lopat into his Stadium office.

"I can see that you are not the pitcher you were last year in Chicago. You are trying to throw the ball too hard. I want you to just relax and pitch normally. If you go back to the way you pitched last year you will be a big winner for us. I'm not worried about you. I don't want you to worry about yourself," Harris told the lefthander.

"That really helped me," says Lopat. "I realized I wasn't pitching for my job every time out there. I was just trying to get some guys out. If I relaxed I would win."

Lopat's next start was against the struggling St. Louis Browns. They were a bad ball club but they did have some good hitters in Al Zarilla, Bob Dillinger and Gerry Priddy.

"Certain righthanded hitters gave me trouble. Tom McBride, who had a short career with Boston and Washington, used to kill me. The other guy I hated to see was Hoot Evers. He was very tough on me," Lopat says.

Before the game against the Browns, he discussed the St. Louis hitters with his roommate.

"The Chief had just pitched and won and I wasn't pitching for a couple of days. I think we had dinner one night and then went up to the room. We must have gone over the hitters a thousand times all that night, probing weaknesses on every one of them. Of course, I couldn't throw hard the way the Chief did but it was always helpful to know weaknesses of the hitters. Everything the Chief said made sense. I went out to the mound for my next start, just relaxed, and found my rhythm and won the game easily, something like 8–1. After that I just settled down."

Lopat would go more than two months without losing another game for the Yankees. He would win seventeen games, lose eleven and finish with a respectable 3.65 ERA. Lopat was smiling broadly as the season ended. Ben Epstein would write in late September in the *Mirror*, "Ed Lopat, the Junk Man, has made New York fans sit up and take notice. He teams perfectly with the hard stuff offered up by Vic Raschi and Allie Reynolds. This appears to be a Yankee Big Three that will be very productive for years to come."

Epstein could hardly know as he wrote that late in 1948 just how right he would prove to be. A new manager would gain the benefits from New York's Big Three.

The Yankees had won the World Series in 1947 under manager Bucky Harris. They finished third in 1948 as Boston and Cleveland tied at the end of the regular season. Cleveland won the playoff in Fenway 8–3 with manager Lou Boudreau hitting two home runs into the Fenway screen. Joe DiMaggio was a Fenway visitor as his brother Dom played center field for the Red Sox.

While that was going on, a decision was being made about the 1949 season in the Yankee offices at 521 Fifth Avenue in Manhattan. Owners Dan Topping and Del Webb had instructed general manager George Weiss to fire Bucky Harris and hire a new manager. Weiss knew the man he wanted.

Weiss and Casey Stengel had been friends for more than twenty years, dating back to their days together in the Eastern League when Stengel managed the Worcester club and Weiss ran the business of the New Haven club.

Stengel had just completed a first-place season at Oakland in the Pacific Coast League. When Weiss called, Stengel was ready for a return to the big leagues. Not all the Yankee front office people were as thrilled with the selection as Weiss seemed to be.

"The general consensus," said Lee MacPhail, the Yankee farm director then, "was that we had hired a clown."

"Casey soon proved he was no clown," says Lopat. "He knew an awful lot about the game and he knew a lot about pitching. He often would cite something he remembered from sitting on the bench next to John McGraw with the Giants. Another thing about Casey. He could give the press that double-talking Stengelese but when it came to the players he could be as clear as could be."

Stengel immediately saw he had three gems in Reynolds, Raschi and Lopat, got a lot of work out of another lefthander named Tommy Byrne and resurrected a relief pitcher named Joe Page who had a strong 1947 season but had slumped the next year. The Red Sox, still hurting from losing the 1948 playoff, got off to a big lead. Joe DiMaggio was out of the Yankee lineup with a heel injury and did not return until June. He hit four homers in a big Fenway series as the Yankees moved closer to Boston in the standings.

The race seesawed all season. Boston came into Yankee Stadium for the final two games of the year. They were one game up and needed only a split for their second pennant in three years (they had won big under Joe Cronin in 1946) and third in thirty years. They had won in 1918. A big left-hander named Babe Ruth won thirteen games that year and hit eleven homers and batted .300 for that team. Reynolds won on Saturday for the Yankees and Raschi won on Sunday as the Yankees became American League champions.

Said Stengel, in a deliriously happy Yankee clubhouse, "I never coulda done it without my players."

Lopat, his red hair turning gray, continued to be a vital cog in the Yankees pitching wheel. He won eighteen games in 1950, twenty-one in 1951, ten in 1952 and was a sixteen-game winner with only four losses in 1953. The Yankees beat the Dodgers again for their fifth straight World Series title and the famed 5 diamond rings arrived shortly thereafter for the twelve members of those teams. The other players on the 1953 squad received their handsome diamonds with only the year 1953 inscribed on the ring.

Lopat, now a spot starter, won twelve games in 1954 as Cleveland ran away with the American League pennant. On July 30, 1955, Lopat was sent by the Yankees to Baltimore on waivers.

"I was released by the Orioles at the end of the year. George Weiss called me and offered me the job of managing the Richmond farm club. It was a great opportunity to stay in baseball. I had never done anything else so I grabbed it before they changed their minds," he says.

In three seasons at Richmond, Lopat helped supply the Yankees with the young players who would continue their winning tradition through the next eight years. The Yankees would win their last pennant with farm system players from Lopat's time in 1964 and not win again until the George Steinbrenner–Billy Martin era of 1976.

Lopat and his wife, the former Mary Elizabeth Howell, married in 1940, bought a home in Hillside, New Jersey. They raised their children there and Lopat found that the life of a baseball minor league manager wasn't all bad.

"I worked hard all season. Then I came home for the winter, spent a lot of time with my family and enjoyed the relaxation," he says. "I like to putter around the house in the off-season. I don't go to a lot of dinners. The reason I can take all the baseball travel is that I don't have to travel at all in the winter."

In 1959 the Yankees brought Lopat back to New York as a big league scout. The following year he was named the pitching coach. The Yankees won the pennant and lost the seven-game World Series to the Pittsburgh Pirates when Bill Mazeroski hit Ralph Terry's one-and-oh pitch in the bottom of the ninth inning over the wall in left field. A stunned left fielder named Yogi Berra was under the last fly ball of the season.

"The Yankees lost so they had to make changes. That is always the way it works in baseball. Everybody knows that. They decided to fire their three key guys, Stengel, Weiss and me. We all went together after the 1960 season," he says.

Lopat coached for the Minnesota Twins for two seasons, managed in Kansas City for Charles O. Finley, was the general manager of the A's and did some scouting.

"I had a lot of those players, Reggie Jackson, Catfish Hunter, Rick Monday, Sal Bando, who would go on to become great stars in Oakland. Charlie had decided to make a change in managers when the team moved west to Oakland. He offered me a job in the organization. I just decided I didn't want to move that far away from New Jersey. I got along with Charlie. I've worked for Charlie and I've worked for George Steinbrenner and survived to tell about it. Not many others can make that statement," he says.

He was soon scouting for the new Montreal Expos team and remained in that position for seventeen years. He was offered a scouting job with the Yankees in 1986 and was able to come back home again.

When he turned seventy in June of 1988, he seemed no less enthusiastic about the game and his part in it than he was half a century ago when he started.

"I have had an awful lot of fun and a lot of success in baseball. I have done about everything a person can do in baseball so I've seen baseball from every angle. I never once had a regret about staying in the game. It has really been a fulfilling career. I've done well enough financially for my family and we have traveled and enjoyed the country. When you think about a kid from Manhattan without a college education, the son of a shoemaker, doing this well, you just have to give all the credit to the game," he says.

Eddie Lopat was a class act on the mound. He took his pitching turn without complaint. He never was a clubhouse lawyer. He shared some marvelous moments with teammates and he was quick with a bouquet for his colleagues. He got along well with the press and the public. He appreciated the good fortune of his life and made the most of his talent.

"I once pitched a World Series game against Brooklyn and beat them 4–2. I think that was the most exciting game I ever pitched. Just the idea of pitching for the Yankees, my hometown team, and beating the hometown Dodgers, well that was something. As a kid, I had this dream of playing in the big leagues for the Yankees, of being on the same field that Babe Ruth and Lou Gehrig had walked on, and that day in 1953 I won a Series game for that team."

Lopat never made the big salary in baseball as a player but he has worked every year for more than half a century in the game. He has also been a class act off the field; a real Good Soldier of the game.

9 Jack Rogers

TRAVELING MAN

ON OCTOBER 2, 1978, ONE OF THE MOST IMPORTANT and thrilling baseball games ever played was completed in Fenway Park, Boston. The New York Yankees and the Boston Red Sox played for the American League East title after ending the season the previous day in a tie.

Boston had built a huge lead that summer reaching to fourteen games over the fourth-place Yankees as late as July 19. The Red Sox soon slumped and the Yankees roared forward. By August 1 the lead was down to six and a half games. By September 1 it was still at six and a half with little hope the Yankees would catch Boston in the last month. By October 1 the Yankees were actually in first place by one game. They lost that last Sunday, Boston won, and a playoff, the second in Boston baseball history (they had lost to Lou Boudreau's Cleveland Indians in 1948), was scheduled for the following afternoon, Monday, October 2.

Mike Torrez, a hard-throwing former Yankee, was in command until the seventh inning. The Red Sox were ahead 2–0.

Jack Rogers, the traveling secretary of the Boston Red Sox since 1969, and Bill Kane, the traveling secretary of the New York Yankees since 1963, exchanged glances across the press box. One of them would fly out of Boston's Logan Airport in a few hours with an uproariously happy team. The other would have his season at an end.

"The playoff happened so fast that we weren't prepared," says Rogers. "We were playing at home and the Yankees were coming in to Boston. One of us would go on to Kansas City. I knew the Yankees would be coming up to Boston by charter. I called Killer [Kane is so called because of his mildness] and worked out the deal."

The two traveling secretaries agreed they could charter one airplane for Kansas City and the American League Championship Series the next night. There was no need to have two airplanes waiting at Logan for the same journey. Only one group of baseball players would be going on.

"We always prepared for the playoffs," says Kane. "It was bad luck not to."

The year before the Yankees were playing the Kansas City Royals in the American League playoffs. Kane had instructed the players to bring their bags into the hotel lobby before the fourth game. If the Yankees lost, the series would be over and the Yankees would fly home. Gabe Paul, the Yankee general manager, saw the bags piling up in the lobby.

Paul, who had been a traveling secretary for the Cincinnati Reds, exploded at Kane.

"Don't you know that's bad luck?"

"I just wanted to be ready," explained Kane.

"Don't ever be ready for a loss."

Kane took the advice to heart. He always assumed victory and prepared his travel plans in that fashion.

"As soon as we made the arrangements for the playoff in Boston I made the arrangements at the same time for the Championship Series in Kansas City. I assumed we would win," he explained.

Rogers hadn't been as quick. Now he was stuck for a plane as the Yankees flew in for the one game that would settle the pennant.

"I figured we could get a plane the next day if we needed it," Rogers says. "I didn't want to waste the money if we wouldn't use it."

Then he came up with the glorious idea that the plane waiting to take the Yankees to Kansas City could be used by his team if the Red Sox won. The Yankee players would go to their own homes around the country or return to New York by shuttle or even commercial plane to LaGuardia Airport in New York.

"Then Bucky Dent hit that home run," Rogers was saying now.

In Boston, ever since that day in October in 1978, the Yankee shortstop has been known as Bucky Bleeping Dent. It is the worst curse Boston fans can come up with for the man who ruined their dreams.

Dent hit a three-run home run off Torrez, the Yankees scored again in the seventh for a 4–2 lead, added another in the eighth for a cushion. The Red Sox came up with two in the bottom of the eighth and left two men on base in the ninth as Carl Yastrzemski popped up for the final out against Rich Gossage.

"I remember that pitch like it was yesterday," Gossage says. "I was real nervous before I let it go. Then I turned around and looked out toward center field and thought about the worst possible thing that could happen. I figured if Yastrzemski hit a home run to beat me I would be back home in Colorado the next day. That wasn't so terrible."

Gossage says he has one other memory from the final out that makes him laugh every time he thinks about it.

"Just before I let go of the ball on that final pitch to Yastrzemski I heard Graig Nettles at third base yelling over at me, 'Pop him up, pop him up.' I threw a good hard fastball inside and Yastrzemski did pop up the ball foul to third. As it takes off for that area I hear Nettles screaming, 'Not to me.' The ball was caught by the comedic third baseman and the Yankees were the Eastern Division winners.

Pandemonium broke out in the press box with that last out as sportswriters scurried for the clubhouse, officials raced down to the locker rooms to be with their teams and plans were completed for a trip west by the Yankees.

"I just nodded over to Killer that he had the plane back," says Rogers.

The Yankees took the waiting aircraft from Logan Airport to Kansas City. They eventually beat the Kansas City Royals for the third straight time and marched into the World Series against the Dodgers. New York would win the Series in 1978, the last championship they have achieved.

While the Yankees were dressing for the trip to Kansas City late that October afternoon, Rogers was finishing up his business for the season in the executive offices of the Red Sox under the stands at Fenway Park. It was a melancholy experience.

"That had to be the toughest day I ever had in baseball," says Rogers. "I think it had to be the toughest day anybody associated with the Red Sox had. That was a crushing blow. We had blown a big lead that year, as everybody knows. What people forget is that we had fought back to tie the Yankees on the last day of the season. When we got up 2–0 into the seventh with Torrez looking as strong as he did, we all thought sure we would win."

Instead Rogers was in his office in an hour writing out travel checks for the members of the Red Sox for travel to their winter homes, the saddest chore a traveling secretary has to face each season.

Traveling secretaries may well be the most important people in baseball. They get their teams there on time.

"I think our most important job is to show up for the scheduled game," Rogers says.

They seem to be the only baseball people who work 365 days a year. Their season begins early in January with the logistics of spring training. They must arrange for hotel headquarters for the club. They oversee the spring training schedule of their teams. They hire the bus and buy the lunches for spring training games. They handle the gate receipts and write checks for living-out expenses for married and veteran players. They arrange for all airline flights to distant games.

When spring training ends, they handle the logistics of shipping personal bags and equipment back to the hometown park. Woe to the traveling secretary who leaves a baby carriage or a stroller behind when the team breaks camp. In the hometown, they arrange for hotel rooms for players not yet settled and prepare logistical arrangements for reaching the park each day. Then there are tickets.

"Taking care of the tickets is really a chore," Rogers says. "No matter where they are located in the stands, somebody likes a different location."

When the team travels, the traveling secretary is the man responsible for hiring the bus to the airport, chartering the plane, seeing that there is sufficient beer on the craft for the thirsty players, arranging for the bus to the team hotel and checking that the hotel rooms are adequate and available.

He then must arrange for a bus each day to the ball park and a bus back. Players sometimes get upset if they have to wait for the bus to leave after a game; few of these millionaire players would ever imagine hiring a cab for five dollars back to the team hotel.

One of the most shocking experiences for a traveling secretary occurred when pitcher Joe Hoerner of the St. Louis Cardinals stole the team bus.

The Cards were playing in Atlanta. On a hot summer afternoon, the players boarded the bus for the ride to Atlanta Stadium, about two miles away. Players straggled onto the bus. The driver went inside the air-conditioned hotel to await the word from the Cards traveling secretary to move. Hoerner became impatient.

"Let's go," he bellowed.

Without a driver, the bus remained in place. Hoerner suddenly leaped from his seat, moved to the driver's seat, put the bus in gear, shut the doors and drove forward. His ride lasted only about twenty yards as the bus crashed into a hotel pillar.

"OK, we're here," shouted Hoerner.

The flaky lefthander was fined for his trouble and warned not to try the same thing with the team plane.

Ball clubs have often had trouble on bus rides. There is the tale of the Los Angeles Dodgers riding a bus to old Forbes Field in the heat of a late summer afternoon in 1963. This was the team of Sandy Koufax, Don Drysdale, Maury Wills, Tommy Davis and Frank Howard. They would go on to win the pennant and sweep the Yankees in the World Series. On this day they felt like overheated Little Leaguers. Traveling secretary Lee Roth had been unable to get an air-conditioned bus and as the vehicle became stuck in traffic up a Pittsburgh hill near the park, the players began growling about the conditions.

Usually mild-mannered Frank Howard began roaring. He threatened to tear up the bus with his bare hands and to tear apart every Dodger executive who had anything to do with hiring this terrible bus.

"If you don't like the conditions, let's go outside and settle this in the street," bellowed manager Walter Alston.

The Dodger manager got up from his front seat and walked off the bus. Howard sat down quietly in his back seat. The Dodgers waited out the heat and traffic without another word. They also learned that day who was in charge of their team.

The following year another team bus incident made headlines in sports pages across America. The New York Yankees were struggling in August of 1964 under rookie manager Yogi Berra. They had just lost a doubleheader to the Chicago White Sox. This was a Yankee team with Hall of Famers Mickey Mantle and Whitey Ford, with home run king Roger

Maris, with class players such as Elston Howard, Bobby Richardson, Tony Kubek and Clete Boyer. It also had Joe Pepitone as the first baseman and Phil Linz as the backup shortstop.

Linz sat in the back of the quiet bus as the players sulked about the twin defeats. Suddenly Linz pulled out a harmonica he had purchased that day and began playing "Mary Had a Little Lamb." Berra ordered him to stop playing. He halted his concert for a few moments. As Berra returned to his seat in the front of the bus Linz began playing again. This time Berra was enraged. He stormed back to where Linz was sitting. Before he could reach him, Linz flipped Berra the harmonica. Berra caught it (after all, he was a Hall of Fame catcher) and threw it back at Linz. It caught Pepitone, sitting next to Linz, on the right knee. Pepitone immediately feigned a crippling injury.

There was much shouting, many obscenities and a tension-filled ride the rest of the way to the airport. Kubek and Richardson later met with general manager Ralph Houk and complained about Berra's handling of the team. They suggested he had lost control of the club. In a few days a decision was made that was irrevocable: Berra would be fired at the end of the season.

The Yankees rallied from that August day to win the pennant. They lost the World Series in seven games to Bob Gibson and the Cardinals.

"I went into the Yankee offices the next day to discuss my next year's contract," recalls Berra. "Instead, I was fired."

"I always made sure we had air-conditioned buses to take us to the ball park and the airports after that incident," says Kane.

John R. Rogers began his baseball career with the old Boston Braves in 1948 after graduation from college. He had grown up in Somerville, Massachusetts, and had always been a Braves fan.

"I joined the club in the season Boston won the pennant. That was the year of Spahn and Sain and pray for rain. It was very exciting," he says.

The Braves won the pennant in a bitter fight with the Brooklyn Dodgers. Warren Spahn, the Hall of Fame left-hander, and Johnny Sain, the crafty righthander, were the mainstays of a very fine pitching staff. It was a team of some notable characters, not the least of whom was a young assistant in the public relations department named Donald Davidson.

"Nobody who ever met Donald could ever forget him," says Rogers.

Davidson is a forty-eight-inch-tall midget with all the stamina, skill and strength of a man twice his size. He began his career in baseball as a schoolboy in 1935 when Babe Ruth was finishing out his playing career in Boston. Davidson stayed with the club as a traveling secretary and public relations director, moved with them to Milwaukee, moved again to Atlanta with the Braves and finally settled in Houston with the Astros as an administrative assistant. He wears a ten-gallon hat that is almost as large as he is.

Davidson knows everybody in baseball and everybody in baseball knows Donald. He is also kidded mercilessly by ball players. He was once hung up on a hook by his small jacket in a spring training clubhouse. He was unable to press an elevator button on a high floor and was tortured by the players as they left the elevator one by one without pressing the button for him. He was a small raging bull when he wound up back at the lobby level. He soon remedied that situation by never traveling without a walking stick.

Davidson has always been partial to outrageous clothing. He buys his clothing in the boys department of the finest stores. He once walked across a spring training field wearing a red jacket, red pants, red socks, white shoes and a red cap. A San Francisco Giants scout, a huge man named Tom (Clancy) Sheehan, passed him on the field.

"What's the matter, you too stuck up to say hello?" barked Davidson.

Sheehan looked down on the little man.

"Oh my gosh," he said, "I just didn't recognize it was you in that red cap."

"That 1948 team was a wonderful collection of people," says Rogers. "John Quinn was the general manager and a finer man you couldn't find. Billy Southworth was the manager and he was one of my very closest friends. It was a great bunch of players with Spahnie, Sain, Alvin Dark, Eddie Stanky and all the rest. Earl Torgeson was the first baseman on that team. He also became one of my closest friends. The year after the 1948 team won the pennant I got a call from a local television program. Television was just beginning in those days and they wanted Torgeson to host a sports show. They called me and asked if I could set it up. We got it going with Earl giving his opinions on baseball matters and answering questions from the audience. It was really the first sports show of its kind in Boston. I think it was really the forerunner of all the sports shows that have followed since in Boston and around the country. Oh, yes, it had a creative title. It was called *The Earl Torgeson Show*."

Rogers enjoyed every minute of his association with the Boston Braves.

"I was doing some public relations work, filling in as the traveling secretary when Duffy Lewis chose to skip a trip and learning all about the baseball business," he says. "Then they pulled the bottom out from under us."

Despite their pennant-winning year of 1948, the Braves were losing money steadily. Braves Field was in disrepair and the Red Sox, playing across town in Fenway Park, were drawing more people and becoming Boston's favorite team. They weren't winning pennants but they seemed to be in exciting pennant races every season with the Yankees. They had a major draw in the great Ted Williams and they had a park that was more conducive to exciting home run baseball.

In 1953 the Braves franchise moved to Milwaukee, Wisconsin. It was the first franchise move in big league baseball since the Baltimore Orioles had moved to New York in 1903 as the Highlanders and eventually became the New York Yankees. Baseball fans had learned their geography by following the baseball map. National League fans knew the teams in the East were Boston, Brooklyn, Philadelphia and New York and the teams in the West were Pittsburgh (believe it or not), Chicago, Cincinnati and St. Louis. American League fans followed New York, Boston, Philadelphia and Washington in the East with Chicago, Cleveland, Detroit and St. Louis in the West. That's just the way it was. That's just the way it would always be. The shocking move of the Braves to Milwaukee changed the landscape of baseball forever and clearly led to the franchise shifts in later years, especially the opening of the West Coast after the 1957 season when the Brooklyn Dodgers moved to Los Angeles and the New York Giants moved along with them to California and settled in San Francisco.

"I figured that was the end of my baseball career," says Rogers. "Some of the Boston people moved with the team to Milwaukee. I simply was not interested. I was born and raised in the Boston area, had my family and friends there, felt comfortable there and saw no reason to move to Wisconsin."

Rogers was out of work only a short while before he got a job in the public relations department of Pan American Airlines. He remained there until 1969 when he returned to baseball as the traveling secretary of the Red Sox.

"I always loved baseball. I wanted to stay with the Braves forever. When they left I figured my baseball days were over. I still remained a good fan and attended several Red Sox games, especially when the Yankees were in town. One game I attended was historic. I was sitting in the stands when Ted Williams ended his playing career with a home run off Jack Fisher in Fenway Park. Few memories of mine would be as exciting as that," Rogers says.

Williams remains a Red Sox vice-president and a good friend of Rogers to this day. "I never know when I might get a call from Ted for a score. He calls from Newfoundland in the summer and Florida in the fall."

When the Red Sox needed a traveling secretary, they hired Rogers.

"I had been traveling for Pan American so that part of the job was not a major adjustment. We had two children, a son and a daughter, and my wife, Ellie, was busy with them at home. I enjoyed being back in baseball and we also had spring training to look forward to. That is always the nicest part of any baseball official's life," he says.

Rogers returned to the game with much enthusiasm. By 1975 the Red Sox were rebuilding strongly and when two rookies named Fred Lynn and Jim Rice arrived on the local scene, the fortunes of the Boston Red Sox began looking up. Rice and Lynn would lead the Red Sox to a pennant. There were high hopes for the first World Championship in Boston since 1918 when a young lefthander named George (Babe) Ruth led the Red Sox to a title. It was not to be. The Cincinnati Reds, the Big Red Machine, won the Series in seven exciting games.

"I remember the sixth game of that Series as just about the most dramatic I have ever witnessed," says Rogers. "That's the game that was won by Carlton Fisk's twelfth-inning homer. What people forget is that the Red Sox were down in the eighth when Bernie Carbo hit a three-run pinch homer after looking so bad."

The Red Sox, true to their history, lost the title the next day to Cincinnati. Three years later Rogers and all Boston Red Sox fans would have their hearts broken in the loss to the Yankees at Fenway Park.

"I can still see Mike Torrez making that pitch to Bucky Dent," says Rogers. "It was just a little fly ball and when he hit it nobody could imagine it would carry. It was just a little fly ball."

There would be all sorts of front office and player turmoil in Boston after that season. The Red Sox finally got going again with another strong team in 1986. They won the pennant, came back to defeat the California Angels in the American League Championship Series and had the Mets down three games to two in the 1986 World Series. In the tenth inning of the sixth game, there were two strikes on Mookie Wilson when his routine ground ball went between Bill Buckner's legs, allowing the winning run to score.

"We have certainly had some very disappointing losses," says Rogers.

With his children grown and on their own, Rogers's wife, Ellie, makes many of the team's trips now with him.

"We really have a good time visiting the cities around the league and going to the fine restaurants and enjoying ourselves shopping in different places. It has been a wonderful life," he says. "I owe everything I have to baseball."

The tall, lanky, gray-haired New England Yankee looks forward to many, many more years with the Red Sox.

"When I worked for the Braves I didn't miss a game. When I started working for the Red Sox in 1969 I knew I wouldn't miss a game. Baseball is just too much fun. You don't stay away unless you can't move," he says.

Rogers is proud of his attendance record, his relationship with the players and front office and the friends he has made in the game.

"You just sit back and think of all the wonderful games and the exciting moments and you know there can't be a better job around," he says.

Rogers did have a major disappointment a couple of years ago when burglars broke into his home and stole his 1948 Boston Braves Series ring and his 1975 Boston Red Sox Series ring.

"Those things are not replaceable. That was upsetting," he says. "I still have the memories and nobody can ever take that away from me."

He has some sour memories, such as the sad October 2, 1978, when Dent hit the screen in Fenway with his soft fly and the October day when Mookie Wilson's grounder went between Buckner's legs and the crushing loss to the Oakland A's in the 1988 American League Championship Series.

"I wear the 1986 ring," he says. "I don't want that stolen. I may not have a ring from those other years anymore but I still have the pleasant experiences of those seasons."

Through all the delayed flights and the lost suitcases and the cramped hotel rooms, Rogers has fulfilled a fantasy.

"There's nothing like working in baseball," he says. "Nothing like it."

10 Denny Sommers

HAVE TEAM, WILL COACH

■■■■ THIRTY YEARS AFTER HE ENTERED PROFESSIONAL baseball as a frightened seventeen-year-old farm boy out of the tiny town of Hortonville, Wisconsin, Dennis Sommers was out of work for the first time.

He had played in the minor leagues for ten seasons, managed in the low minors for another ten years and coached and scouted on the big league level for the next ten until the winter of 1987.

"I was an advance scout for the Minnesota Twins in 1987 when they won the World Championship. I was as excited and happy as I'd ever been. The club gave all the scouts that big World Series ring and I wore that thing everywhere. I slept with it, ate with it and worked with it. Then they let me go," he says.

Baseball is that way. Job changes are built into the system. The Good Soldiers accept it all graciously and move on. Sommers moved on to San Diego.

"It was the time for the baseball convention in December and I went out there hoping somebody might need a bullpen coach or a scout or a batting practice pitcher or somebody to shine shoes. Anything to stay in the game," he says.

Sommers was at the luncheon given every year at this event. He suddenly spotted Charles (Chub) Feeney, who only that season had been named president of the San Diego Padres. Feeney had retired as the National League president the previous year, stayed out of baseball for a few months and then accepted a job as the club president in a management shake-up. Sommers, who had coached for the Mets in New York, had seen Feeney often around Shea Stadium.

"I didn't know if he knew who I was. I just went up to him and introduced myself. He recognized me and asked what I was doing. I told him I had just been let go by the Twins in a scouting shake-up and was trying to find a job. I told him I had read that a couple of the San Diego coaches had been let go and that manager Larry Bowa might be looking for coaches," Sommers says.

Feeney said he wasn't sure what plans had been made for the 1988 coaching staff of the Padres.

"Write your phone number down and I'll get back to you if we have anything," Feeney told Sommers.

"I looked around for something to write on. I didn't want Feeney to get away without my number. The first thing I saw was a cocktail napkin. I grabbed a pencil from one of the guys and scribbled my number down. Chub stuffed it into his pocket. We shook hands and that was it. I went back to Wisconsin the next day," he says.

About a week later the telephone rang in the home of Sommers's seventy-five-year-old mother. Dennis, a bachelor who spent his winters with his mother and his summers in hotel rooms, was out back chopping some wood. She called to him and said it was a "Mr. Feeney on the phone."

"We'd like you to come aboard with us," Feeney told him.

Sommers was thrilled. He was back in the game, back in uniform and back working in the assorted baseball jobs every team fills with a loyal man.

"I told Chub what I've told everybody who has ever hired me," Sommers says. "All I ever wanted to do was be in baseball and I'll give my team all my time, all my energy and all my loyalty."

If it sounds as if Dennis Sommers is married to the game, he admits that he is.

"I guess when you have been in baseball thirty years the way I have and traveled to all the small towns I have there isn't much time for any other life," he says.

Born July 12, 1940, the husky crewcut Sommers is among the legions of baseball workers who have made a career out of their devotion to the game. No job is too menial. Sommers will carry a bag of baseballs from the bullpen to the dugout with as much joy and satisfaction as he would get out of a detailed scouting report sending his team to the Series.

"I just love everything about the game, the people, the competition, the travel, the hotel rooms, the fans, the noise, the excitement, everything. This is what I do, what I love, where I always want to be," he says.

As the bullpen coach of the San Diego Padres, Sommers finds himself in a most enviable position. His new boss, manager Jack McKeon, was Sommers's top boss when McKeon was the club general manager.

"After Chub called me and said the job was open I had to talk to Jack. I've known him a long time. We get along great. I'm very happy to be working for him," he says.

It would probably be accurate to say that Sommers is the Will Rogers of baseball coaches. He has never met a manager or a general manager he didn't like.

Dennis James Sommers began his baseball playing days in the small farming community of Hortonville, some ninety miles north of Milwaukee. His father, James, worked on the county highway crew and his mother, Alice, stayed home and raised five children.

"We had a small dairy farm as a sideline and raised a few milking cows. I was always used to getting up early and doing those farm chores," he says.

Sommers began playing baseball in Little League and went on to American Legion baseball.

"My father had to drive me ten miles to the nearest baseball field," he says. "We played about eight games a year in

American Legion ball. Four of them were played with ice and snow still on the ground. We just didn't have enough kids for too many games and we couldn't get all the farm boys out."

After graduation from Hortonville High, Sommers won a scholarship to Marquette University. He never got to go because a scout for the San Francisco Giants came around looking for him.

"His name was Dave Garcia and he was from up in Oshkosh and he had seen me play Legion baseball and a little basketball and he told me the Giants were interested in me. I was crazy about baseball but I didn't think any scouts would ever find me in a little place like Hortonville," says Sommers.

As he would later learn in the business himself, scouts tend to find ball players everywhere. Garcia watched Sommers in a couple of those Legion games and finally told him the Giants were interested enough in him to pay him a twenty-five-hundred-dollar bonus if he signed.

"I was a third baseman and a catcher then. Dave suggested I should concentrate on my catching. He thought that would be the fastest way to the big leagues. They must have thought I was a prospect. They paid me eight hundred dollars a month," he says.

In June of 1958, Sommers reported to Michigan City, Indiana, in the Midwest League. He was seventeen years old.

"I couldn't believe I was in professional baseball," he says. "This was a dream and now I was living it. The whole thing was right out of the storybooks. It didn't seem as if it was really happening to me."

It almost didn't. Professional pitching, even at that level, was a little too much for the inexperienced kid from Wisconsin. He struggled with the bat, could only record a .167 average and was in danger of being released before he finished his first season.

"Buddy Kerr, the old Giants shortstop, was my first manager. He was very understanding and helped me a lot. He worked with me and tried to improve me. He also worked on my catching. He told me that if I concentrated on my catching and got really good defensively, there would be a place for me in baseball. I really became dedicated as a catcher that year," he says.

Sommers went back to Michigan City the following year and hit .214. It wasn't much to write home to Wisconsin about but it was a step in the right direction. While he continued to struggle with the bat, his defensive ability behind the plate and his strong arm kept him in the game. He believed they would lead to a big league chance.

"I never did develop the bat speed you need to hit big league pitching. I was big enough but I wasn't quick enough with my hands for some strange reason," he says.

At six foot two inches tall and weighing over two hundred pounds, Sommers certainly had the physical tools. He simply didn't hit enough. The Giants kept moving him up in their organization but the reality was setting in after his fifth or sixth year in professional baseball that he would not be a big league player.

He played in Eugene, Oregon; Victoria, Washington; and Springfield, Massachusetts for four seasons from 1962 through 1965. The Giants, still hoping his bat would come around, sent him to Tacoma, Washington, in late 1965. The following season he made his only appearance at the San Francisco Giants big league training camp in Phoenix, Arizona. When camp ended, he was assigned to the Giants Triple A club in that Arizona city.

"Bill Werle, the old pitcher, was my manager. My first roommate there was Don Larsen, the guy who had pitched a perfect game for the Yankees in the 1956 World Series. He was something else. He sure did love to socialize. He was pretty hard to keep up with. I never really tried. He would come in late sometimes after a long night and storm through the room. He was a very physical guy and he would slap my bed or squeeze my toe when he came in the room. You always knew he was there. He was a great guy to be around, could tell wonderful stories and had a lot of fun playing baseball. He just didn't think sleep was very important so he didn't do too much of it. I enjoyed being his roommate and I learned a lot of baseball from him," Sommers says.

The other fairly well-known pitcher on that Phoenix club was Bob Garibaldi. The Giants had paid the big handsome kid from Stockton, California, a huge signing bonus. He could throw very hard but he never found control or consistency. He had several chances with the Giants. He got into only fifteen games in four separate seasons and never won a big league game.

"He was another guy who liked to party," says Sommers. "One night the three of us went out to dinner together in Phoenix. After dinner we had a couple of beers, nothing serious, and jumped in a cab for the ride back to the hotel. Garibaldi was sitting in the front seat and me and Larsen were in the back. We had only gone a few blocks when a guy drove through a red light and struck our cab. It later turned out it was a drunken driver. Garibaldi was cut and Larsen was bruised but I was thrown against the side of the cab. I suffered a severely bruised deltoid muscle. I was laid up a long time. The accident ruined my shoulder. The bone deteriorated and I never could throw well again," he says.

When the injury healed and Sommers returned to the club in late July, Rosy Ryan, the farm director of the San Francisco Giants, summoned Sommers to his office.

"I figured that would be it in baseball," he says. "I never was much of a hitter and now I couldn't throw so I couldn't catch. All I could think of was that I would go home to Wisconsin, try to go back to school and maybe I could teach and coach someplace. I knew I wanted to be around baseball some way or other."

At the age of twenty-six, without any big league time, after nine years in professional baseball, Sommers was released by the Giants as a minor league player. There was still one surprise left for him that fateful day in 1966.

"Rosy gave me the bad news about my playing days being over. I expected it so it was not a terrible shock," Sommers says. "Then he did shock me. He asked if I had ever given any thought to managing."

Big league managers are usually experienced minor league managers, former stars, long-rumored potential skippers. Few managers on the big league level surface without name recognition. Minor league managers are picked at random. No one really knows how it happens. They just look at a kid, see something in his desire or dedication, recognize he may be a good baseball teacher and offer him the opportunity. The won and lost record will decide how far up the baseball ladder he will go. One other thing about rookie minor league baseball managers: They will work cheap. They are just so grateful for the opportunity to get into the field, they rarely, if ever, argue price.

"Rosy said if I was interested, he was prepared to offer me the job of managing the Lexington, North Carolina, club in the Western Carolinas League. I would start immediately and my salary would be a thousand dollars a month for the last two months of the season. I told him I would catch the first plane down there," Sommers says.

He flew to North Carolina and began a minor league managerial career that would last through 1976. Sommers managed at Lexington; Decatur, Illinois; Fresno, California; Amarillo, Texas; Lafayette, Louisiana; and Midland, Texas.

"I really enjoyed managing in the minors," he says. "You do about everything yourself in those low minor leagues. I drove the bus, I worked as the trainer, I wrote letters to the front office, I did reports, I took care of the kids when they were lonely and depressed, I answered phone calls from their mothers. I think the minor league managers really are very important to baseball. The way a kid is handled at that level may have an awful lot to do with how he relates to managers all the way through his career," he says.

The club Sommers managed at Decatur in 1968 won the pennant in the second half of the split season. He also won again with Fresno in 1971. His best team was in Lafayette, Louisiana, in 1975. The key guy on that ball club was a big first baseman–third baseman by the name of Jack Clark. He hit .303 for Lafayette, had twenty-three home runs and batted in seventy-seven runs. He would later go on to stardom with the Giants, the Cardinals, the Yankees and the Padres. As the baseball wheel turns, Clark and Sommers were reunited in San Diego in 1989 with Clark being traded over from the Yankees and Sommers returning for his second season as a coach for the Padres.

"You didn't have to be a baseball genius to see that Jack Clark was going to be a great big league hitter," says Sommers. "He was just a kid when I got him, nineteen years old, out of Pennsylvania, with raw talent. He was a little moody when he had a bad day but he worked very hard. I figured he would be something special. I think it's great for the Padres to have him back. He was a tremendous hitter when he was with the Giants and Cards in the National League. I'm sure he'll help us a lot."

After the success with the Lafayette club, Sommers thought he deserved a raise for the 1976 season. He was still grateful for the opportunity but after ten years in the Giants organization and no chance for a big league spot, he felt a little more money was in order.

"I told Rosy Ryan I had heard the average salary for managers in the league was nineteen thousand dollars. He offered me fifteen thousand dollars. I told him I had been around a long time and we could split the difference. I would take seventeen thousand and be happy. Instead, he fired me."

Sommers wasn't out of work very long. He soon received a call from the Chicago Cubs and they offered him a job as the manager of their minor league club in Midland, Texas. It would be a sideways move in the same league, something very common to baseball, but he was happy to have it.

"I got a raise from the Cubs to sixteen thousand dollars," he says. "I felt very happy to be with them."

While Sommers was moving to the Cubs organization, Joe Frazier, a longtime manager in the Mets organization, was being promoted to the big league job. Frazier was named manager of the Mets October 3, 1975, for the 1976 season. He was succeeding an ousted Yogi Berra and interim manager Roy McMillan. Sommers hardly noticed the change in New York.

"I knew Joe slightly. We had managed against each other in the Texas League when Joe was at Memphis and I was at Amarillo and again in 1974 when he was at Victoria and I was back at Amarillo. We talked, as opposing managers do, but you wouldn't say we were friends. I don't think we ever had dinner together or spent a social evening out together. I knew him about the same way as I knew a hundred other people in baseball."

New Mets general manager Joe McDonald hired Frazier after working with him several years as the Mets farm director. He brought Frazier, a low-key, unpretentious, unknown sort of baseball guy, to New York for the 1976 season. The name coaches—Gil Hodges holdovers Joe Pignatano, Eddie Yost and pitching coach Rube Walker—were retained; McMillan, who had finished out the 1975 season as the skipper, was brought back and Willie Mays, working off a ten-year contract, was added for identification and fan recognition.

The Mets finished third in 1976. Frazier was asked back in 1977. On May 31, 1977, with the team in last place, Frazier was fired and replaced by his veteran third baseman Joe Torre.

Shortly after the 1976 season ended, Frazier met with GM McDonald. He was told he was being rehired. He asked if he could have a couple of his own coaches. Eddie Yost and Roy

McMillan were let go. Frazier told McDonald he had the guy he wanted as first base coach. He put in a call to Hortonville, Wisconsin.

"You're in this game," Sommers says, "and you never really lose hope that somehow, somewhere you will get a big league opportunity. I probably would have stayed in the minors all my life if it hadn't happened. Baseball was my life. I just wanted to get that chance. I just wanted to see what the big leagues were all about."

Sommers picked up the phone and Frazier identified himself.

"I thought he was calling to ask about some player I had down there. We knew each other and guys often do that. I figured that's what he wanted. I couldn't expect anything else."

Frazier got right to the point. Sommers almost fell off his chair.

"We're making some changes in New York," Frazier told Sommers. "We'd like you to join us as our first base coach."

Sommers glows even now and a smile breaks out on his face when he recalls that wondrous day.

"I felt," he says, with a huge grin, "I had died and gone to heaven."

Three months later Sommers was in the spring training headquarters of the Mets. Frazier told him that he wanted him to work with the young catchers, pitch batting practice, stay on the stragglers, coach first in the games and handle chores on the field that no one else seemed to handle.

"I didn't care what they wanted me to do," he says. "It was all terrific."

With an ever-present smile, with a thinning crewcut, with a bubbly personality, Sommers quickly became one of the best-liked members of the Mets entourage. He seemed to be everywhere that spring, pitching batting practice on the field, checking on injured players in the clubhouse, sitting with the manager after games, socializing with the press, signing autographs for the fans, working on scouting reports, soaking up all the juices of big league play.

"After all those years in the minors it was outstanding to have my bags taken care of on a trip, to be flying in charter planes, to be getting all that meal money, to be staying in the finest hotels. You don't realize what the big league life is like until you have put in about twenty years in the minor leagues on those dirty buses and dingy hotels."

Less than two months into the 1977 season, Sommers's first in the big leagues, Frazier was fired. Torre became the skipper and Sommers knew his Mets days were numbered. There was, however, a pleasant surprise. Torre kept him on.

"I really liked Joe and it was fun to be working with him. He had been around the league a long time. Joe knew everybody in baseball. More important, he knew every Italian restaurant in America. I don't think there was a major Italian restaurant we missed in the years I was with Joe in New York. Win, lose or draw, every meal out was an adventure," Sommers says.

Sommers remained with the Mets through the 1977 season and again in 1978. The team finished last again in 1978 as the franchise seemed to be breaking up under the careless management of Mrs. Joan Payson's daughter, Lorinda de Roulet. Mrs. de Roulet brought in her own two young daughters, Whitney and Bebe, who decided they knew more about baseball in their few months at Shea than all the people who had spent their lives in the game. So many Mets people heard the line, "Mummy will hear about this," that morale was as low as it can get around a ball club.

Somehow Torre was able to hang on through the end of the de Roulet regime after the 1979 season and for two years under the new Nelson Doubleday ownership with general manager Frank Cashen. He finally was fired and replaced by George Bamberger.

After the 1978 season, Torre and the front office decided to make some more coaching changes. Sommers was quickly

Bill Rigney. (*Courtesy of the Minnesota Twins*)

Herb Stein. (*Courtesy of the Minnesota Twins*)

Yosh Kawano. (*Courtesy of the Chicago Cubs*)

Larry Bearnarth. (*Courtesy of the Montreal Expos*)

Vada Pinson. (*Courtesy of the Detroit Tigers*)

Bill Buhler. (*Courtesy of the Los Angeles Dodgers*)

Bob Sheppard. (*Louis Requena*)

Eddie Lopat. (*Courtesy of the New York Yankees*)

Jack Rogers. (*Courtesy of the Boston Red Sox*)

Dennis Sommers. (*Courtesy of the San Diego Padres*)

Harry Wendelstedt. (*Louis Requena*)

Eddie Layton. (*Louis Requena*)

Alvin Jackson. (*Courtesy of the New York Mets*)

Ed Liberatore and friend.
(*Courtesy of Ed Liberatore*)

Chuck Hiller. (*Courtesy of the New York Mets*)

Al Pascarella. (*Author*)

Enzo Limongelli. (*Author*)

Bob Brown. (*Courtesy of the Baltimore Orioles*)

Buddy Kerr. (*UPI/ Bettman Newsphotos*)

Tony Ferrara. (*Courtesy of the New York Yankees*)

Bob Quinn. (*Courtesy of the New York Yankees*)

Phyllis Merhige. (*Courtesy of the American League Office*)

and quietly told he would not be rehired for the 1979 season.

"I had been around long enough to appreciate the big leagues. I didn't want to go back to the minors. I called around but there was nothing available. I finally accepted a job as the manager of the Montgomery, Alabama, club. It was a very depressing season being back in the minors after that long struggle to get to the big leagues. I think that season was the low point of my life. I was almost forty years old, I had realized my dream of making the major leagues and now I was going in the other direction again. It was very hard to take," he says.

Sommers went back to the minors, worked hard, brought the Montgomery club home in second place and returned home to Wisconsin. Another magical phone call would rescue him again.

"I have to be the luckiest guy in the world," he says.

The turnover in baseball can be incredible at times. Only two teams can win pennants, only one can win the World Series. After a season, all the losing clubs think the way to October success is through a managerial change. Refusing to recognize they had few quality players, the Cleveland Indians fired manager Jeff Torborg and replaced him with veteran coach Dave Garcia.

It was the same Dave Garcia who had been scouting for the San Francisco Giants in the Oshkosh, Wisconsin, area and signed a kid catcher out of Hortonville named Dennis Sommers.

"We had stayed friendly all these years," says Sommers. "I would see him at a banquet in the Milwaukee area over the winter or at some other baseball event along the way. We always managed to pass a few words and check up on each other's career."

Garcia rallied the Indians for a while late in 1979 and was offered a contract for 1980. This time, unlike the situation with Joe Frazier in New York, Garcia was allowed to pick his own coaches from the start. One of those he picked was Dennis Sommers.

"I had just returned from the longest baseball season in my life. I was not certain if I would go back to Montgomery or not, or whether they even wanted me back. I was out of the big leagues a year so I didn't think too many other teams would be calling me. All of a sudden Dave called. What a thrill. He wanted me with him in Cleveland."

Sommers would last a lot longer in Cleveland than Garcia did. Good first base coaches, who can pitch and catch batting practice (though not exactly at the same time) and hit the highest fungoes in the league, are obviously a lot harder to find than managers.

Sommers stayed on in Cleveland through the three full years of Garcia's stay on the shores of Lake Erie, for the 1983 start of Mike Ferraro's regime and on into the next two seasons under Pat Corrales.

By now Sommers had clearly identified his skills to big league people. He was a qualified coach. He was liked by players, press and fans. He had a cheery personality. He did not rock the boat. Most important, he did not have the identification among the fans or the executives of the club as a potential manager. That made him a safe bet around other managers who do not enjoy looking down at first base or third base and seeing coaches who are too well known, too popular or too successful. Such men present distinct threats to the security of a managerial position. Especially on a losing ball club.

Sommers had about realized all his baseball dreams by 1985. He had made it to the big leagues, had traveled through all the National and American League cities and knew good restaurants in most locations.

"I hadn't been in a World Series but I had been involved in two All-Star games. Sparky Anderson took me to the 1977 All-Star game in my rookie year as a coach and Jimmy Frey took me to the 1981 All-Star game. I pitched and caught batting practice before both games and it was some thrill serving them up to those guys," he says.

The Indians changed the coaching staff again after the 1985 season. This time Sommers caught on with the Minnesota Twins as an advance scout. He did that in 1986 and 1987.

"I finally got the big ring, the World Series ring, after the Twins beat the Cardinals in the 1987 Series. Nothing could quite match that," he says.

After that season ended, he was let go by the Twins and managed to run into San Diego GM Chub Feeney in the San Diego hotel site of the annual baseball convention. He was hired as the first base coach of the Padres for the 1988 season and rehired, under new manager Jack McKeon, for the 1989 season after McKeon agreed to come back as the team's skipper.

"I really love it out in San Diego. I have a lot of pals around that club. Pat Dobson is the pitching coach and he's a little wacky but he's great fun to be around. I'm close with all the other coaches, Greg Riddoch, Amos Otis and Sandy Alomar. I really enjoy sharing my time with those guys," he says.

Sommers was given a raise to thirty-five thousand dollars for the 1989 season. He considers that a decent, liveable salary for a single man.

"My mother is seventy-five years old and she is home alone in Wisconsin now. My sisters and brothers watch out for her but they are on their own. I spend the winters there and do all the chores around the house. It's a great change to be up there in the winter after spending the summers in San Diego. It's very restful for me, very pleasant. I don't start getting itchy for baseball until the first of the year. When we get the big snows and the cold weather I begin to think of the next season and start preparing myself for spring training," he says.

As he begins his fourth decade in baseball, Sommers is as content with his life as a man can be. He is anxious to remain active in the game he loves as long as he can.

"It has been a great ride," he says. "I have enjoyed every minute of it. I'm not campaigning for any other job in baseball. I'd be happy coaching the rest of my life. Of course, I'm only forty-eight years old, young as baseball managers go, and I wouldn't turn down the opportunity. A couple of young managers, Jimmy Leyland at Pittsburgh and Tom Trebelhorn at Milwaukee, have had about the same baseball background as me and they have done very well. I think I could handle a big league club if it came along. If it doesn't, I won't be very unhappy about it. I have already gone a lot further in this game than I ever thought I would. I have no complaints, no regrets about my time in the game."

Sommers is probably too nice a man, too gentle, too sincere to ever get an opportunity to manage on the big league level. Running a baseball team filled with vain millionaires hardly seems a chore he could handle.

But who knows. The kid catcher couldn't hit and he lasted ten years as a player. The young manager lasted ten more years. No fewer than four big league clubs have hired him for the most recent ten years of his career. Denny Sommers may have another decade or two in a job he could hardly expect. It has happened before with him.

"I know one thing," he says. "If it is in baseball I'll love it."

11 Harry Wendelstedt

UMPIRE, TEACHER

◼◼◼ IN THE SPRING OF 1961 A HUSKY, PINK-CHEEKED high school teacher of mathematics and science in Baltimore visited an old buddy named Gary Jackson. He began talking about a school he was soon to attend in Florida.

"The more he talked the more fired up I got about the idea," says Harry Wendelstedt. "I had always loved sports. When I played at Kenwood High in Baltimore I knew all the old stories about Babe Ruth. I knew the Babe had come out of Baltimore and had been a catcher and had gone on to fame and fortune. I was from Baltimore, I was a catcher. Maybe I could go on to fame and fortune. Then they started throwing curveballs at me in high school and my baseball career was over."

Harry Hunter Wendelstedt, Jr., did not become the next Babe Ruth. He still has a chance to become the next Bill Klem, one of the most respected, dignified, successful umpires in the history of the big leagues.

"I had played baseball and football and soccer around the Baltimore area. I was a pretty good athlete but not good enough to make a career out of it. I decided I would teach school, maybe coach a little down the line. That would be about it. When Gary told me about the umpire school in

Florida I was twenty-four years old. I had never thought about umpiring for a second. I figured I was a schoolteacher and that was what I would always be," he says.

Wendelstedt thought about it for a couple of days. Then he walked into the office of his high school principal and announced, "I'm quitting. I'm going to become a professional baseball umpire."

Wendelstedt was making sixty-five hundred dollars a year as a schoolteacher. He couldn't expect to make even that much as a minor league umpire. Chances of making the big leagues were about ten to one against him.

"I suddenly realized that was what I wanted to do. I wanted to be part of the game, part of baseball. I enjoyed teaching but I wasn't excited and stimulated every day. One day was pretty much like the next. In baseball no day is exactly the same as another, no game is exactly the same. I just love every day, every game. I'm thrilled to be part of professional baseball," he says.

The six-foot-two-inch two hundred pounder was soon on his way to the Al Somers baseball school in Florida. Somers had been a professional umpire for many years and had established the school in Daytona Beach many years before. Wendelstedt would emerge as one of his prize pupils and many years later would actually take over the operation of the school as Somers moved toward retirement. The Harry Wendelstedt school for umpires is now considered the finest training ground for big league umpires.

Wendelstedt grew up in Baltimore where his father drove a truck.

"He's Harry Wendelstedt, Sr., and my son is Harry III. My father was always supportive. When I told him I was quitting school to become an umpire he told me that if I thought that was what I wanted to do, I should go right ahead and do it," he says.

Graduation from the Al Somers school did not guarantee a job in baseball, as graduation from the Harry Wendelstedt school does not. It does guarantee that the graduate will be trained in the fundamentals of umpiring and have the skills, stamina and style to make it as an umpire.

"All we can do in the school is prepare a person as best we can. It is really up to them if they make it or not," he says.

While more than seventy graduates from Wendelstedt's school are in the big leagues, one who did graduate and has not yet made it seems to get the most publicity. That is Pam Postema, a female umpire who has progressed to the American Association and Pacific Coast League level without a big league chance. She has umpired in spring training games for big league teams over the last four years.

"There is a lot of pressure on any rookie umpire," says Wendelstedt. "There is enormous pressure on Pam. I think she is qualified. I also think she will make it if the media leave her alone. I think the players have accepted the idea of a female umpire. I watched her work in the spring of 1988 and she was quite professional. It was all the attention she got that I think caused the league to shy away from her. She is getting up there in age, about thirty-two, thirty-three years old, so if she doesn't make it soon, I think they will reach down for younger umpires. I hope she gets her chance."

Wendelstedt's size and strength were significant factors in his early success as a big league umpire. Physical people such as professional athletes tend to have more respect for physical officials. It is a little tougher for a smaller umpire, a Dutch Rennert, a Bruce Froemming, a Billy Williams to make it as successful big league umpires.

"Pam has a lot to overcome," says Wendelstedt. "Every umpire does."

Wendelstedt began his career in the Class A Georgia-Florida League in 1962. The next year he was promoted a notch to the Class C Northwest League.

"At the end of that season the president of the league called the umpires together. He started to tell us how lousy we all were, how none of us knew the first thing about umpiring, how all of us should look for another line of work. 'You're all fired,' he screamed. I figured that was it and I would go back to school in Baltimore, as much as I hated to do that. 'Except you. The National League has an option on you. I don't know why but they do.' I didn't know who he was talking to. I looked around and looked back at him and he was looking straight at me."

Wendelstedt went to the Texas League in 1964, the International League in 1965 and the National League in 1966. He has been there ever since.

"I remember the first game I ever worked in spring training that year. It was the Yankees against the Braves in Fort Lauderdale. I was nervous, of course, but I did all right the first couple of plays. Then the third guy came up. It was Mickey Mantle. I just wanted to do a good job and make sure I didn't embarrass myself. I tried not to stare at him and be too obvious. I just couldn't help it. Here I was a guy who had been a schoolteacher a few years earlier watching this great player on television or once in a while in a game in Baltimore and now all of a sudden I was standing behind the plate and he was swinging a couple of bats and getting ready to step in. I broke into a cold sweat. I kept it all inside. He just didn't know how I felt," he says.

Before long Wendelstedt had become a successful umpire. The players respected his calls and the managers didn't give him too much heat.

"I guess my toughest time in those early days came with Leo Durocher. I knew he was an umpire baiter and I had prepared myself for his attacks. I decided I wouldn't listen to what he said from the dugout and when he came out to argue on the field I would give him his time and then I would heave him out. I didn't want any prolonged arguments with Leo on the field. Anyway, it became very uncomfortable. Any time I got a game with the Cubs with Leo managing I just hated to face it. From the minute I broke into the league Leo wouldn't let up on me. I heaved him a few times but the next day he would be just as loud-mouthed. One day I got him real early and that night I got a call in the hotel from the league president, Warren Giles.

" 'Harry, this is Warren Giles.'

" 'Yes, Mr. Giles. How are you, sir?'

" 'Well, Harry, I'm not real good. I got the report that you had a tough time with Durocher again.'

" 'Yes sir, I did. He just won't let up on me.'

" 'I understand that. You just have to get this thing settled down. We can't keep having this kind of fuss every time you are on the field with Leo.'

" 'I'm doing my best, sir.'

" 'Maybe I'll speak to Leo.' "

Giles decided to confront Durocher. Leo had never been known to budge an inch but he did admit that he was getting on the kid because he was new. It was simply his style.

"I finally proved I belonged and Leo finally let up on me a little bit," Wendelstedt says.

In 1980 Wendelstedt was working the All-Star game in Los Angeles. Many of the Dodger stars were on hand and Durocher, now seventy-five years old, marched up to Wendelstedt.

"I thought it was going to be more of the same old garbage. Anyway, this time," Wendelstedt says, "Durocher grabbed me in a big bear hug and said, 'How you doin', old buddy?' He was some character."

Tom Gorman, one of the most respected and entertaining umpires of all time, was a frequent after-dinner speaker at sports dinners until his death two years ago. One of his favorite stories concerned Durocher.

"I was working this game between the Cubs and Mets," Gorman would say, "and Billy Williams hit a grounder behind first base. The first baseman fielded it and threw to the pitcher. The pitcher, the runner and me all arrived at the same time as the ball. We all crashed and the ball flew free. I was knockcd flat. I'm on the ground and I hear this voice screaming, 'Is he safe or out? Is he safe or out?' Then I scream, 'Is that you, Leo?' Durocher says it is him and I immediately scream, 'Then in that case, he's out.' Then they carried me off the field with a broken leg."

Wendelstedt and most umpires who have worked games against Durocher's teams always considered Leo a burr under their skin.

"I'll tell you who was the worst guy I ever met in baseball. That was Alex Johnson. He was born mad. He had a foul mouth and he would argue every pitch. I got sick of him. He was just a terribly aggravating player. Another guy who always gave me a hard time was Tim Foli, who was with the Mets and Expos. He was very combative, liked to scream at everything. That went on for a few years and all of a sudden his entire personality changed. I thought it was an act at first. But it turned out he had married, found religion and really changed his lifestyle. After that it was always, 'Good evening, Harry, how you doin', Harry?' Things like that. I never saw anybody change as dramatically as he did," says Wendelstedt.

Umpires care for the game and Wendelstedt says the biggest problem is concentration.

"You have to separate yourself from the action. You know what the score is and the game situation and what's going on at all times, of course, but you have to concentrate on your job. A guy hits a homer, you have to watch him touch the plate. A guy strikes out, you have to be sure the next hitter is at the plate. You have to stay up with the count, the outs, everything about the game, and you have to do it without any consideration whether it's Pete Rose at the plate going for a streak or some kid in his first big league at-bat. You always have to keep in mind the integrity of the game," he says.

Wendelstedt is by nature a pleasant, gregarious, outgoing man. There are some pains to the job with a man of that nature.

"We come on the field sometimes after a game the previous day with a controversial play. The fans boo us. It is as if they had waited all night and into the next game for that opportunity. I hate that. I want to be liked. I know the fans are for the home team but I expect baseball fans to understand that we are calling the plays as we see them. We have no interest in who wins or loses. Only the players can decide that. We are there to make the calls and represent the league. I always hope that fans are better educated on the role of the umpire. I think there is far too much criticism of the umpires. When we do a good job nobody knows we are there. When there is a tough play and it goes against the home team, the press plays it up. I'm very unhappy when they exaggerate a play's importance or our role in the outcome of a game. The players settle the game, not the umpires," he says.

Wendelstedt turned fifty last year. He has made one concession to his age.

"Now I wear reading glasses off the field," he says.

When umpires are hired they go through a rigorous physical and mental exam. This includes an investigation into their private lives.

"I can't imagine a job where there is a bigger investigation of somebody's life. When I was hired they sent people around to talk to my friends, my relatives, my schoolteachers, my coworkers. I couldn't believe how thorough it was. I got home after that first year in the big leagues and one of my friends said that he had heard how I collected bottles off the stoops of the homes in my neighborhood and sold them for a few dollars to help out at home. Another friend said he told the investigators about the fight I had when I was in sixth grade and tore this kid's jacket. There wasn't anything about my life that the National League did not know," he says.

Four years after he joined the National League, Wendelstedt married Cheryl Maher, a former airline stewardess. They have two children in school in their Florida home at Daytona Beach.

"That's the toughest part of the job. I miss my family very much," he says. "Not a day goes by that we don't talk on the telephone and I get home every chance I get. In 1979 the umpires won a two-week vacation during the season in their contract and that makes all the difference in the world. Unlike other umpires, I don't live in a big league city so I'm on the road all the time."

The travel and logistics for umpires are much more grueling than they are for players. Players may have a two-week home stand. Umpires may have a two-day stand in the same town. Then it could be off to Houston, Los Angeles, San Francisco, Cincinnati, St. Louis and Pittsburgh over a two-week period.

"There are lots of nights when we come to the ball park with maybe an hour or two of sleep. It isn't the most comfortable feeling in the world but we have to do it. There just aren't enough planes to get out when you want," he says.

Umpires are given an allowance for meals, rooms and travel. With careful managing of their funds, the expenses can be kept to a fair amount. When they take a side trip home or splurge on a big meal it can cut into their own salaries. They try to keep a steady budget through the season. Traditionally, they have friends who will drive them to airports and save the cab fares. That usually costs a signed baseball or a couple of tickets to the game.

Most umpires make those compromises to their integrity without any feelings of conflict. In some cases it is an abused privilege, but the clubs get to know quickly which umpires ask for too many autographed balls, too many complimentary tickets or too many free seats at the local theaters.

There is no rule against it but by common practice umpires tend to stay in hotels away from the hotels with the teams.

"Nobody tells us we can't stay in the same hotel. It just isn't a good idea. It is the kind of thing where appearance could be as important as anything that is actually done," says Wendelstedt.

In many cities umpires will get lower rates than the average guest, sometimes because they represent steady business for the hotel, especially over a weekend when downtown big city hotels are not quite filled to capacity.

One other unwritten rule of umpiring crews pertains to their own logistics. The junior man on an umpiring crew handles the arrangements. That means he makes all the flight reservations, all the hotel bookings, all the rentals of cars or cabs. It is the rite of passage that moves quickly to the junior man in the next crew in the following season. Umpires have no official traveling secretaries as teams do but they get the same services.

Salaries have also increased dramatically in the past years since the umpires became more militant in negotiations under their union leader, Philadelphia attorney Richie Phillips. They are generally paid according to seniority, with salaries approaching one hundred thousand dollars a year for senior men like Wendelstedt, with extra money for playoffs and World Series work. No matter how much he makes, though, it is never enough.

"Every umpire has to maintain a home away from work and has huge travel and phone expenses," he says. "I can't imagine how the umpires made it in the old days."

While working conditions have improved tremendously in the past ten years, the umpire's lot is still not an easy one. What keeps them going in the brutal July heat of St. Louis or the frozen nights of San Francisco is merely their love for the game.

"When you are one of only sixty guys in the world who do what you do," says Wendelstedt, "that is a great thrill. I come home on vacation or at the end of the season and my friends and neighbors come over and they tell me how much they admire me or how much they want to be me. That's a great kick. Everybody is a baseball fan and they always want to know about the great stars of the game and what kind of fellows they are and who's the best hitter. Actually I try not to talk too much about baseball. I like to get away from it when I'm home. I'll talk fishing with anybody."

Wendelstedt says that good umpires also know how to spot a phony right off the bat.

"There are times you are in the hotel lobby or at the airport and a guy comes up to you and starts a conversation. We get our pictures in the paper once in a while, so people know who we are and they'll ask about this player or that. We just don't discuss it. We don't give out any information. I try to be respectful but I also make it clear that I'm here to travel or to stay in this hotel and I'm not here to discuss the game. You never know who you might be discussing it with," he says.

One of the most impressive records in sports has to belong to big league umpires. There has never been a hint of a scandal about umpires dealing with gamblers or giving out information to outsiders about the game. Wendelstedt says there will be no Black Sox scandal among umpires.

"We are not that much better as human beings than anybody else. It is simply that this aspect of our job is what our lives are based on. After the way we are screened and examined at all times we understand the conditions. If we accept that job of being a big league umpire we accept the responsibilities and the pressures. If it gets too much guys can get out. Some of them do," he says.

One of the provisions of the latest umpire contract was mandatory testing for illegal drugs. On this day at Shea Stadium, while Wendelstedt was being interviewed, representatives of the league office arrived to perform tests on the four umpires in his crew.

"I don't see it as a very big deal if I have to urinate into a bottle once in a while to prove that I am clean," he says. "I don't see that as a violation of my constitutional rights. I see it as a duty and an obligation. I owe that much to my employers and I owe that much to the fans. I'm proud that they know I have been tested and that I'm clean. Our profession has been built on years and years and years of integrity. This is part of it. I may miss a play because I had a bad angle or I had a bad day. I want them to know I didn't miss a play because I was under the influence of an illegal drug."

In his twenty-three seasons in the big leagues, Wendelstedt has been involved in some dramatic games. He remembers the Don Drysdale scoreless string, five no-hitters, two more games that went into the last out in the ninth inning, batting streaks, World Series games and dramatic playoff homers. Mostly he remembers doing a good job.

"People are always asking at banquets and baseball occasions about the great players. How did Koufax throw? Was Marichal better than Gibson? I have opinions but I try not to offer them. I'm more interested in how I did my job. Was I concentrating? Did I control the game? Was I bearing down on every play? There are times I'm concentrating so hard in some games I have no idea who wins or loses," he says.

While calling balls and strikes may be the most difficult technical chore of an umpire, controlling the game and controlling one's own emotions may be the measure of a successful umpire. Wendelstedt can often be seen chatting with ball players at home plate or on the bases. Most players seem to like him.

"He's a very capable umpire, works very hard and hustles on every play," says Mets first baseman Keith Hernandez. "All you can ask of an umpire is that he be consistent and bear down. Harry always bears down. He's into the game."

Hernandez has been talked about as a future manager. He is tough, he knows the game and he can lead and teach. He will argue with umpires when he believes they are wrong. He will not bait them.

Mets catcher Gary Carter is another star player with ambitions in the game down the line. He seems more the general manager type.

"I have always gotten along well with Harry. Even when I'm having a tough time at the plate or my pitcher is having a tough time in the game Harry is pleasant," says Carter. "He's a nice man and he is a good umpire."

Unlike some umpires, there are no indications Wendelstedt favors veteran players over younger players, a traditional complaint of younger players.

"I think you have to call the game as you see it. I try not to consider the identity of the player involved. It might happen that Pete Rose gets more close pitches than a rookie. That isn't because you favor Pete Rose. It is because he has such a good eye at the plate himself that you usually agree with him when he takes a pitch," he says.

Wendelstedt says he tries to keep his personal feelings about a player far removed from his calls.

"I have always admired Rose. Most people in baseball do. He has done an awful lot for the game. That doesn't mean I won't throw him out when I think he is wrong. I've done it and then greeted him the next day as if nothing happened. That's the only way to get along with people in this game," he says.

When the season ends, Wendelstedt returns to his Florida home for quality time with his family.

"I just love it down there. I find it very relaxing to get away from the game after a long season. I throw a football around with the kids and I have a lot of fun with all the neighborhood kids. Sometimes when they meet me and know I'm an umpire, some of the kids are a little shy. People sometimes have trouble figuring out what to say to an umpire. We're just like anybody else. They can ask me how my water heater is working. The neighbors who know me never talk baseball. They know I'm tired of that after the year is over. We just enjoy the sun and the fresh air and have a good time," he says.

Wendelstedt owns a boat and can be found most afternoons in the water around Daytona Beach with friends.

"I'm an absolute fishing fanatic. I can go out and sit there all day until I pull in a marlin or some other big fish. I find that very satisfying and very relaxing after a long season in big stadiums with lots of noise. I think when I retire that's what I'll probably be doing every day, just sitting out in the sun and waiting for that one real big fish to jump on my line," he says.

Only two National League umpires, Doug Harvey and John Kibler, have seniority over Wendelstedt. He expects to remain in the game another half dozen years at least before he begins thinking of that full-time fishing job.

"For now I think I have the best deal in the world. From February until October I'm in the National League. I'm doing what I love. Even though I miss my family and the travel is rough and those blistering summer days can wear you down, I wouldn't trade it in for anything else. Then I am home with my family until the next spring training. I run my school for a month in the winter and I'm very proud of that. We help bring young, qualified umpires to the game. I feel that is very important. I know I'm not as quick as I used to be and my eyes aren't twenty-fifteen as they once were but my experience makes up for the slow-down in reflexes. But I feel I'm as good as I ever was," he says.

He knows retirement will be coming within a few years. He also knows he will leave behind a proud career as a National League umpire, more than two decades of honesty and accuracy, as good a record as any man in his profession has ever had.

"You can't do this work unless you love the game, really love it. It is just too hard to do it simply for a living. I'm still excited every time I walk out on the field and look up in the stands at a full house and hear the National Anthem being played. I know I'm part of all that, important to the game with the respect of all of my peers. I see baseball as one of the most important, historic institutions in this country and I'm always concerned about doing my share to keep that reputation deserved."

It was time for Harry Wendelstedt to go to work. There was a lot of gear to put on before he would take the field at Shea on this hot afternoon. The most important piece of equipment he carried to home plate was a wide smile and a happy disposition.

Even Leo Durocher had trouble keeping from hugging this dedicated bear of a man.

12 Eddie Layton

THE MAN WHO'S PLAYED FOR THEM ALL

■■■■ ON A SUMMER AFTERNOON AT YANKEE STADIUM OR-
ganist Eddie Layton was practicing for the night game that
evening against the Tigers. The ball park was still empty
save for some cleaning personnel and a few groundskeepers
down on the field working on the mound. Layton hit a few
keys, B flat, F, G—making the familiar boom, boom, boom,
boom sound of the Stadium charge—as he tuned up his
sparkling Hammond organ.

"I do that every day just to make sure everything is in
working order. I can't come to the ball park just before the
game, sit down and put my fingers into a dead organ," he
says.

Layton played his charge music, worked in a few familiar
tunes linked to the players, such as "I'm Just Wild About
Harry," for Yankee catcher Ron Hassey, or the "Trolley
song," for Wayne Tolleson, the player his teammates call
Tolley, or the ballet "Dance of the Hours," for the graceful
Don Mattingly.

Layton did not notice a man walking toward his small
booth on the press level at the Stadium.

"Move over," said the commanding figure of the Boss.

"I looked up and there was George Steinbrenner," says Layton. "I had no idea he was in the park, I had no idea he knew I was there and I certainly didn't imagine him sitting down at the organ."

Steinbrenner moved his ample girth onto the organ stool as Layton rose to the occasion.

"All of a sudden he began playing 'I'm in the Mood for Love,' and it was a professional job," says Layton.

The Boss's music echoed through the empty Stadium. He finished the piece with a flourish, looked up at the famous organist and asked, "What do you think?"

"I think you're fired," says Layton, a man who clearly does not need the job to survive.

Steinbrenner, a man as famous for his firings as for his hirings (often of the very same people in a very short period of time), started to laugh heartily.

"He really took it with a big laugh," says Layton. "All I know is he hasn't been back since and I'm still at the organ."

The small, dark-haired, middle-aged man has been at the organ in Yankee Stadium for more than twenty-one years. He started out not knowing a foul ball from an infield fly.

"When I first heard the term 'sacrifice fly,' I thought it was some baseball ritual in which they sacrificed flies for good luck or something like that," he says.

When he first joined the Yankees in 1967, Mickey Mantle was in his declining years as a Hall of Fame star. Layton did know a ball hit into the stands counted for a run. He also knew the fans screamed one day when he saw Mantle do just that.

"He hit the ball out of the field, into the seats, and I could see the crowd applauding and screaming. Then I looked up and he was running counterclockwise. I thought that was wrong. He was batting lefthanded and facing third base. I thought he had to run clockwise in the direction he was facing. I'm not kidding when I say I knew nothing about baseball," he says.

Layton may not know the infield fly rule after more than two decades at the Stadium but he does know a fair ball from a foul ball now.

"What I still don't understand is how teams win games when they are three or four runs down. I pull for the Yankees to win but I'm a giver-upper. If they are down a run or two in the early innings I always figure they have no chance to win," he says.

While Layton may not be ready for a winning record in baseball trivia, he does add much to the enjoyment of the game with his melodious play between innings or when some of the Yankees are serenaded to the plate. He is good without being intrusive.

"There was only one time that I can remember that I held up the game. I was playing a tune and not looking down on the field for some reason. Reggie Jackson was with the Yankees then and all of a sudden I looked up and he was in the batter's box. I was just about to pull my hands from the keys. I was very embarrassed. Jackson just looked up at the press level and began to do a little dance with his bat. I continued it for a few more moments just to entertain him and the crowd," Layton says.

The organist had the right guy. Jackson would never miss a chance to entertain the fans. He was probably baseball's most infamous showoff, a hot dog, in ball player terms.

"There isn't enough mustard in all America to cover that hot dog," Oakland teammate Darold Knowles once said of Jackson.

Jackson is one of the few players ever to notice the music. Most players seem too intent on their march to the plate to march to Layton's music.

"I try to play something fitting for all of them but I very rarely have any contact with the players so I have no way of knowing if they like what I do or not," he says.

In all the years he has been around the Stadium, Layton figures he has had a meaningful conversation and relationship with only one Yankee, veteran pitcher Tommy John.

"I was up in the Stadium office one day and he came in and we began talking about the organ. He's really a very wonderful fellow, very curious about other people, and we became good friends after that," he says.

Layton hasn't been able to play a tune on the field for John. Pitchers don't bat in the American League.

"About the only way you can serenade a player is when he comes to the plate. I play only between innings or when the batter walks to the plate. I know maybe fifty or a hundred thousand tunes by heart but I don't know what I'd play for Tommy if he came up to hit," he says.

After all these years at the Stadium, Layton has become as much a fixture around the ball park as the monuments in center field or the feuding, fussing and fighting with Steinbrenner and his players.

"I just love it. I know that I couldn't be as happy if I didn't have the ball games to play at. I have no thoughts of retiring. I just want to keep playing for the Yankees as long as I can," he says.

Eddie Layton was born in Philadelphia, attended Frankford High and graduated from Westchester State Teachers College outside Philadelphia.

"My father, Bill, was in the grocery business in South Philadelphia. He did very well and we grew up comfortably. He owned four supermarkets by the time I was college age and there were no problems sending me off to school. I majored in meteorology and minored in music. I had been playing the organ ever since I was twelve years old," he says.

Layton entered the Navy in the early 1950s. He was trained as an X-ray technician and began thinking in terms of that skill for a career.

"When I got out of the Navy I really was undecided about what I wanted to do. I had a choice of three careers because I had improved my organ-playing skills in the Navy, I had learned X-ray technology and I was still interested in meteorology," he says.

As often happens, circumstances had more to do with his career decision than any conscious choice.

"While I was trying to figure out what I wanted to do," he says, "a friend of mine told me that a club in New Jersey was looking for an organ player. I went down there, auditioned for the owner and got the job for twelve dollars a week playing nightly at the exclusive Wannamassa Club in New Jersey, across the river from Philadelphia. I enjoyed it very much and after a couple of weeks I decided that was what I wanted to do. I also decided I'd better get more proficient with the instrument if I was to support myself playing the organ."

After a few months at the Wannamassa Club, Layton decided to move to New York and enroll full-time in the organ classes taught by Jesse Crawford, one of America's most renowned teachers of the classical organ.

"This was the best decision of my life," he says. "I knew how to play well enough but I had to learn harmony, theory and arranging if I was ever to do anything with the instrument except entertain a few people in a nightclub with some popular music."

For more than a year Layton attended Crawford's classes in Manhattan, spent many hours practicing and studying theory, talked with the master about the history of the instrument, developed a passion for the music and what the organ could do and soon felt qualified enough to strike out on his own as a classical performer of one of the most difficult instruments in the musical array.

"I got a job playing at a few other places but the real breakthrough came when I was asked to make a classical organ record. It was a great success and I went on to make twenty-four single records of organ performances with great sales on each of them. That was the start of my very successful professional career. After that I knew I could always make a living with the organ," he says.

Layton was becoming one of the most distinguished performers on the organ in the country. People in the field knew of his work and his appearance at any hotel or club was a guarantee of a successful turnout.

"My work came to the attention of the Hammond Organ Company. One day a representative called me and asked to meet with me. I knew this had to be the start of something big," he says.

Layton could not even begin to imagine just how big this gig would really be. Hammond wanted him to travel across the country as their representative, give pop concerts and help sell Hammond organs in every city, town and village in America. He would do more than seven hundred concerts in large auditoriums and small ones, arenas, schools, churches and offices before ending the tour a few years later.

"I have no idea of the sales figures but I am certain I had a great deal to do with the surge of sales for Hammond organs. I would guess that a good percentage of the people who bought Hammond organs in those early years of the 1960s heard me in concert or on record," he says.

Shortly after winning a pennant in 1964 and firing manager Yogi Berra for not being successful in the World Series against the Cardinals—George Steinbrenner is not the only impulsive Yankee-firing owner—Yankee owners Dan Topping, who had inherited millions, and Del Webb, who had earned millions in the real estate business in California, Nevada and Arizona, decided to sell the team. They saw it in decline and were no longer interested in the operation.

Topping and Webb knew William Paley, the successful broadcasting mogul from the Columbia Broadcasting System. Paley assigned a young, long-haired troubleshooter and former World War II OSS hero named Michael Burke to explore the possibilities of the sale for CBS. Burke had been a football star at the University of Pennsylvania, a naval officer, a writer, a movie actor and the operating officer of the Ringling Brothers circus. Paley had hired him a few years earlier and Burke's main focus was the company's diversification of investment.

On Burke's recommendation, CBS decided to purchase the Yankees from Topping and Webb for a price estimated at something over 12 million dollars. They would hold it until January 3, 1973, when the struggling team would be sold off to a group headed by a Cleveland industrialist and shipping company owner named George M. Steinbrenner III. The purchase price, some ten years after CBS acquired the team, was barely 10 million dollars. Steinbrenner has reportedly turned down bids in excess of 150 million dollars for the team as late as 1988.

The CBS Yankees, under Burke, fell apart. Their stars, Mickey Mantle, Whitey Ford, Elston Howard, Roger Maris, Tony Kubek, Bobby Richardson, were all past their primes. The team finished sixth under new manager Johnny Keane in 1965, fell to tenth under old manager Ralph Houk in 1966 and would bounce around the bottom of the league until the first pennant in Steinbrenner's regime in 1976.

Burke was more successful off the field than his team was on the field. He quickly became a well-known figure around town, seen at the opera, at the Broadway theaters, at the finest restaurants, at the A list parties, at charity balls and at major sporting events. After his Yankee years he would resurface as the operating head of Madison Square Garden during that sports emporium's down time, which may or may not have been coincidental with Burke's arrival. He did arrange for the sale of the Stadium to New York City and its needed refurbishing. He upgraded the atmosphere around the team and he added color and drama in some unique ways. He once had famed poetess Marianne Moore, an inveterate baseball fan, throw out the first ball on opening day. Burke continued to look for ways to liven up the Stadium while the team rebuilt slowly.

Layton's touring days for Hammond were finished by now. He had taken a steady gig at the Mermaid Room of the flashy Park Sheraton Hotel on Manhattan's East Side. One night Michael Burke walked in to listen to a performance.

"I didn't know he was there and I didn't know who he was," says Layton. "All I knew was that a few days later I got a call from somebody at CBS. They wanted to hire me to play live organ music for their soap operas."

Television was moving then from the early days of live shows into taped programs. One of the few genres that would remain live was the afternoon plays, or soap operas, so called because when they were first presented on radio in the 1930s and 1940s they were often sponsored by soap companies.

"My job was to play background music. They would outline the story for the day, sometimes even give me the script and ask me to play appropriate background music. All the shows were performed live in the CBS broadcast center. Sometimes the final writing of the script would continue right until the opening of the show and even after it started. This was clearly a live performance, so live it often changed right until airtime," he says.

The shows Layton performed on included some of the most popular afternoon entertainments, watched by millions across America from New York to Los Angeles, from Minneapolis to Miami and most points in between—such shows as *Secret Storm*, *Love of Life* and *Love Is a Many Splendored Thing*. There were many, many more and their names changed constantly after the story ideas didn't. It was always boy meets girl, boy beds girl, boy loses girl, boy murders girl, boy saves girl from murder by other boy or some combination thereof.

"While I was doing that in the daytime at one or two in the afternoon I was also working at night. I would be performing at the Mermaid Room or once in a while I would get a job at the Radio City Music Hall. That was always a thrill because Radio City has the world's largest organ. It was very exciting to perform before several thousand people live even though I was performing before millions live on television that I couldn't see," he says.

Burke had listened to Layton's work at the Mermaid Room and he had watched him and listened to his performances on these CBS shows. He approached Layton one night after a show at the Mermaid Room.

"How would you like to play at Yankee Stadium?" he asked.

"I've never even been to Yankee Stadium," Layton said.

Burke explained that he could entertain the fans between innings without knowing much about the game. When there was no action on the field he could assume it was proper for him to play.

"I explained to him I had grown up in Philadelphia and had never been to the ball park and I said that I had lived in New York and had not been to the ball park here, either," he says.

Burke told Layton that most of the Yankee games were at night. He could keep his CBS job on the soap operas, play his gigs when the Yankees were on the road and perform for the baseball audience when the team was home.

"He was very persuasive and I agreed to give it a chance," he says.

Burke had an old organ delivered to the Stadium press level, set Layton up in a booth and told him he was on his own.

"I had all these thousands of songs in my head but I certainly didn't know what I would play. I figured I could come up with something. I also knew that if I heard an appropriate song I could play it again on the organ. I didn't need music to repeat a melody if I once listened to it," he says.

Layton played a few tunes on the organ. The fans seemed to applaud respectfully. Then he noticed a Yankee player walking to the plate with a steady stride.

"It just came into my head that I could accompany him to the plate with some rousing music and help generate some excitement in the ball park. I came up with that charge sound, the boom, boom, boom, boom that is now so familiar. I played the notes, the crowd began applauding to the beat and the players seemed to walk to the plate with an energetic bounce. I looked over at Burke in his box seat and he was applauding like the average fan. He looked up at me and gave a hearty smile and a thumbs-up sign and I knew I was a hit in Yankee Stadium. It was a great feeling even though I didn't know a sacrifice fly from a sacrificed fly," he says.

Layton was soon a fixture at the Stadium. He performed at every night game as well as every day game. Most of the time he could continue his CBS soap opera schedule but if there was a conflict—for example, a Thursday afternoon game when *Love of Life* was in one of its most dramatic climaxes—he would hire a pinch hitter for the television show.

"Young organists would be thrilled to play for a soap opera. They did it many times through the years. I wouldn't do that at the ball game. I enjoyed the games too much, I felt a stronger obligation to offer my own music and style and I liked being a part of the Yankees," he says.

There was only one catch to Layton's daily performances. He had to get there. He didn't know how to drive and he certainly wouldn't take the subway from CBS's mid-Manhattan offices to Yankee Stadium. He got around the city by cab but didn't expect to have to deal with cabdrivers in the long ride from CBS to the Bronx.

Michael Burke solved that problem immediately. He said, "We'll get you there and back by limo." That was a nice side benefit to the job. Every afternoon a limousine would be waiting for him at the CBS broadcast center for the ride to Yankee Stadium. He was there until the last out of the game whether it was nine innings or eighteen innings with a rain delay. Then the limousine would be ready at the Stadium entrance to take Layton to his luxury apartment in Forest Hills, Queens, about a half hour ride from the Stadium at those late hours after night games and devoid of traffic.

"I really love my place in Forest Hills. It is beautifully furnished and when I want to have some fun I can just press a button and about three quarters of the ceiling comes down with a display of electric trains. Collecting electric trains is my hobby and I have one of the finest displays in the country," he says. "I bring them down electrically almost every day."

Several years ago Steinbrenner purchased a giant new Hammond organ for Layton's use at the Stadium. The beautiful instrument can be heard for miles.

"The average home stereo set has anywhere from thirty-five to fifty watts in electrical power. The new organ has over fifty thousand watts in power. It could be heard on the Triboro Bridge about three or four miles away if I turned it up. The main speaker comes out of center field and bounces back into the ball park. There are no dead spots in the Stadium. It can be heard equally well from any seat in the house," he says.

In all the seasons he has been with the Yankees, Layton said, he has never missed a performance.

"The closest I ever came was a few years ago when I injured a finger while working on my boat. It was severely damaged and swollen. I had it taped and I came to the park and played with nine fingers. I don't think anyone heard the difference," he says.

While the small, slight, middle-aged bachelor enjoys playing at the Stadium and spends a good part of the winter now playing at Madison Square Garden for basketball and hockey crowds, he probably enjoys his boat even more. He owns a twenty-six-foot diesel tugboat, which he berths at the Tarrytown Yacht Club. He often motors with friends from the Forest Hills Yacht Basin to Tarrytown and back during a pleasant summer afternoon. He gets home in time to change from his sailing jacket and captain's cap into his sedate business suit for Stadium work. He usually takes off his jacket and performs in shirtsleeves in the booth next to the press box on the mezzanine level at the Stadium.

"I've been around so long now that fans are getting to know me. People wave and sometimes call out my name and ask me to play a certain tune. They often ask to hear some of the tunes I play for the players," he says.

Layton is dropped off in the Yankee Stadium parking lot just across the street from the ball park. The players and team executives also park there.

"I came to the game one Saturday afternoon and a small boy, about nine or ten, was waiting outside the gate behind the fence. He stared at me for a while, since he had seen that I had come out of the players' parking lot. As I crossed the street to the park he walked up to me.

" 'Are you anybody?' he asked.

" 'Yes,' I said. 'I'm Eddie Layton. I play the organ at the ball park.' "

Even though it wasn't Don Mattingly or Dave Winfield or even the Boss himself, the youngster seemed satisfied it was somebody connected to the Yankees. That was good enough. He pulled a baseball from a brown paper bag and asked Layton if he would sign it.

"I'll sign it," Layton replied, "if you can give me the last two words of the National Anthem."

Layton performed that number every day and always tried to get the Stadium audience to sing along.

The boy just paused for a second. He was deep in thought. Finally, a smile came to his face. He announced that he knew the last two words of the National Anthem.

"OK," said Layton, waiting for the proud announcement that he had remembered "home of the brave."

"Play ball," said the boy resoundingly.

While the story seemed more apocryphal than accurate, Layton reaffirmed its truth and accuracy.

"That's exactly how it happened," he says. "If I'm not

telling the truth, the whole truth and nothing but the truth, may my boat sink."

No more convincing was necessary.

After more than two decades around the Yankees and their famous ball park in the Bronx, Layton admits he still isn't what any objective observer would call a finished baseball fan.

"There are still too many things about the game that I simply don't understand," he says. "People who have played baseball and been around it all their lives probably have no trouble understanding its intricacies. People like me who came to it late still have difficulty understanding a lot of the rules," he says.

Layton's knowledge is clearly adequate for the performance of his duties. He knows how to play the organ and he certainly knows when to play the organ. He says he has not played at any inappropriate time save for the one episode with Reggie Jackson. He already has become one of the longest-standing Yankee employees in the George Steinbrenner regime.

"I have never had a single problem with George. I get along with him very well. He has never told me to play anything special and he seems to understand and appreciate everything I do. I have invited him out on my boat but he has been too busy to come. Maybe one of these days he will join me on the boat and we can talk about boats and the organ playing as well as the Yankees," he says.

Layton says that his playing in the Stadium gives him great pleasure. A few years ago he gave up all his other evening performances and simply plays at the Stadium.

"About three or four years ago I decided to stop playing for the soap opera and now I just spend most of my summer afternoons before the game on the boat. I don't do anything else anymore but play at the Stadium," he says.

Some ball parks have been carried away in the electronic era and the noise level becomes overwhelming as the sound is turned up to incite the fans. There was even a case of the scoreboard at Houston being accused of interference in the playing of the game as the electronic chants against the opposition and the hand-clapping and charge noises performed by electronic wizardry became disconcerting for the opposing teams. After many complaints this electronic noise finally was turned down.

The Yankees say they have never had a complaint about anything Layton has played in the ball park.

"I'm employed by the Yankees and I want to see them win," he says, "but I'm most interested in entertaining the fans in the park. Some of them root for the opposing teams so I try to serenade them with fitting numbers if I can."

He tries for fitting music such as an Irish jig for Oakland slugger Mark McGwire or a lilting Cuban number for Havana-born Jose Canseco. He reads the papers and talks to the sportswriters of the visiting teams to get ideas about the opposition players.

Layton is a daily fixture in the press room at Yankee Stadium. He arrives early, usually sits at a corner table with public address announcer Bob Sheppard and a couple of sportswriters, makes his way to his mezzanine-level booth about a half hour before game time, pulls out a few pieces of organ sheet music, entertains with some easy numbers shortly before game time and gets into the action with the first pitch.

"I'm so glad Mike Burke asked me to work here. It has been a joy from the first day I walked through the Stadium gate. I enjoy every minute of it and I think the fans have enjoyed hearing me play," he says.

Layton has cleared the decks of all his chores except for the Yankee job. He sees no reason why he can't still be entertaining fans well into the twenty-first century. The job isn't very wearing and he doesn't get any emotional pressure from the Boss.

"I've done a lot of wonderful things in my life and had lots of successes," he says. "I can honestly say that being part of the Yankees is really the most wonderful thing. I love the game and the people and I wouldn't trade a minute of it."

It was time for Layton to get the Hammond organ in gear. He takes the elevator to his mezzanine-level studio and office and entertains the fans for another evening. No matter the outcome of the game many people would leave the House That Ruth Built with an overall impression of having a good time in the ball park.

"That's tremendous satisfaction for me," he says. "I know they are enjoying my work and I enjoy bringing it to them."

There was one other thing that Layton was proud to display as he bragged about his Yankee career.

"Look at this," he says. "I'm very proud of it."

Layton was showing off his 1978 New York Yankee World Series ring with the large diamonds and his name engraved clearly on the side.

No soap opera organist ever had anything like that.

<u>13</u> **Alvin Jackson**

CASEY STENGEL'S
MAIN MAN

■■■■ HE SAT THERE THINKING MIKE TORREZ WAS THROW-
ing too many sliders.

"He was a big, strong guy with a live fastball. That was
his best pitch. If he hung one of those sliders he could get
hurt. Then he threw that one to Bucky Dent. I thought it
would hit the screen for a single, that would be the worst of
it," says Alvin Jackson.

Jackson was the pitching coach of the Boston Red Sox
under manager Don Zimmer on October 2, 1978, a date, for
Boston fans from the Fens to the Common, from Charles
Street to the Charles River, that will live in infamy. He can
still see that slider flying over the screen now as he sits in
Miami Stadium as pitching coach of the Orioles under skipper Frank Robinson.

"Even after it cleared the fence I didn't think it was
any big deal. You spend time in Boston you know a lot of
them are going to land up or over that net. I knew we were
down a run now but I was sure we'd score again off the
Yankees. The hit that really hurt was when Reggie Jackson
doubled for a two-run lead and then hit a homer later
for a three-run lead. That's when I started worrying,"
he says.

The Yankees won that memorable 1978 American League playoff game, went on to beat Kansas City in the League Championship Series and won the World Series over the Los Angeles Dodgers.

"When we didn't win the next year I knew they would have to make some changes. They kept Zimmer into the start of the next season but they had to fire somebody. I was the guy they picked as the scapegoat for the Torrez homer. It wasn't unexpected. You gotta take the bad with the good in baseball," he says.

Alvin Neil Jackson, a Christmas baby born on December 25, 1935, in Waco, Texas, the ninth boy and thirteenth child of a Texas sharecropper, has always handled adversity well.

"When you come from the kind of background I came from, you are grateful for anything you get and not too disappointed for what you don't get," he says.

He has spent thirty-five years in baseball, some of it hard time, dating from the prejudice directed at him as a young black player in the Texas League.

"When I broke in black players still took a lot of abuse. My first professional year was 1955 and that wasn't that long after Jackie [Robinson]. A lot of people still didn't like the idea of blacks playing with whites. Then there was the housing and the restaurants and the travel problems all of us had to deal with back then."

Through it all, this small lefthanded pitcher with the heart of a giant has been a smiling, friendly presence on any club he played with through the years.

"Sometimes it was tough, sure," he says. "But it was baseball, it was all equal on the field if you could get them out. I always knew it would have been a lot tougher if I hadn't worn that uniform. I was thrilled I could play. I never stopped enjoying the game. Still haven't."

Jackson played ten years in the big leagues and was a losing pitcher, with a 67–99 record. He was with baseball's worst team ever, the 1962 Original Mets, stayed with them three more years and then was with the Cardinals, Mets again and Reds. He began his career in the Pirate organization.

"I think if there wasn't racial prejudice I would have been with the Pirates a lot earlier. They held me back because of the quota system. They just had too many of us in those days. I could have been a lot more advanced as a pitcher if they had given me a better chance," he says.

Jackson laughs easily, has a high voice and talks with that drawl of Texas still in his system. He doesn't complain about the baseball facts of life. He just states them.

"I look back at everything and I know I was pretty lucky," he says. "I got a nice home, wonderful family, enough security and a job I love. There isn't much to complain about."

Jackson began his baseball career with his own brothers.

"My mom used to call me Baby because I was her last child. We'd all go out to play in the fields and she would yell, 'Now don't any of you let my baby get hurt.' The others all protected me. I was the youngest and the smallest," he says.

Jackson says that food, clothing, shelter were adequate in those early days back in Texas.

"We all farmed, raised a lot of our own food and had plenty to eat. We had a big family but that was not something that anybody really noticed. Most of the families in the black areas of Waco were big families. You needed a lot of kids to work those farms."

He played at Moore High School and then at Wiley College. He soon distinguished himself as a football star quarterback with a strong arm and a baseball pitcher with an even stronger arm.

"I started pitching for a semiprofessional team in the area, the Waco Pirates—the Pittsburgh club had some investment in it—and then I toured with the Jasper Steers, an all-black team, that traveled through many of the small towns in Texas, Alabama, Mississippi, Arkansas and up into Kansas. Those were tough places in those old days. You ate where you could and slept where you could. Lots of times it was in the bus or somebody's old jalopy. I don't know how those old cars made it on those dusty roads but we never missed a game," he says.

In 1955 the Pirates signed Jackson for a four-thousand-dollar bonus. He was 8–5 with a 2.79 ERA. The next year they wanted to move him at the age of twenty to a Double A club in New Orleans. That would have put him in line for the Columbus Triple A club the following season with a chance at the big club in 1956.

"I was told over the winter I was assigned to the New Orleans club and I was all excited about it. That was a big step up. Then I got a call from Branch Rickey, Jr., the Pittsburgh farm director, and he told me I couldn't go to New Orleans. They weren't ready for any black players."

Pittsburgh assigned him instead to the Mexico City club in the Mexican League. They had a working agreement with that team. Jackson had another strong year, with a 14–10 mark, and found a hospitable climate.

"I went to spring training with the big club in 1957. I knew I didn't have a chance to make the club but it was a good experience. They sent me to Columbus, didn't pitch me very much and then sent me back to Mexico City. They said I needed more work on my breaking pitches and dropped me down to the Lincoln, Nebraska, club in an A league," he says.

In the late 1950s, most teams would not allow their total of black players to go over three or four. Pittsburgh was one of the more progressive clubs but still wouldn't take any fringe players north out of spring training unless they thought they could be stars like Roberto Clemente or hard-throwing Bob Veale.

"In 1959 I was 15–4 at Columbus. I was certain I would make the team in 1960. That was the year the Pirates won the pennant. Halfway into spring training I was reassigned to Columbus again," he says.

Jackson was 10–14 in 1960 after being discouraged by the return to the minors and 12–7 the next season there again. Pittsburgh called him up in late September.

"I went in to see Mr. Rickey and I asked him if I had a future with this club or not. I was tired of being bounced around like a basketball. I told him I wouldn't go back to the minors. He said, 'You know expansion is coming. I promise you that you will be pitching in the big leagues next year with us or with somebody else. Just have a good finish.' I won my first big league game and went home to Texas with much optimism," he says.

A month later Jackson was among twenty-two players selected by the Mets for their first team in 1962. He was a $75,000 selection along with such well-known New York names as Roger Craig, Gil Hodges, Gus Bell and Hobie Landrith. Don Zimmer, later to be his Boston boss, was selected by the Mets for $125,000. Zimmer got one hit as a Met before he was traded.

"I was real excited about the opportunity of coming to the Mets," says Jackson. "I knew I would get a chance to pitch. I also looked forward to playing for Casey Stengel. I had heard a lot about him."

Stengel clearly was the life of the party around those Original Mets. His enthusiasm, loquaciousness and verve did an awful lot to sell that team to the public, making the losingest team in baseball history one of the most beloved franchises of all time. It was Stengel who involved the fans in the fortunes of the team and earned them a nickname, the New Breed, as created by sportswriter Dick Young of the *Daily News*.

"It was a joy to be around Casey. He always admired and respected me. More important, he pitched me," says Jackson.

Stengel, born in Kansas City in 1889 (hence KC and later Casey), was proud of how Jackson improved under his instruction.

"My bantam rooster," he would describe Jackson, who then weighed 160 pounds and stood five feet nine inches tall.

"One day I was doing my running in the outfield during that first spring training. I was doing my laps with Ken MacKenzie [later to be a baseball coach at his alma mater, Yale] and after three or four laps we paused to catch a breath. Mac suddenly looked over at me and asked, 'Do you know how many lefthanders there are in this camp?' I told him I didn't think there were too many. He said there were only two and he pointed at me and then at himself. Then he said, 'Don't say anything about it.' "

MacKenzie became the only winning pitcher in that first season, with a 5–4 record. Jackson, of course, became the only lefthanded starter, with a record of eight wins and twenty losses. He had a 4.40 ERA, which meant the high-scoring Mets (they played in the high-scoring Polo Grounds) were just about in every game Jackson started.

The Mets managed to lose a record 120 games that first season but with Jackson and Roger Craig, another competitive starter, who lost twenty-four games to lead the league, they often scared the other clubs.

"I really enjoyed playing for that team," says Jackson. "Casey made us feel as if we could win every game. When we did actually win one it was like New Year's Eve. The guys really celebrated our few victories."

Despite his lack of size, Jackson threw hard, struck out 118 batters in 231 innings and earned respect around the league.

"Even though I had a losing record with a bad ball club I convinced everybody I could pitch in the big leagues. I wondered, sometimes, how well I would have done with a good club like the Pirates. I had no regrets about being with the Mets. Casey pitched me. The Pirates didn't," Jackson says.

Jackson was 13–17 with a 3.96 ERA in his second season with the Mets. With Craig traded away to the Cardinals, Jackson quickly became the ace of the New York staff. There was one game in the 1964 season that typified his status.

"We were going into St. Louis for the last three games of the season against the Cardinals. Casey told me he would give me an extra day of rest and pitch me on Friday night in St. Louis," Jackson says.

The 1964 pennant race in the National League was one of the wildest ever. The Phillies, leading most of the way, were six games ahead with ten to play. Only a complete collapse could keep them from the pennant. They collapsed completely.

Philadelphia lost nine in a row as the Cardinals, Reds and Giants all had a chance to win on the final Saturday of the season. The Cards led by a game going into Friday night.

St. Louis skipper Johnny Keane had his ace, future Hall of Famer Bob Gibson, primed for the Friday night game. He felt if he could win that one as the Phillies and Reds lost it would give the Cards a two-game edge and he could clinch Saturday and save Gibson for the Series opener against the New York Yankees.

Gibson and Jackson became involved in a titanic scoreless struggle. The Mets scratched out a run in the sixth inning on a single, a bunt, a Cardinal error and a fly ball. Jackson made it stand up through eight.

In the bottom of the ninth Stengel asked Jackson if he had one more strong inning left in him. Jackson wanted the ball.

"He's the best I got," Stengel would tell the press later. "Why wouldn't you want him in there?"

Jackson retired the Cardinals in order in the bottom of the ninth. Stengel lunged from the bench to congratulate his little lefthander.

"I remember the game but it wasn't my best of the year," Jackson says now. "I shut out Cincinnati on two hits a few weeks earlier. I had a great sinking fastball that day. Against the Cards I made some bad pitches. They just didn't hit me."

That Friday night after the victory, Stengel held court in the Tenderloin Room of the Chase Park-Plaza Hotel where the Mets were staying. He told baseball stories that dated back to his own playing days starting in 1912 and even earlier when he rooted for Christy Mathewson, Cy Young and Pop Anson.

"My little lefthander is as good as any of them," Stengel said.

There were few compliments Stengel, then seventy-four years old, could pay a player that meant more. He was saying that Jackson was good enough to play with the old legends of the game, the players Stengel grew up admiring and rooting for from the turn of the century when he was a small boy in Kansas City to that very day.

Jackson had earned a place in Casey's heart forever. The grizzled old manager had few big wins in that sorry season. This was about as big as they come. Stengel beat the Cards again the next day but couldn't do it three times in a row. The Cards had to use Gibson in relief on Sunday to beat the Mets and clinch the flag. Few clubhouses in modern times were as raucous as that of the winning Cards that Sunday afternoon, led by utility catcher Bob Uecker, later to go on to television fame, dancing barefooted in his shorts in a tray of melted ice.

Jackson came back for another year as a starter with the Mets in 1965. His record was 8–20 again, as it had been in 1962. He was finally traded to the Cardinals where he posted a mark of 13–15 with an outstanding 2.51 ERA in 1966.

He was with the pennant-winning Cards in 1967 but failed to make an appearance against the Red Sox in the Series. The following season he was traded back to the Mets.

"The Mets were really starting to build with young pitchers then," he says. "They had [Tom] Seaver and [Jerry] Koosman and [Nolan] Ryan. My old teammate Gil Hodges was the manager and he put me in the bullpen. That really hurt my career. I just couldn't pitch out of the pen. I didn't like it, I couldn't adjust to it and I never accepted it. I lost my pitching rhythm."

While Hodges brought along his young stars, Jackson started only nine times and played in only twenty-five games. He sat in the bullpen without work for long periods of time.

"I never really said anything about it. I had learned that in baseball you can't often change people's minds. I went along with the program. I was only thirty-two years old. I know I could have pitched a lot longer if I started," he says.

Jackson began the 1969 season in the New York bullpen. By June, he was passed over for young lefthander Tug McGraw and two veteran righthanded relievers, Cal Koonce and Ron Taylor. The message was clear.

"They traded me to the Reds but I had nothing left," says Jackson. "I had lost all my stuff sitting most of the 1968 season."

Although Jackson had a losing record in his ten big league seasons, he clearly impressed his peers. No one ever took Jackson lightly. Around his teams, he was always friendly, outgoing, chatty, pleasant. He never was a problem on any ball club and he thought his devotion to the game might earn him a job. Nothing happened.

"Nobody wanted me as a player and I guess nobody thought of me as a coach at that time," he says. "I loved every minute I was in the game. Now I was out of the game. I had a wife and two sons to support. I went to work."

Jackson became part owner of a restaurant and bar and also became involved in a shipping business near New York's Kennedy Airport.

"I kept thinking about the game. I wasn't about to call anybody. That wasn't my way. If they wanted me they knew where to find me," he says.

New York Mets farm director Joe McDonald found Jackson shortly before the start of the 1971 season. The team needed an experienced pitching instructor.

"When Joe called I wasn't sure I wanted to do it," Jackson says. "I had been out of the game a year and I was making that emotional transition. That part is never easy. I was also starting to earn some money for my family. I knew he wasn't going to pay me very much."

Jackson talked it over with his wife, Nadine, who had supported him through all those tough early years. She knew he was part of the game and the game was part of him.

"Joe McDonald said that the job started in June and would be over in September. I would travel to the minor league clubs and I wouldn't be away all that much," he says. "I told Joe I would take a chance."

For the next five seasons, Jackson helped and evaluated young pitching prospects in the organization. He improved their motions and worked on their pitch selection. He offered advice and counsel. Mostly, he worked on their heads.

"Kids don't know if they can get hitters out or not. I tried to convince our pitchers they could get good hitters out. I told them they wouldn't be here if we didn't think they could. I knew I didn't become a successful pitcher until I stopped worrying about the big hitters I was facing and let them worry a little about facing me," he says.

In the winter Jackson stayed in his restaurant and kept up on his other business interests. He made frequent appearances at charity dinners in the area. He was seen at many ball club events in the off-season.

"I wanted to be part of the game but I wasn't sure if I wanted to make that full-time commitment," he says.

In 1976 McDonald asked Jackson to be the full-time minor league pitching coach of the Mets. That would demand more travel, larger responsibilities and a total commitment.

"What had changed by now was the fact that my kids were older. They were pretty much on their own now and I felt I could be away more. I wanted to see if I would enjoy being a full-time baseball instructor. This was the time to find out. I told Mac I would take the job for one year. After that we would see where we were," he says.

He worked with some youngsters, helped some kids, including Neil Allen, one of his earliest projects, and enjoyed every minute of it.

"That was the summer I learned just how much I needed the game," he says.

Late that year Don Zimmer was hired to manage the Boston Red Sox. Jackson hardly noticed.

"I finished with the Mets minor league job and a few days later got a call. It was Zim. He said, 'How would you like to come to Boston with me as my pitching coach?' I told him I would talk it over with my wife and let him know," Jackson says.

Nadine Jackson and the two Jackson sons were all in favor of getting back into the big leagues.

"Zim and I had played together on the Mets in 1962. I got along real well with him and I knew I could work for him. It was a lot of fun. We didn't win but I really enjoyed the town and that team," he says.

Jackson helped build a strong pitching staff. The Red Sox thought it had gotten much stronger in 1978 when they signed Mike Torrez as a free agent. He was 16–13 with them and teamed with Dennis Eckersley to give the Red Sox two powerful righthanders in Fenway. Zimmer and Jackson felt confident when it was playoff time against the Yankees with Torrez as their starter.

"He had real good stuff that day. I remember he was throwing too many sliders. I didn't say anything to Zim about it. The guy was pitching a shutout. Then he made that mistake to Bucky Dent. The rest of the game was a downer," he says.

Jackson had one more season in Boston. When the Red Sox failed to win in 1979 despite a Yankee collapse, Boston fans jumped all over Zimmer. The front office was forced to make changes and Jackson was fired. Zimmer would follow early the next year.

"I really thought I was finished with baseball then," he says. "You can love the game but you don't love the heartaches. You accept them but it is never easy. When I got fired I figured that was it."

Jackson says he took the year off, spent time with his family, rested up and thought about his future.

"I was on the beach a lot and it gave me a chance to think that summer. I kept thinking of things I wanted to do. Nothing seemed as much fun as baseball," he says.

The Mets had been sold early in 1980. Joe McDonald was gone. Chris Kaeger was the new farm director. He called Jackson at his Dix Hills, Long Island, home one winter afternoon.

"He told me he had two jobs open, one as a pitching instructor and one as a manager in Kingsport. I thought I'd try my hand at managing. That was fun but it was also a headache with young kids," he says.

He spent 1981, 1982 and 1983 in the minors. When the Mets made a change of managers to Davey Johnson in 1984, he thought he had a chance to get back into the big leagues.

"If you are going to work in baseball, that's the only place to be," he says.

Johnson brought in Mel Stottlemyre, the former Yankee, as his pitching coach. It did not sit well with Jackson.

"It was disappointing. They knew I was there. I never campaigned for the job. That just wasn't the way I do things," he says.

Stottlemyre made a big success of the job, helped by the likes of Dwight Gooden, Ron Darling, Sid Fernandez, Bob Ojeda and other quality young pitchers.

"I had Gooden, Darling and Walt Terrell down there," he says. "I knew the Mets had pitching depth and would soon be winners."

Jackson continued to work in the minor league organization of the Mets in the good years from 1985 through 1988.

"I don't know how much longer I would have stayed in the job if I hadn't moved to Baltimore. You get a little stale at that level if you don't move up," he says.

Late in September of 1988, Tom McCraw of the Orioles, a coach under manager Frank Robinson, asked Jackson if he would be interested in coming to Baltimore. Robinson was about to change pitching coaches and he would talk to Jackson if he showed interest.

"Tom is a good friend of mine so I had to listen. Robinson was a different story. I never talked to him when we were opposing players in the National League. I remember one time after he moved to the Angels and I was out in Anaheim. I went up to say hello to him and he just walked away. I thought he was a pretty vicious guy. Tom told me he was like that with opposing players. It was a lot different when you wore the same uniform," he says.

Jackson accepted Robinson's offer and will serve as the pitching coach in 1989 for the rebuilding Baltimore Orioles. The task will be a lot tougher than the one he had in Boston.

"The Orioles have a lot of good kids," he says. "I don't know how well they will do in the big leagues but from what I'm told they have strong arms."

Jackson will jump into the challenge with his eyes open. After more than thirty years in the game, few things come as surprises.

"I'm really looking forward to the Baltimore situation. I think I can help Frank and improve that team. They certainly can't get much worse."

Al Jackson, the little dynamo who made Casey Stengel so proud of him, laughed hysterically.

"At least nobody expects us to win the pennant. I hope I don't get fired if we don't win," he says.

Jackson has come quite a distance from those days at the crowded dinner table in Waco, Texas.

"Nothing is ever perfect," he says. "But I think baseball comes as close to it as you can get. I had some tough times and a few setbacks. But I'm still in the game. I love it as much now as I ever did."

14   Ed Liberatore

A LOYAL SCOUT

■■■ IT WAS ONE OF THE MOST CELEBRATED AND NOTORI-
ous baseball stories in years. It had some innocent victims.
Ed Liberatore, a career baseball scout, was one of them.

In the early spring of 1987, in the fortieth anniversary year
of Jackie Robinson's 1947 arrival in Brooklyn as the first
black major leaguer, Ted Koppel was doing a *Nightline* show
on the event. He had originally requested an appearance by
Don Newcombe, the former Brooklyn Dodger pitcher and
teammate of Robinson's, with several others. As time for the
show grew closer, Newcombe was delayed by a mixup in
airline schedules. He would not arrive in Los Angeles in time
to be filmed live for the Koppel program. Production assistants scurried around hurriedly for a substitute. One suggested Al Campanis, the seventy-year-old general manager of
the Los Angeles Dodgers.

Campanis had been a teammate of Robinson's as a player
with the Dodgers farm team in Montreal during the 1946
season. They had played alongside each other at second and
short, with the veteran Campanis helping the younger man
learn many of the subtle skills of infield play.

After some early animosity, Robinson's road in Montreal
was made smoother by many of his teammates, including

Campanis, outfielders George Shuba, Tom Tatum and Marvin Rackley and, especially, manager Clay Hopper.

Campanis and Robinson remained cordial through the years until Jackie's death in 1972.

On the night of the interview, Campanis, like most baseball people, had a couple of drinks in the press room after the game and before going on the air from Houston where the Dodgers were playing the Houston Astros. His segment lasted less than three minutes. It shattered his career.

When asked why there were so few blacks in managerial or executive positions in baseball, Campanis referred to their lack of "necessities," a baseball code word for intelligence. He also made some strange reference to the differences between blacks and whites by suggesting blacks couldn't swim or float in water. Robinson, of course, could swim. He had learned in a neighborhood pool near his home in Pasadena, California, opened one day a week in summer to blacks on a segregated basis when Robinson was growing up there in the 1930s.

The story exploded in the press, especially after California officials of the NAACP leaned heavily on the Dodgers. Within twenty-four hours, Campanis, who had been with the Dodgers organization forty-four years, since his graduation from New York University, was out. Owner Peter O'Malley, whom Campanis had known as a teenage boy working for his father, Walter, in the Brooklyn offices of the team, would not stand up for his faithful employee. Campanis was forced to resign.

Baseball organizations, especially in the front office, are built on loyalty. Players need not be loyal as long as they can hit .300, win twenty games or bat in a hundred runs. There is always free agency. Front-office people have no such protection. They simply work on a handshake. When that hand is gone, they are usually gone.

"I don't know for sure that I was let go because Al was let go," says Liberatore. "All I know is that after nineteen years in the Dodger organization I was told I would not be back the next season."

Liberatore, a short, stocky, smiling, bald man, seemed as much a part of the Dodgers as Campanis for those many years, as much a part of the team as Tommy Lasorda, as much a part of the tradition as any athlete.

"I loved every minute of being with the Dodgers," he says. "It was a very proud time of my life. That was a terrific organization with much success in the years I was there. Scouts don't get a lot of attention or a lot of honors so they take their pleasure where they can get it. One way of getting it, one sure way of recognition, is to see your big club winning. The Dodgers were in contention or winning all the years I was there. I was always made to feel part of that success. Tommy talks all the time about family. If you worked for the Dodgers you really did feel part of the family. That's why what happened to Al was so upsetting. He had been part of that family for a long time. Then that situation comes up and they drop him like they didn't even know who he was. It was a shame."

One of Liberatore's great strengths as a scout had to be his contacts. He had been around baseball more than half a century and he seemed to know everybody on the big league level. He was close with players, he knew the executives, he spent time with sportswriters and broadcasters, he was friendly with stadium personnel. All of this added up to information.

"You never know where you might pick up a useful tidbit about a player," he says.

The scouts are a group of men who spend an awful lot of time together. They may or may not be contributing to the success of their colleagues with some of the gems they drop over a press room sandwich. Liberatore always understood the system.

"If you keep your eyes and ears open you will leave a ball park a lot smarter than when you came," he says.

Edward Liberatore was born in Parkersburg, West Virginia, in the summer of 1913. His father worked at a woolen mill and he was the sixth of nine children.

"Things were always tough but my father was able to make a decent enough living. He worked his way up to superintendent at the mill and we always had adequate food and clothing. Times were different then. People didn't seem to need as much. If you had food on the table and a roof over your head that seemed to be enough. People didn't worry about big cars and big houses. There were no such things as fancy machines or television sets or the latest in machinery. You just worked hard, made a living, spent a lot of time with your family and enjoyed everyday things," he says.

When the boys in West Virginia weren't working on farms or going to school or helping out some way at home, they were playing sports.

"We just played ball anyplace we could. There was no such thing as Little League in those days so you played in the nearest lot or nearest open field as a kid. Then I made the high school baseball team as a second baseman. I was pretty good and I started thinking about a professional career when I graduated from high school in 1931. I soon got an offer to play semiprofessional baseball around my hometown. There were a lot of teams around there in those days," he says.

Liberatore joined his local semiprofessional team for five dollars a game. The teams would make the salary costs by passing the hat around the stands. Whatever they didn't make in fees from the fans, they collected from the concessions. It was enough to get by and most of the time it was enough to get another game for the following week. Baseball wasn't played in small towns because it was a big money-making proposition. It was played because young boys loved to play it and because older fans loved to watch it being played. The expenses and income involved seemed quite incidental to the operation, a far cry from baseball in the 1980s with salaries in the millions of dollars and club payrolls sometimes reaching above twenty million dollars per season.

"I followed the big leagues and rooted for guys like Lefty Grove and Jimmy Foxx. They were my big heroes. I read the newspapers about them and I would see them once in a while in the newsreels with the picture show on Saturday afternoons," he says.

Liberatore had high hopes for a distinguished baseball career as he reached the age of twenty. He had filled out a bit, could hit the ball hard, was an excellent fielder and began to get some interest from baseball scouts. Then came a huge setback.

"I was playing second base and a guy slid into me. We made contact and I went down. I twisted my knee and could feel something snap. It turned out I had torn ligaments in my knee and a slight fracture. Today that probably wouldn't be much of a big deal. In those days they really had no way of treating you when you did that kind of damage. They sort of snapped it together and taped it all up. Most doctors believed nature would heal most of those injuries. They would heal, all right, but you never could exert any pressure on the knee. After that accident I knew that I would never play professional baseball," he says.

Around the time, Liberatore ran into a well-known scout for the Washington Senators by the name of Joe Cambria. It was Cambria who introduced many Cuban and Latin players to the attention of the Senators. He worked in Central and South America and when he saw a kid with ability, he would simply meet with the family, tell the parents he was going to give the boy a chance to get rich in North America and sail north to Florida with the prospect. Then he would hand deliver the frightened young man—very few of them spoke a word of English—to Washington owner Clark Griffith. Griffith would arrange a tryout for the boy and if Cambria's prospect was as good as the old scout said he was, the boy would be on his way up the ladder, a few leagues at a time and for very little pay.

"There wasn't much money around baseball in the 1930s. There wasn't much money anywhere. It was Depression time and people were selling apples on the streets. If a guy could get a job in baseball where they would pay his room and board while he was traveling, that was a pretty good deal. Competition for jobs was very tough," says Liberatore.

Cambria took a liking to the youngster from West Virginia and soon hired him as his assistant. He would work mostly as a go-for as the old scout searched for players.

"I remember when we first made the deal he said he would take care of me. He gave me two quarters as my first salary. He said I would have to learn to take care of money if I was going to make it in this business," he says.

Scouts are still probably the lowest paid employees in the baseball chain. They learn to exist on very little and they learn to stretch their dollars. One way of expanding salaries is by spending as little as possible on food. Scouts manage to get almost as many free meals as sportswriters. They also manage to grab an extra sandwich, an extra bag of cookies from a press room luncheon for a late evening snack. Hotel room service is a fortune.

Liberatore was learning the nuances of the scouting profession as he followed Cambria around. He also learned how to deal with young players.

Early in the 1930s, Cambria brought a youngster from Cuba named Roberto Estalella to Washington. Estalella would later become a big leaguer with Washington, the St. Louis Browns, the Senators again and finally, the Philadelphia A's. He lasted nine years in the big leagues and had a lifetime mark of .282. When Joe Cambria first laid eyes on him in the Cuban provinces, he was raw and hungry. Estalella was a fire pump of a fellow, weighing 185 pounds but standing only five feet six inches tall.

Coming from the town of Cárdenas, he was overwhelmed by the luxury of downtown Washington. Cambria sent him up to Washington on a bus from Florida after he arrived there by boat. He checked him into a fleabag hotel on the south side of the city and met him there to arrange for the tryout before Griffith and the other Washington scouts.

"I was with Joe when we went to see Roberto. He was in this seedy hotel but he hadn't known how to check into the room. He just walked in, sat down on some small chair and stayed there. He fell asleep in the chair and when Cambria came to claim him, the owner wanted Joe to pay for cleaning the chair. There was quite an argument," Liberatore says.

After that was straightened out, Estalella himself became the next problem.

"Joe was from Latin America and they could communicate all right. I got the drift of the thing that Cambria wanted Roberto to go with him right away to the ball park. Roberto refused. He kept pointing to his stomach and showing that he was very hungry. He wasn't going to move until he was fed. He was pretty stubborn about it," Liberatore says.

Cambria finally broke down. He reached into his pocket and pulled out a dime and a nickel. He handed them to Estalella and that seemed to make the young outfielder happy. They had a quick conversation before Roberto took off for a nearby lunchroom.

"What did you tell him?" Liberatore asked his boss.

"I told him not to eat too much. You can't play ball on a full stomach," Cambria told his young assistant.

Liberatore stayed with the Senators through the years of World War II. In 1946, with baseball rebuilding its farm system, Liberatore got his first full-time scouting job, with the Cincinnati Reds.

"Warren Giles was running the Reds then and his farm director was Fred Fleig. They hired me and I was assigned to scout young players in the Eastern part of the country," he says.

Giles would late become the president of the National League and Fleig would work many years as his assistant and the league official in charge of the umpires.

Liberatore scouted ball players everywhere he went. It was a time when all baseball teams were competing heavily for young prospects. There was no draft system yet so teams worked hard to discover prospects, sign them and develop them as rapidly as possible. From 1946, the first year after the end of World War II, through 1949, more ball players were signed by the sixteen big league teams than in any other time in baseball history.

"All the big league clubs were rebuilding with young players. Most of the stars had gone off to the war and a lot of them came back without the same skills," Liberatore says. "We started concentrating on the younger players and most clubs did the same. The peak year was 1949. By that time there were fifty-nine leagues operating across the country."

Most big league clubs had more than a dozen farm teams of their own or had working agreements with many. In contrast, the late 1980s showed teams owning no more than five minor league clubs each with working agreements with maybe one or two more. The level of play moved from the Triple A leagues all the way down to D leagues. Few players with ability would be missed in a system with that many teams.

Giles left for the National League job when former National League President Ford Frick moved up to the job of baseball commissioner, succeeding the ousted Albert B. (Happy) Chandler. Giles's assistant in Cincinnati, Gabe Paul, became the general manager of the Reds. He was a career baseball man who had ventured down from his home in Rochester, New York, in 1926 to watch his favorite team, the St. Louis Cardinals (Rochester was a Cardinal farm club), play the New York Yankees.

"I was sitting in the bleachers next to the St. Louis bullpen when they got up Grover Cleveland Alexander to pitch against Tony Lazzeri," says Paul. "Legend had it that they had to wake up Alexander from a drunken stupor. That isn't true. He was sleeping on the bullpen bench. A lot of them did in those days. But he got right up and threw a few pitches. Then he went into the game to strike out Lazzeri."

Paul was a fascinating character for Liberatore to work for in those days. He was an intelligent man, very smart about the game and a wonderful storyteller. Paul seemed always to have a good line for any situation. One of his favorites concerned rainy days, a constant annoyance for operators of baseball teams in the days before indoor or enclosed stadiums.

"I never worry about rain," Paul once said. "It will stop. It always has."

Paul started his career with Cincinnati as the traveling secretary of the team. In 1940 Paul was the man who forcibly entered the hotel room of a small Cincinnati catcher named Willard Hershberger when Hershberger failed to show up for a game at Braves Field against the Boston club.

"When our manager, Bill McKechnie, couldn't find Hershberger I told him I would go back to the hotel to look for him. I had the hotel security open the door. I walked in and saw Hershberger dead in the bathtub. He had slit his wrists. It was a very sad occasion," says Paul.

Paul left Cincinnati in the early 1960s to go on to Houston, stayed there for a short while and then moved to Cleveland. He was the man responsible for introducing George Steinbrenner, a Cleveland shipping magnate, to baseball. Paul was part of the management team in New York when Steinbrenner bought the Yankees from CBS in 1973.

By that time Liberatore had settled into his favorite baseball job. He was the head scout under Los Angeles farm director Al Campanis. Campanis had been a field scout for many years for the Dodgers and had risen rapidly in the organization. By the late 1960s, he was the righthand man for Dodger owner Walter O'Malley. He was in charge of supplying the talent that year after year would keep the Dodgers at or near the top of the National League standings. Campanis signed a young man named Sandy Koufax in 1955.

"I had seen him as a schoolboy in Brooklyn at Lafayette High School," Campanis says. "Then he went on to the University of Cincinnati and played basketball. We knew he could throw very hard and even though he was wild and inexperienced, we decided to take a chance on him. He certainly paid off. The signing of one boy like that can make you a very successful scout."

While other Dodger scouts worked with younger prospects, Liberatore soon was concentrating his efforts on big league players.

"I did mostly advance scouting. That meant I would see a team for a few days before the big club played them, scout all the players, compile my report, hand it over to Al and move on to the next team," he says.

Liberatore soon became one of the most popular baseball personalities around the spring training headquarters and home stadiums of many clubs. He would often wear a Dodger cap in the Florida sun and talked often of how much pride he had working for that organization. The Dodgers and Yankees were clearly the two most successful baseball teams of modern times.

"I just enjoyed watching baseball players perform," Liberatore says. "It is a great job. I never really minded the travel and I didn't mind being away that much. You do it for so many years that you just get used to it. That's your life. That's how you make a living. My family understood that. I don't think they would know what to do if I was home every day."

Liberatore has lived with his wife and two children for many years in the Philadelphia area in the town of Abington. His daughter is a psychologist and his son is an industrialist.

"I think if you are happy in what you do, the family is happy," he says. "We all understood how much I loved baseball and how I wouldn't ever want to do anything else. My family was very supportive of my career."

Liberatore has seen them all over the last half century. He admits that he has some favorites.

"Al Simmons was probably the best hitter I ever saw. He was a magician with the bat. There just wasn't a pitcher around in those days who could handle him," he says.

Liberatore says that two young players, Pete Reiser and Mickey Mantle, were the best young all-around players he had ever scouted.

"They both could do everything you look for, hit, hit with power, run, field and throw. There's no telling how good Reiser would have been if he hadn't got hurt. He was just an explosive player and beautiful to watch. He started running into walls real early in his career, so he never became the player he could have been," he says.

As for Mantle, the Yankee home run great, Liberatore blames injuries for his loss of skills.

"When I first saw Mantle as a nineteen- or twenty-year-old kid I told people he had a chance to become the best player to ever play the game. He was so strong, so quick, so intense the way he played the game. He was the best switch hitter there ever was because he could hit the ball as hard from each side of the plate. Very few switch hitters come close to that. They usually have a strong side and the other side isn't quite as good," he says.

Liberatore saw one other switch hitter, Garry Templeton, who truly excited him.

"He didn't have Mantle's power, of course, but he was very good. He was an excellent hitter from both sides of the plate, a wonderful shortstop and a great baserunner. He fought himself a lot and he fought with other people. He just never became the kind of player I expected when I first looked at him. You can look at a player's skills. You just can't look inside his head," he says.

At the end of the 1987 baseball season, the Dodgers told Liberatore they were retiring him. He had seen the handwriting on the wall ever since those early spring days after Campanis popped off about "necessities" and buoyancy. The Dodgers were making fast work of all the people in the organization who were linked to Campanis. His stable of scouts began disappearing rapidly.

"I had been with the Dodgers nineteen years and I loved every minute of it," he says. "I know if Al stayed I probably would have stayed. Once Al left, the only thing the Dodgers saw for me was retirement."

Good scouts are hard to find. Liberatore was out of work a very short time when the phone rang at his Abington home.

"It was Roland Hemond and he said he wanted me to join him in Baltimore and see if I could help bring that team back," he says.

Hemond had been hired to take over a failing franchise. Baltimore had been going downhill ever since Earl Weaver retired and Hank Peters moved on to Cleveland as the GM there. Hemond was hired by owner Edward Bennett Williams and given full authority to rebuild. He was a strong believer that you rebuild with a strong farm system and wise trades. Liberatore was soon hired to scout on the big league level with a heavy emphasis on young players the Orioles might obtain in deals.

"It's just about the same job I had with the Dodgers. The Orioles are down now but Roland feels they can come back in two or three years. I will do what I can to help him," he says.

Still energetic and enthusiastic after nearly six decades in baseball, Ed Liberatore will be a smiling presence in spring training camps in Florida, in press rooms in baseball's stadiums and in confabs with his fellow scouts wherever he goes. He believes he still has a lot left to offer the game.

If he picks up a helpful tidbit over a press room lunch, so be it. It is a fraternity rite.

15   Chuck Hiller

IRON HANDS, STOUT HEART

▬▬ THE KID WAS A FEW DAYS OUT OF HIGH SCHOOL WHEN he landed at the small airport in Kingsport, Tennessee, to begin his professional career. His reputation had certainly preceded him. Everybody knew "the black Ted Williams" was in town.

Darryl Strawberry, a few months past his eighteenth birthday, tall and lean and already famous from his exploits as a star player at Crenshaw High in Los Angeles, was reporting for his professional debut with the Kingsport Mets. The manager was Chuck Hiller.

"The organization didn't give me any special instructions about handling him," Hiller remembers. "He was supposed to be treated like any other new young player. Run him out there and see what he could do."

Hiller, a friendly, smiling, bald man, took the youngster aside for a few minutes when he arrived at the small Class A league ball park.

"Darryl," he told the tall young man, "go out there and have a good time. Just relax. If they didn't think you could do this they never would have given you all that money."

Strawberry had been signed by the rebuilding New York Mets—the first amateur free agent signed by the new

Doubleday ownership of the team—and quickly dispatched to Kingsport.

"I knew there was a lot of pressure on the kid. I had heard all about him by then," says Hiller.

Working with him about the same as he worked with the other youngsters, many of whom were away from home for the first time, Hiller soon eased Strawberry into professional baseball. He hit five homers with a .268 average and twenty RBIs that first season on his way to big league superstardom.

"I enjoyed managing down there," says Hiller, now a roving minor league infield instructor in the New York Mets organization. "We had a lot of good kids, Jay Tibbs, Johnny Gibbons, Doug Sisk as well as Straw. I think he learned a lot with me."

Hiller is a former big league infielder without overwhelming ambition or massive ego. He just loves being part of the game, putting on the uniform, pitching batting practice, laughing with other baseball people in the clubhouse, talking about the game.

"I've been in it more than thirty years and it would be all right with me if I was in it another thirty years," he says.

Hiller is proud of his contributions to Strawberry's success. He does not look for rewards.

"When you have a kid in the minors and you help him a little and he goes on and has a great career it is very rewarding. Nobody comes around and tells you that you contributed. You just know those things and you just enjoy being part of the kid's success. It's one of the reasons we all stay in the game," he says.

Hiller was a journeyman player with a decent bat and bad hands. He led the league in errors one season. His teammates tagged him with the negative nickname Iron Hands and some sportswriters cruelly called him Dr. No (after a James Bond character of the same name) for having No Hands.

"Aww, that was all invented," he says. "I was a pretty good fielder until I made a couple of errors my first year as a regular and the sportswriters began writing about it. The next thing I know is I had a reputation for having bad hands. That was pressure. All I could think of when a ball was hit to me was 'Don't blow it. Don't blow it.' It's very hard to play baseball that way."

Hiller did have one incredible moment in the baseball sun. It made all the other negatives worthwhile. Hiller could always glow in the aftermath of October 8, 1962.

The San Francisco Giants were playing the New York Yankees in the fourth game of the World Series at Yankee Stadium. No fewer than six Hall of Famers, Juan Marichal, Willie Mays, Willie McCovey, Mickey Mantle, Yogi Berra and Whitey Ford, were on the two teams. For one shining moment Hiller outshone them all.

It was a tie ball game, the Giants had the bases loaded, there were two men out and Marshall Bridges, a successful lefthanded reliever that year, was on the mound for the Yankees.

"I think Marshall got behind me one and oh and wanted to make sure he got the ball over with the bases loaded," says Hiller. "He had a good screwball but he threw me a fastball just on the outside part of the plate. I was able to get my bat on the ball and pull it hard on a line to right field."

The famous right field stands in the Stadium, which had been the home of so many famous lefthanded home run hitters from Babe Ruth to Lou Gehrig to Berra and Mantle, were now beckoning for Hiller.

"I don't think it got in there by more than a foot or two. It probably landed in the first or second row of the stands. That didn't matter. They don't pay off on how far it goes. It was a home run and we had four runs," says Hiller.

The Giants won the game (the Yankees were to win the Series in seven games) and the press was around Hiller as never before after the game.

"They kept asking me if I knew about the record and I had no idea what they were talking about. Finally they explained that I was the first National League player to hit a grand slam in a World Series game. Considering all the great players, the Hall of Famers, who had been in the Series, that was quite a thrill. It's one of those records they can never take away from you no matter how many guys hit World Series grand slams after that," he says.

That Series homer was certainly big news back in Johnsburg, Illinois, where all five hundred residents of the tiny farming community north of Chicago were suddenly interested in the game. The local boy had made good.

Charles Joseph Hiller, son of an Illinois construction worker and small farmer, was born there in Johnsburg on October 1, 1934. He grew up with an older brother and sister, was interested in sports from his earliest memories and starred in football and baseball at the local high school.

"I wasn't very big, about five-ten and 170 pounds or so when I finished high school. Nobody was interested in me as a player. I went on to St. Thomas College in St. Paul, Minnesota, and majored in business. That was a small school and I played a lot of ball there. I got a little bigger and a little stronger (five-eleven, 175 pounds) and a Cleveland scout became interested in me," he says.

The scout was Cy Slapnicka, one of the most famous scouts in the game. It was Slapnicka some twenty years earlier who, while roaming the Midwest for the Cleveland Indians, discovered a young high school fireball pitcher by the name of Bob Feller. A scout could live on one signing like that all his life.

"When I graduated from college they signed me to a contract and sent me to Cocoa, Florida. I was just thrilled to be there," he says.

Hiller spent a couple of seasons in the Cleveland organization. He had trouble fielding but he hit .293 at Cocoa and .281 at Minot, North Dakota.

"Hoot Evers, the old Detroit outfielder, was the farm director of the Indians. He came to our club once, watched me play for a few games and then told me I would never make it. I was pretty depressed. All I ever wanted to do was play baseball in the big leagues. He hadn't really seen enough of me but he was convinced I was not a prospect. I hit the ball hard, I could run well, I hustled every minute I was on the field. I did have some fielding deficiencies but I knew that would improve. I thought they gave up on me too quickly," he says.

Evers made it known that the Indians had no plans for Hiller. The San Francisco Giants, finishing their first season in California after moving west, decided to take a chance on the balding youngster. They drafted him from the Indians organization and assigned him to the Eugene, Oregon, club in the Northwest League. He responded with a spectacular season. Hiller not only hit .341 but led the league in fielding at second base with only twenty-two errors and a .970 fielding average.

In the following season, 1960, he led the Texas League in hitting with a .334 average and also led in fielding by a second baseman with a .980 mark. Hiller was definitely a big league prospect now, no matter what Hoot Evers thought.

Hiller spent one more season in the minors before being called up by the Giants. He was the regular second baseman a good part of the 1961 season and all of the 1962 season. The Giants won the pennant in an exciting playoff with their rivals from Los Angeles. Alvin Dark, the San Francisco manager, had been a player on the Giants team that beat the Dodgers in a playoff in 1951.

"We really had a great team that year. I wasn't surprised we won. Actually I thought we would win a lot more pennants before I left San Francisco," says Hiller.

Hiller, his wife Pam and their parents all made the trip to New York for the World Series. Not even a Giants defeat could diminish the joy and pride they felt in Hiller's play, especially after that fourth-game grand slam.

In 1965 Hiller was traded to Casey Stengel's New York Mets. He fit in perfectly. He was not a very accomplished fielder on what was not a very accomplished team. His good nature, balding head and friendly personality made him one of the more popular players on those terrible teams.

Hiller batted .235 in 1965, had his best big league season ever at .280 the following year and, for some strange reason, couldn't buy a hit the next year. He was batting only .093 for the Mets in 1967 before being traded to the Phillies. He finished out his active career after the 1968 season with the Pirates as a pinch hitter. His lifetime average for eight seasons was .243.

His stay with the Mets was even more significant for another reason. One of Stengel's favorite people, Whitey Herzog, was a coach on the 1966 Mets. Herzog hoped to manage the Mets someday but was put in charge of the farm system the following year. Herzog was as much responsible for the championship team of 1969 led by Tom Seaver, Jerry Koosman, Gary Gentry and the rest of that brilliant pitching staff as Gil Hodges, the manager, Johnny Murphy, the general manager or anyone else.

Herzog was an intelligent, glib, astute baseball man who could recognize talent. He would go on to a wonderful managerial career at Texas, Kansas City and St. Louis, where he remains with the Cardinals as field leader. Hiller would benefit from Herzog's skills.

"When Whitey was coaching the Mets and I was a player we got real friendly. We weren't that far apart in age [four years] and we were both from Illinois and we both wanted to stay in the game as long as we could," he says.

Herzog would hire Hiller as a coach in Texas, Kansas City and St. Louis. In between he was always working for the Mets.

Herzog hired Hiller after his playing days ended to work in the Mets minor league organization. He worked for the Mets at Marion, Virginia, as a coach and later at their top club at Tidewater.

"When Whitey got the job in Texas in 1973 as the manager he called me before he actually was announced publicly.

I was thrilled to accept the position. I figured being a baseball coach on the big league level was heaven. It was certainly a lot better than working construction back in Illinois," he says.

Hiller stayed with Herzog in the American League again when the manager moved on to Kansas City. Those were frustrating years for that team.

"We were always running against those tough Yankee clubs in the playoffs with Reggie and Thurman and Sparky and Goose and we just couldn't beat them. That really got to Whitey. He kept saying that next year he would get them, next year was the time to win. It just never happened. I think not winning a pennant in Kansas City with the Royals was just about the most frustrating baseball experience Whitey had. I know it was very frustrating for me and I didn't have the responsibility," Hiller says.

Herzog was finally fired by the Royals. Hiller went to work for the Mets again.

"That was 1980 and they asked me if I wanted to manage in the low minors or be a roving instructor. I thought it would be fun to see if I would take to managing. It was a great experience. I managed only for that one season of 1980 when Strawberry joined us. That was good enough. He should go to the Hall of Fame and I can say I managed a kid that wound up as a superstar. I didn't have much to do with it, of course, but it is still a satisfying thing," he says.

Hiller says that most of Strawberry's ability is God-given. He is just big and strong and quick and baseball is easy for him.

"I gave him the same advice I give every kid I come into contact with in the game. I tell them that baseball isn't all that difficult if you have ability. There are only two things you gotta do all the time, hustle and be on time. Those are two of the things that seem to have given Strawberry a lot of trouble," says Hiller.

Hiller stayed with the Cards from 1981 through 1984, worked in their minor league organization in 1985, went back to the big leagues in 1986 with the San Francisco Giants as third base coach and returned to the Mets for the fourth time in 1987 as a minor league instructor. He is looking forward to serving the Mets in that capacity for many years.

"Things have changed for me in the last couple of years. We bought a home in Largo, Florida. I enjoy being there as much as I can, I like to go fishing and play golf and I don't think I want to travel as much as you have to in the big leagues. I don't think you should ever say never in this game because there is no telling what may come up next. Just say this. I'm working with young players, I'm having a great time doing it and I'm home in Florida with my wife and kids most of the time. I don't think you can have a better life than I do. I just thank the Good Lord every day for my lucky breaks."

Hiller says he still enjoys putting on a baseball uniform, sweating under the Florida sun, working with young kids, being around the park as much as he did when he was a player starting out three decades ago.

"I putter around the house, fix things, go fishing as much as I can, play golf, share time with my family. But what I love to do, really love, is the game. I even enjoy it in the winter when I help the Mets out at their dream camp and these rich businessmen come down for a week to play baseball. They love the game as much as I do and I do what I can to see they have a good time. I pitch batting practice to those guys nice and easy and hit a few ground balls to them and answer their baseball questions as best I can. They always want to hear about the grand slam and they always ask about those games with Kansas City against the Yankees. It's just fun talking baseball and being around guys who love the game," he says.

At the age of fifty-five, Hiller still has much of the boyish enthusiasm and dedication to the game he had years ago.

"I was not a great player," he says. "I know that. I did the best I could with my ability. I had a few big hits and helped my team win a few games. I got into coaching because I loved the game so much and I think I have helped a lot of young players along their way. That's reward enough for me. My family is healthy and happy and we all enjoy being together. That's very important in my life. My wife, Pam, has just been great about all the difficulties of baseball, being away, being on bad ball clubs, never knowing if you will have a job the next year or what. I really admire her."

Hiller never made much money in the game. Now he is drawing a baseball pension that pays something like three thousand dollars a month. With his baseball salary as a coach and his wife's salary as a registered nurse they can live comfortably in southern Florida.

"I go back to Johnsburg in Illinois once in a while to visit my mother, who is still living there, and I hardly can believe that a kid like me from that town has traveled all over America with baseball teams, been in the finest restaurants, stayed in the best hotels, traveled on first-class flights. Not much has really changed there since I left thirty years ago. If I didn't have that God-given ability to hit a baseball I would probably still be up there, working construction like my father, fighting those winters, watching those cows, hanging around with the same guys I worked with and went to school with. If that was what I was supposed to do I would have made the best of it. I wouldn't have complained. That's not in my nature. I just took things the way they came. But I'm sure glad I was able to play ball and have all the fun I had," he says.

It is nearly time for another baseball season and Chuck Hiller is as excited about this one as he was about the first one so many years ago.

"I still live by my own motto, the creed my father told me. I arrive on time and I hustle. I do the best I can in whatever job I'm assigned. I think I have been a pretty lucky guy. I enjoyed every minute I have spent in the game. If it ends tomorrow and I never get on the ball field again I won't have any regrets. I'll know that while I was out there I did the best I could and I had the best time I could possibly have," he says.

Hiller was never a Hall of Fame player. He was still a good guy to have on the club for his ability and his attitude. He will probably never be a Hall of Fame manager. He is still a good guy to have on any club for his ability, his generosity of spirit and his cheery personality. A Good Soldier. Any team with Chuck Hiller is better for having him.

NO BAD HOPS HERE

▬▬ EVERY SUMMER MORNING AL PASCARELLA MOVES TO the center field flagpole at Shea Stadium in Flushing, New York. He gingerly unfolds an American flag, places it on four hooks, unwinds the cord bound to the pole and pulls the flag to its full height.

Before he leaves work for the day, he repeats the ritual in the opposite direction, taking the flag down, folding it neatly in the prescribed order and storing it under the stands with the rakes and shovels and wheelbarrows.

It is simply one of the endless chores that Al Pascarella, Enzo Limongelli and a dozen others perform almost daily under the direction of their boss, Pete Flynn, head grounds-keeper at Shea Stadium.

As long as baseball has been played, this skill has been a significant part of the game. There could hardly be a game on a professional level without these artisans painting foul lines, smoothing the infield dirt, seeing the grass growing full, locking the bases in place, drawing the batter's box and maintaining the integrity of the playing field.

"It is exciting to be part of the game," says Pascarella, a stocky middle-aged grandfather. "Anything I can do to make the field better and help the Mets win is really satisfying to me. I just love looking at the field before the game begins when everything is so neat and clean and the bases are white and the batter's box hasn't been rubbed out and the rubber on the mound is so clean you could almost eat off it."

Baseball legend is filled with incidents of the fields becoming factors in play. Alvin Dark, when he managed the San Francisco Giants, would order his Candlestick Park groundskeepers to water down the basepaths heavily to make the field muddy. This would create mud spots between first and second, noticeably hampering the speedy Maury Wills, Willie Davis, Tommy Davis and other Dodgers base stealers. It clearly worked in the 1962 season when the Giants edged the Dodgers in a playoff for the title. The games at Candlestick found the Dodgers unable to run, a vital asset of their game.

Perhaps the best known groundskeeper incident occurred in Pittsburgh in the seventh game of the 1960 World Series between the Pirates and the New York Yankees. It was October 13 and the Pirates, trailing 7–4 in the final game, came to bat in the eighth inning. Gino Cimoli singled and Bill Virdon (who ironically would be a future Yankee manager) hit a sharp ground ball to shortstop Tony Kubek. The future NBC broadcaster went down for the hard-hit ball, which was launched suddenly into a pint-sized rocket.

"The ball hit a pebble," Kubek recalls, "and suddenly came up at me faster than I could react to it. I was soon down and out."

The baseball hit Kubek's throat and forced his removal from the game. When Bill Mazeroski homered off Ralph Terry leading off the home half of the ninth, the Pirates had the dramatic victory. Mickey Mantle, who had played brilliantly, was brought to tears by the sight of his teammate being ministered to on the training table. Kubek was bleeding from the throat area. The injury would cause his early retirement from the game after the 1965 season. He was twenty-eight years old.

It became one of the most famous pebbles the game has ever seen.

"You have to use crushed pebbles on baseball diamonds or else the dirt won't stay down. A good wind would take it all away before you could play a game," explains Pascarella.

Pascarella was born and raised in Brooklyn, New York. When he was a kid he attended many games at Ebbets Field. He had wanted to work there as long as he could remember.

"I loved everything about Ebbets Field. It was just a wonderful ball park. It was small and close and the fans were all part of the game," he says. "I'm still sad about the Dodgers moving out of Ebbets Field. I don't think anyone who ever went to a game there could ever forget what a thrill that was. There was just something special about that park and the fans and the surroundings that made it unique in baseball. Shea Stadium is fun and the fans are involved and the excitement is pretty good here when the Mets are doing well. But Ebbets Field was just different. I don't know. It's hard to explain it. You ever been there?"

When I told Pascarella that I was also a kid from Brooklyn and loved going to Ebbets Field and watching the Dodgers, his eyes lit up.

"See, it was different, more part of the team, the game, I don't know. I talk about Ebbets Field all the time to these young kids around here and they look at me like I'm crazy. Ebbets Field, what about it? They didn't know. They never saw a Brooklyn game there."

The Dodgers weren't a very successful team when Pascarella was growing up there in the 1930s. It would be 1941 before they won their first pennant since the 1920 season. The 1930s were a dreary time in Brooklyn baseball.

"There were a lot of good players. I remember Babe Herman when I was a kid and I remember Leo Durocher playing shortstop and a lot of names like that. My real thrill came one day when I was at the game early and Babe Ruth came out on the field and moved to the fence to talk to us kids. Whew, I didn't know if I would survive that," he says.

Ruth had completed his magnificent Yankee career in 1934 and had been sold to the Boston Braves for the 1935 season.

He was forty years old by then. He hit three home runs in one game for the Braves against the Pirates at Forbes Field. About a week later he retired. He was out of baseball in 1936 and 1937 and was hired as a Brooklyn Dodger coach in 1938. When Leo Durocher was named player-manager of the Dodgers for the 1939 season, one of the first to be fired was Babe Ruth.

Ruth and Durocher had been adversaries going back to their New York Yankee days together in 1928 and 1929. One of baseball's unproven legends had it that Ruth's gold watch was stolen from his locker in Yankee Stadium and he accused the pugnacious kid, later known as Leo the Lip, of doing the stealing. True or not, it seemed to have added some tension between the great slugger and the weak-hitting shortstop. With Durocher's Brooklyn promotion, Ruth was gone.

Before he went, he thrilled thousands of kids in Ebbets Field as he had thrilled many thousands in Yankee Stadium.

"I got his autograph," says Pascarella, "and I just remember leaning up against the fence at Ebbets Field and staring at him. He was bigger than any man I had ever seen and he was just greater than anyone for sure. Babe Ruth. Even now I just get chills when I think about him or mention his name. People don't know how big he was if they weren't around in those days. You think some of the guys of today cause a fuss. He was making so much money as a Yankee player nobody believed it. If he was playing now, there probably wouldn't have been enough money in baseball to pay him. There was nobody like the Babe."

Pascarella attended Erasmus Hall High School in Brooklyn. That was the school that sent the great Sid Luckman to the Chicago Bears of the National Football League. It was Luckman who engineered the biggest championship triumph ever when his Bears beat the Washington Redskins of Sammy Baugh by the incredible score of 73–0 in the 1940 championship game. Baugh uttered one of football's most memorable lines after the game when he was asked if the score would have been different if an early first-period pass he had thrown had been caught instead of dropped in the end zone.

"Sure," said the drawling Texan known as Slingin' Sam, "the score would have been 73–7."

"I played ball at Erasmus but I wasn't that good. I knew that I could never make a career of sports but I was always determined to watch it," says Pascarella.

Shortly after he graduated from high school, he got a job as an attendant at a Brooklyn hospital. He stayed at the hospital in a variety of jobs for thirty-seven years.

"The hours were great. I would come in early and go home early. Sometimes I would work overnight and that always gave me free time in the afternoon. In the late 1940s I got a job in the afternoons on the grounds crew at Ebbets Field. I knew the groundskeeper, Jimmy Esposito, and he asked me if I wanted to help out. It was a good way to pick up some extra money and I told him I would be happy to do it. I think we made about two bucks an hour then. Now we make about thirteen bucks an hour," he says.

Pascarella was soon learning his baseball trade. He learned how to work on the grass. He learned how to smooth out an infield without damaging it. He learned the fundamentals of caring for a field after a rainy day.

"The grass that grows in a ball park is no different than the grass that grows in your front yard. It needs a lot of care if it is to grow properly. If you get a dry summer like we had in 1988 you have to water it extensively. If you get a wet summer then you just have to watch that it doesn't get too soaked," he says. "If it does, you try to drain off as much as you can."

Shea Stadium was built on marshland across from Flushing Bay. In the early days of the stadium, a heavy rain would damage the field and cause soft and lumpy spots throughout the outfield. James Thomson was the stadium manager and he was constantly involved with the city in hassles over the cost of maintenance of the ball park.

"We had tested the field for drainage," Thomson once said, "but we could not determine just how much water it would hold. We found out that the water didn't run off as fast as we had calculated. We realized we had to build more drainpipes to get it off faster."

It took several years of battling with the city, the owners of the municipally built stadium, but the Mets were finally able to improve the drainage situation.

In 1974 the Yankees were playing at Shea Stadium while their famous old ball park, Yankee Stadium, was being upgraded and remodeled. One of their outfielders, Elliott Maddox, played right field on a rainy night. He damaged his knee going after a fly ball on the mushy field. He later claimed in a huge lawsuit against the city that the condition of the field had caused the injury. The courts later ruled that there were some inherent risks to his profession and he could not prove negligence on the part of the Mets or the city. His case was thrown out of court.

"Actually we do very little with the outfield these days," says Pascarella. "We might throw a little extra dirt on the warning track after a heavy rain but the rest of the grass is simply treated naturally. The best care for a ball park outfield is still lots of sun and just enough rain."

The Brooklyn Dodgers decided to leave Ebbets Field and Brooklyn after the 1957 season. The name of Walter O'Malley, the Dodger owner, became one of the most hated in city history. He was burned in effigy at locations as diverse as Canarsie and Cropsey, Bensonhurst and Bedford-Stuyvesant, Flatbush and Flatlands, all Brooklyn neighborhoods, when he took the Dodgers west to Los Angeles. The festering hatred remains to this day.

"Most people around here have never gotten over that move," says Pascarella.

Pascarella attended to his family, his own garden and his job at the hospital in those quiet New York baseball years between 1958 and 1962. He never considered working in Yankee Stadium.

"I lived in Brooklyn, I was a Dodger fan and I loved Ebbets Field, I didn't want any part of Yankee Stadium or the Yankees," he says.

There was one other opportunity to remain in the game when the Dodgers went west. He had an opportunity to go with them.

"Some of the members of the crew were asked if they wanted to go out to Los Angeles and work out there. The Dodgers wanted to take some of the guys from Ebbets Field so they could train people and maybe stay out there if they liked it. I wasn't interested in it," he says.

A few of the grounds crew did go to Los Angeles and worked in the Coliseum where the Dodgers played until Chavez Ravine was ready for Dodger Stadium.

"Too hot out there. I don't know how they make the grass grow. They must spend an awful lot of time watering in Dodger Stadium, I bet," he says.

Pascarella admits that he followed the Dodgers in the newspapers in those years before the Mets arrived. He missed baseball a lot but wouldn't go up to Yankee Stadium.

"I don't think too many Dodger fans went to Yankee Stadium," he says. "That was a completely different ball park with completely different fans."

By 1960 agitation for a new National League team to replace the departed Dodgers and New York Giants had begun. There was some opposition from National League officials.

"Who needs New York?" bellowed National League President Warren Giles, when asked if the league could prosper without a team in the nation's largest city.

A league called the Continental League was making noises about rivaling the major leagues. Branch Rickey, who had run the St. Louis Cardinals and the Brooklyn Dodgers, was in charge. A man named Bill Shea, a Manhattan attorney, had been appointed by New York City Mayor Robert Wagner to lead a committee to return big league baseball to New

York. Shea was interested in building a new stadium in Queens.

In an effort to counter the new league, the major leagues absorbed four of its franchises and expanded in the American League in 1961 with a new team in Washington (the old Washington team moved to Minnesota) and a new team in Los Angeles and then, finally, expanded in the National League. Houston was awarded one of the new National League franchises and New York was awarded the other. Bill Shea had proven that it could be done and the new park—aptly named Shea Stadium—would be built there and opened in 1964. Shea Stadium remains a baseball landmark more than a quarter of a century later.

"I still laugh when some people try to figure out where the name comes from," Shea once said. "I remember walking down the ramp a couple of years ago after a big game. These two kids were arguing about the game and they suddenly began arguing about the ball park and where the name came from. One kid was adamant that he knew and he was calling the other kid names for not knowing. 'How can you call yourself a Mets fan if you don't know that the park was named after this guy Shea who was a hero in the war and got killed fighting in the Pacific?' I almost tapped the kid on the shoulder but I thought that would spoil their fun and end the argument."

Pascarella noticed the story about the new team in the papers but didn't pay it much heed.

"I enjoyed watching the games on television but I had a good job and I didn't think I wanted to work on a field again," he says.

One day he received a phone call from Jack O'Brien, one of the groundskeepers he had worked with at Ebbets Field.

"This new team, the Mets, is starting up at the Polo Grounds. We could use a few experienced guys," he said.

"I don't think I want to work anymore on the job," he said.

O'Brien said that the new team would be fun to watch, the work at the Polo Grounds wouldn't be very difficult because it was mostly patching up an old stadium, not maintaining a new one, and he wanted to surround himself with some of the old faces.

"I decided I would try it for a season and see how it went," he says.

The Mets played the 1962 and 1963 seasons at the Polo Grounds, managed by Casey Stengel, and set a record for most losses in 1962 with a 40–120 mark. Stengel's luminaries included such widely recognized names as Marv Throneberry, Richie Ashburn, Frank Thomas, Gil Hodges, Roger Craig and Frank Thomas.

The Mets finished out the 1963 season and prepared to move to the new stadium in Flushing.

"I thought that would be fun because I had never worked in a new park. I wanted to see what that was like. It was very difficult in the early days because the park wasn't really finished when we opened up in 1964. They had an opening day to meet but there were still plenty of things around the field that needed attending to," he says.

Somehow the field was put in playing shape and all of the scheduled games were played.

"I was glad I came back because the place was very exciting," he says. "I really got to know all these new players and I could see that the Mets were going to have a good team in a few years."

By 1968 Hodges was installed as the new manager, and the 1969 Miracle Mets caught Leo Durocher's Chicago Cubs to win the National League pennant. But the field was destroyed by onrushing fans the night they clinched against the Cardinals, with Joe Torre, later a Mets manager, grounding into a game-ending double play.

"That was a wild night and most of us had to work through the night to get the field ready again for the playoffs and World Series. We made a lot of overtime but we got it all done with new sod and lots of new dirt. We always have bags of sod and piles of dirt available for every emergency," he says.

Like any fan, Pascarella has developed his favorites among the Mets. He likes most of the players from those championship teams in 1969 and 1973 and the modern winners in 1986 and the division winners of 1988.

"If I had to be pinned down and really pick a guy as my favorite I guess I would have to pick Tom Seaver," he says. "He was always nice and kind to me, always had time for a greeting and seemed to be a fine young man. Everybody knows what a good pitcher he was in his time here."

Pascarella sits in the left field bullpen with the visiting team's relief pitchers for all games.

"As soon as I finish my work on the field I go out there and work in the bullpen," he says. "I take care of the mound in the bullpen and see that the conditions are always ready for the pitchers. If they call a relief pitcher into the game I drive him with the cart. I think most of them prefer that to running in. That's a long run. I remember the old days in Brooklyn when the relief pitcher walked in and the Dodger Sym-Phony would serenade the guy if he was ours or make fun of him if he was theirs."

He has retired from his hospital job now, collects unemployment in the winter, spends time with his son in Florida during the bitter cold weather and looks forward to another season at Shea.

"I enjoy what I do and I get excited at the games. I also like it when the players come on the field and comment on how smooth and solid the infield is after we have worked on it for a long time. That's a very satisfying feeling."

When Enzo Limongelli drives in each summer morning from his Hempstead, Long Island, home to Shea Stadium, he thinks of his baseball job as a picnic.

"I work on New York City road crews in the daytime. When you put down asphalt on those hot summer days this is nothing. I'm tired after that asphalt job. I'm never tired after the baseball job," he says.

Limongelli has had various jobs—on the road crew, in a hospital as a mechanic and in construction. He has always had time for a Shea Stadium grounds crew position.

"I just enjoy coming out to the ball park. For me it is a dream come true, just to be out here and get to know the guys and work on the field. I want to do a good job because I don't want anything we do to cost the Mets a ball game," he says.

Limongelli remembers the 1969 season as his favorite baseball year.

"There never was a season like that. We would come to the park early and stay late because the crowds were so big," he says. "All the players were wonderful to us. Jerry Koosman and Tug McGraw were my favorites. McGraw would always crack jokes and say funny things when I drove him in to the mound for a relief appearance. He used to kid me about my driving and always said he wanted to drive the cart one day and I should jump out to the mound. We never did it but he threatened more than once. He wanted to see how the crowd would react."

The 1969 World Series team voted five hundred dollars from their own money for each member of the Shea grounds crew. That was a touching gesture that Limongelli has never forgotten.

"Players weren't making that kind of money in those days," he says. "I don't think a lot of them could afford that. I really appreciated it."

For many of the people who have been around Shea for more than twenty years, that 1969 team always has a special meaning. The 1986 World Champions have their supporters also.

"They were a great bunch of guys and they were really nice to all of us. We got World Series rings that year. They weren't the very expensive ones with diamonds the players get but they were very nice. I think it is one of my proudest possessions."

Limongelli enjoys seeing the infield grass in great shape. It is what makes the field so attractive.

"I can't imagine how they can play on artificial grass," he says. "That isn't baseball to me. I enjoy going out there, smoothing it down, watering it, cutting it, everything you have to do. To me the grass is the most beautiful part of the ball park. Without real grass it isn't real baseball, I think."

Limongelli says he wants to clear up a popular misconception about baseball grass:

"A lot of people, even ball players, who come from the South ask us what happens to the field in the wintertime. That's the time of the year that the grass is in the best shape. Nothing is better for a grass field than a big snowstorm. That keeps it from the dangerous elements like wind. A good snowstorm will cover the grass nicely and keep it fresh and clean. We never cover any part of the grass. That would kill it. We just come in here in the spring, water it, cut it and let them get out there and play."

Limongelli works only at Shea Stadium now, after some thirty-four years with at least two jobs.

"A few years ago I bought a little place up in the Poconos. I go there in the wintertime and I really enjoy walking through the woods and taking care of my house," he says. "Mostly I just relax in the winter and wait for the season to start. That's the best part of the year for me, being around the game. I couldn't think of a better way to spend a summer than doing a little work outside, being paid for it and then watching all those baseball games."

Limongelli says he likes all the players and he also likes the umpires.

"Nick Colosi [retired NL umpire] used to be my favorite. I loved when he yelled at the players for stalling during the game. He always said that he wanted the game to move along and if the players didn't move fast enough, he would scream at them," he says. "He was quite a guy."

Limongelli says he especially likes old-timers days when the former players return and he drives a few of them in from the bullpen:

"They always remember us and they kid around about something in the past like some game they lost or something like that. I just enjoy seeing them and being around them."

It was early evening, a sparkling summer twilight at Shea. Limongelli and Pascarella sat on a couple of boards that they would later use as markers for the batter's box at Shea. After that chore they would rake the infield, plant the fresh bases and smooth out the pitcher's mound. It was time to go to work.

They both found those chores a beautiful way to spend an evening. They're part of The Game, aren't they?

17 Bob Brown

SPOKESMAN FOR THE ORIOLES

▬▬ JIM PALMER COULDN'T HANDLE ROBIN YOUNT IN THE final game of the 1982 season for the Baltimore Orioles. The Milwaukee Brewers won the game, won the division and went on to the World Series against St. Louis.

But there was a final moment of glory for Baltimore fans before they left Memorial Stadium for the last time that year. They had to show their love and affection for retiring manager Earl Weaver. They called for the manager to come onto the field and when he did, they exploded in noise and applause. Weaver had led the Orioles to six pennants since he took over as field manager of the team on July 11, 1968. Now the fans were returning some of that warm feeling with their recognition of the feisty little manager.

"For me," says Bob Brown, the longtime publicity director of the Orioles, "that was my most thrilling moment in baseball. I never felt such emotion. When the fans began to applaud Earl spontaneously after we had just lost a tight pennant race, I felt goose bumps all over. I don't think any Series win, any pennant race, any great game we had through the years could equal that moment for me."

Brown had seen the rise and fall of Weaver. He was there when the fireplug manager became the skipper in 1968, he was with him through all those years until his retirement and he was there when Weaver returned to lead the Orioles again on June 14, 1985. He lasted through that year and the next but showed little interest in managing in his second Baltimore tour of duty.

"He never should have come back," says Brown. "I think it damaged his reputation in the game and it hurt his standing in baseball history."

The history of the Orioles in Baltimore from their first season there after moving the franchise from St. Louis to the present day is almost a history of Brown's time. He has been with the club since 1957, became public relations director in 1968 and is now senior publicity director in the league and a winner of the Bob Fishel award for public relations excellence.

Actually, Brown thought he would be winning Most Valuable Player awards as the right fielder of the Orioles. He was an outstanding college baseball player.

"I attended Amherst and played a lot of baseball there," he says. "It was not a baseball power but it was a competitive school in our category. One of my closest friends was John Lancaster, who went on to work in the front office of the Orioles in the office of Harry Dalton. That was how I got into baseball."

Brown graduated from Amherst in 1953. He soon entered the Army, served in Japan and came back to study the Japanese language at Georgetown University.

"I really didn't know what I wanted to do because my only serious interest was in baseball. I realized I wasn't good enough to play in the big leagues but I did begin thinking that I might be able to come up with something in the front office of a ball club," he says.

While he waited to land a baseball job, he took a position with the Washington *Post* as a copyboy. He remained in that job several years and worked his way up to head copyboy.

"By 1960 I was the oldest copyboy the Washington *Post* had. I could see that I wasn't going to make a career out of that. I kept in touch with Lancaster and one day he invited me to have dinner with Eddie Robinson, who was working for the Baltimore club. Robinson recommended I talk to Harry Dalton, who was the farm director then. I went to see Dalton and he said he could hire me in his department as an assistant but he wasn't sure I wanted the position. He said it didn't pay very well," says Brown.

Baseball salaries, then and now, are notoriously small for people working in the front office of a ball club. Club officials often explain to youngsters that the players get most of the money the budget allows for salaries. Besides that, club officials stress, people are grateful for an opportunity to work for a ball club. Money should not be important. That gimmick has worked well for many years.

Dalton looked Brown in the eye and said, "I'm sorry but all we can pay you is four thousand dollars a year."

Brown never budged. He looked directly at Dalton and said, "I'm only making twenty-five hundred dollars a year with the *Post*."

Newspapers, like baseball teams, count on the so-called glamour of the profession to keep the salaries down. That trick has also worked well for many years.

Brown was hired by the Orioles and was put to work as an assistant to Lancaster. He would stay in that position until Lancaster left the club. He was soon named publicity director and has remained in that position for twenty years.

General manager Lee MacPhail and field manager Paul Richards were in charge of the Orioles when Brown joined the club. The team was just beginning to shake off its negative St. Louis image and by 1960 was actually a serious contender.

Baltimore came into Yankee Stadium in September of 1960 only a half game out of first place. These were the very powerful Yankees of Casey Stengel's final season, with Mickey Mantle, Roger Maris, Yogi Berra, Whitey Ford, Elston Howard, Bobby Richardson and Tony Kubek starring for the team. Baltimore hardly seemed a serious challenger but they were still dogging the Yankees into the final month.

In the opening game of a four-game series, youngsters named Brooks Robinson, the third baseman, and Ron Hansen, the shortstop, got confused on a routine infield popup. Robinson dropped the ball after a collision, and the Yankees, as they almost always did, took advantage of the break and rallied to win the game. They would go on to sweep the series and win the pennant.

"That was disappointing for us," Brown recalls, "but the more important thing really was the fact that we were competitive at all. Here we were, playing the great Yankees and we were still in the race this late in the year. I don't think we focused on losing our chance that year as much as we focused on the fact that we were certainly a coming contending ball club with all those fine young players we had on our team."

Most of the players on that 1960 Baltimore team would still be with the club when the Orioles finally were able to win their first pennant in Baltimore in 1966 under manager Hank Bauer.

"That was the year Frank Robinson joined us. He turned the club into a winner. He changed the way we played ball and he probably changed the way a lot of teams in the American League played ball. Frank was a very aggressive player and he brought that style over from the National League. He was the outstanding player in baseball that year and clearly the MVP," says Brown.

When Robinson was officially named the American League winner of the Most Valuable Player award by the Baseball Writers Association of America, he became the only player to win sport's most prestigious award in both leagues. Robinson had led the 1961 Cincinnati Reds to the pennant and was named the National League's Most Valuable Player that season.

"There was a lot of publicity surrounding Frank's trade over to the Orioles. We probably got more requests for interviews for him than we had for any other player," Brown says. "Frank was very cooperative, easy to deal with and very articulate. He has always been that way and he is that way now as manager of the Orioles."

Robinson, of course, was the first black manager in baseball when the Cleveland Indians hired him in 1975. Maury Wills and Larry Doby were the only other blacks to manage in the big leagues, Wills with Seattle and Doby with the Chicago White Sox. Robinson also managed at San Francisco before returning to Baltimore as a coach and later assistant to the team owner, Edward Bennett Williams, before assuming the managerial position again early in 1988. As of the start of the 1989 season he remained the only black manager in the big leagues again.

Few teams have had as much success as the Baltimore Orioles did from 1969 through 1974. They won division titles in five of those six years, made it to the World Series three straight times in 1969, 1970 and 1971 and won over one hundred games three times in a row.

"Our 1969 team was probably our best ever of that time. We lost the World Series to the Mets and we just couldn't believe it," Brown says. "I think everybody realized we were the better team. They just had a hot Series and beat us. The Swoboda catch really killed me."

With the Mets up two games to one at Shea Stadium, New York led 1–0 in the ninth inning of the fourth game. With one out Frank Robinson and Boog Powell singled. Robinson went to third. Brooks Robinson was up. He hit a hard line drive to right field. The ball clearly seemed headed for the gap in right center for a double. Suddenly, right fielder Ron Swoboda raced to his right, lunged full length and caught the ball inches off the ground for one of the most stirring fielding plays in World Series history. Frank Robinson did tag up and score after the catch but the Orioles were finished. They lost the game in the next inning when pitcher Pete Richert hit pinch hitter J. C. Martin with a throw after

Martin had bunted back to the mound. The Mets catcher claimed the ball hit him in fair territory after he "swelled up," as he was running to the base.

"That Swoboda catch really got us," says Brown. "It turned the whole thing around. If we get that hit and win that game, we are tied in games and I think we certainly would have won the next two games. Instead, he made that catch, they win that game and we were really down the next day."

The Series ended with Jerry Koosman beating the Orioles. Swoboda also had a key double. Some Orioles still bemoan their fate in that Series.

"I can still see Swoboda flying through the air to catch that ball even now," Brown says.

One of the ironies of the catch by Swoboda was that it came against his hometown team. Swoboda was born and raised in Baltimore, was an Orioles fan as a kid growing up there and always wanted to play for Baltimore. He never got any closer than an Orioles-sponsored amateur team called Leone's before the Mets signed the bruiser out of the University of Maryland.

The Orioles came back to win the pennant again in 1970. They beat the Cincinnati Reds with Brooks Robinson having a tremendous Series, especially at third base against Reds slugger Johnny Bench. Robinson took away half a dozen base hits from Bench with incredible plays at third base. It was that Series that brought Robinson to the attention of fans nationally. He had always been a fine-fielding third baseman and solid hitter. But he performed so remarkably well in that Series that he was soon being looked at as the standard for third base fielding excellence.

"I guess if you have to pin me down to my favorite player in all the years I have been with the Orioles it has to be between Brooks and Dave McNally," says Brown.

McNally was the fine lefthanded pitcher of the Orioles who retired from baseball shortly after being traded to Montreal. After his retirement he, along with pitcher Andy Messersmith, sued baseball in a historic case that went a long way toward establishing the boundaries of free agency.

"I admired both of them very much," says Brown. "They not only had exceptional ability and were exceptional players, both of them were exceptional men. They had guts and brains and all the ingredients it takes to be wonderful players. More important, they were both exceptional men, easy to work with and very considerate of my needs."

Through the years the Orioles have had some wonderful players and some wonderful men. Under Earl Weaver, the Orioles were as easy a team for the media to deal with as existed in the game. Both Robinsons were bright and articulate, McNally was very open, Jim Palmer was witty as well as honest, Boog Powell, Paul Blair, Mark Belanger and a second baseman named Davey Johnson, later the manager of the New York Mets, were all very cooperative with the press.

In later years the Orioles were not quite as easygoing. One of the most difficult players to deal with was Eddie Murray, the then star first baseman on the team, who almost never sits still for an interview.

"All a publicity man can do is ask a player to cooperate," says Brown. "Some players simply don't like to talk to the press. Once they get that idea fixed in their heads there is very little I can do about it. Some players like Murray believe their obligation ends with their performances on the field."

One other aspect of improved press-player relations is significant. Players on winning teams tend to be more cooperative with the press than players on losing teams. It has always been that way. The Orioles had not been a winning team since 1983. After a record twenty-one-game American League losing streak in 1988, they may be a winning team again for several years to come.

"I think Earl Weaver had a great understanding of the press and enjoyed the daily press conferences. Some managers don't enjoy that. Earl had a quick mind and he liked the challenge of wits he saw presented in his daily doings with the press. If the manager is free with the press the players tend to be free," Brown says.

With their great success in the 1970s under Weaver, the Orioles became one of baseball's glamour teams. That put more strain on Brown and forced him to spend a great deal of time offering information to out-of-town print and electronic media. The Orioles always seemed to have a large contingent of press following them throughout the season, especially since the Senators moved out of Washington to Texas after the 1971 season.

"Our press corps is not only large, it can be quite critical. We have had some rough times in recent seasons and there has been a turnover among the writers. Some of the younger writers hardly remember the glory years of the 1970s so they are more critical of our current state. We think those things go in cycles. We are in a down cycle now and I believe we will start moving up shortly. As we begin winning again, the press will be more supportive. We certainly hit bottom with the 1988 losing streak so everyone in the organization is quite optimistic about much improvement in the years to come," he says.

Brown says that he misses being around a winning team but still feels the job is the best position he could ever hope to have.

"If you can't play right field for the Orioles, it is almost as good to watch the guy who is playing right field every day," he says.

Brown's new year is measured, as it is by all baseball people, with the first day of spring training in Florida in late February. There are some six or seven weeks in the sun, on the beaches, at the finest restaurants around, in some local hangouts and in a fine hotel suite for the publicity director. The games are mostly in the daytime, unlike the schedule during the regular season, and the intensity and nervousness of a regular season or playoff game are never there.

"I don't think that there is any question that spring training is the most pleasant time of the year around a ball club," he says.

When the season begins Brown travels with the club most of the time. He draws the same sixty-two dollars a day meal money the players draw, he stays in the same wonderful hotels, he prepares his statistics and press releases each day, he answers the queries of his traveling sportswriters and he is available for all sorts of information about the team.

"The traveling gets a little wearisome but after so many years you just get used to it," he says.

Brown and his wife, Jay, whom he met on a blind date, have five children. They have all learned to accept the rigors of the profession as well as the joys.

"After the regular season ends I spend a lot of time at home," he says. "I usually do some work at home before going into the office. I find that I can get a lot more done at home early in the morning than I can if I rush into the office and get tied up on the phone."

Brown lives only eight miles from the offices of the Orioles, in Towson, Maryland.

"We set a lot of family things around the baseball schedule," he says. "We also remember many things in conjunction with baseball. One of my daughters, Carolyn, was born on the same date Bo Belinsky of the Los Angeles Angels pitched a no-hitter against us. It was May 5, 1962. I never forget my daughter's birthday because of that."

Brown has remained trim and athletic-looking through the years. He wears glasses and looks professorial on occasion. Mostly, he is excited when the Orioles win a big game or are fighting down to the final days of a tough pennant race.

"I really couldn't imagine doing anything else," he says. "I enjoy this so much. There are times you get weary from the travel or are forced to stay up late after an extra-inning night game. Some of that can be difficult. But then you get into some great series and win a big game and the excitement just carries you through all the down parts of the job."

With the start of the 1989 season and hopes renewed again that the Orioles are returning to their glory years of the 1970s, Brown feels invigorated:

"It is just so much fun doing what I do. I wish we were winning more than we are now but I still get a kick out of a well-pitched game or a big hit or a great catch. I love watching young players because I enjoy guessing which of them will be the next Robinson, the next Palmer, the next McNally."

If there is such a young player in the Baltimore system, he will be publicized and protected by one of the best in the business. Bob Brown has had some big stars to sell to Baltimore fans. He has always done it with integrity, courtesy and devotion.

Bob Brown is the Brooks Robinson of big league baseball public relations directors. A class act.

THE MAN WHO SERVES THEM UP

■■■ THE PITCH CAME IN ACROSS THE MIDDLE OF THE PLATE. It was at the letters and Don Mattingly swung hard. The ball rocketed off his bat in a huge arc and headed for the third deck in Yankee Stadium. It landed about ten rows from the top, maybe thirty or forty feet from the roof. No man, not Babe Ruth, not Lou Gehrig, not Mickey Mantle, not Don Mattingly, had ever been able to clear that roof in fair territory. This was as close as those big sluggers ever get.

Mattingly dropped the bat casually at home plate and jogged toward first base. He rounded second and looked in at the pitcher. The pitcher was looking back at him with a huge smile on his face.

"That's about as good as I get," says Tony Ferrara.

Ferrara is the batting practice pitcher of the New York Yankees. He is paid fifty dollars a game to throw batting practice before each game for fifteen minutes. He is thrilled when long drives fly off the bats of the hitters.

"Jack Clark hit seven of ten off me earlier in the year. That was great," he says.

There are a couple of other batting practice pitchers around the Yankees, including a former major league catcher named Nick Testa, who played for the Giants, and a former major league pitcher named Vita Valentinetti, who pitched for the White Sox, Tigers and Washington Senators in the 1950s and now works as a court officer in Manhattan. Neither counts batting practice pitches or has made the *Guinness Book of Records* the way Ferrara has.

"When I crossed a million batting practice pitches I applied for the record. They interviewed me and checked the authenticity of it all," says Ferrara. "When they found out that I kept accurate records and had hitters who authorized how many a day I throw, it worked out."

Ferrara has calculated that he has averaged about four hundred pitches a day over the length of a baseball season. This comes to some fifty thousand a year or over a million in the twenty years he has done this batting practice work. The average major league starting pitcher may reach three hundred innings with about four thousand pitches in a season.

"The difference between me and the regular guys is I can do it all without a sore arm," he says.

Ferrara tends to ignore some other differences, such as the fact that most big leaguers are trying to get hitters out while he tries to get them to hit it out.

"My great thrill is when one of the really big guys drives a pitch a long way," he says. "I used to love Ron Blomberg when he was with the Yankees. He was one of the greatest batting practice hitters of all time. He hit some of the most tremendous drives off me I've ever seen. It was wonderful. His problem was he couldn't hit a ball if it curved and he couldn't hit a big league fastball in a tough location."

What makes a batting practice pitcher successful is his ability to throw a ball in the exact spot the batter wants to see it in.

"Guys work on location hitting. Sometimes they are just working out and want to hit some balls out of the park to get their swing down. Then I give them my seventy-five-mile-an-hour fastball right over the middle of the plate. They love to get a good rip at that and drive it out. It's wonderful for a hitter's confidence. There are other times and other guys who want a pitch in a certain location. Mattingly and Willie Randolph can be like that. They may know a certain pitcher tries to get them out down and in or up and away with hard stuff. They ask me to keep the ball in that location so they can adjust their swing. 'Be quick, be quick,' you hear them shouting in the cage."

Batting practice pitchers really only came into vogue in the 1940s. Before that teams would use coaches, managers or pitchers on their off days to throw batting practice. Once in a while high school or college pitchers would be hired to throw some extra batting practice before an important series if the manager wanted to rest the pitcher.

One of the first recognized full-time batting practice pitchers was Bill Boylan of the Brooklyn Dodgers. Boylan was a milkman with a delivery route on horse-drawn wagons in the 1930s and into the 1940s around Ebbets Field. He had played some semiprofessional baseball and knew many of the Brooklyn players.

"I used to start my milk delivery route about three or four in the morning," Boylan once said. "I would get it all done by noon. Then I could go over to the ball park and watch the Dodgers play. This one time I was in the stands before a Brooklyn game against the New York Giants. It was in the 1930s and Casey Stengel was the Brooklyn manager. He came over and said hello."

Stengel knew Boylan was a milkman when he wasn't playing ball.

"Did you put the cows to bed?" he asked.

"Sure did," said Boylan.

"Then why don't you come down here and throw a little for my guys. You could tell they need help," he said.

Boylan walked onto the field, was ushered into the Dodger clubhouse, suited up and threw a half hour of batting practice. He would throw batting practice every day the Brooklyn Dodgers were home at Ebbets Field or visiting the Polo

Grounds in Manhattan until the Giants and Brooklyn Dodgers moved west after the 1957 season. He became well known to avid Brooklyn fans as the Pitching Milkman. His career highlight came when a wartime youngster named Tommy Brown, who joined the Dodgers at the age of sixteen, counted 142 home runs in 1945. Two of them actually came in big league games.

One other familiar arm around the Yankees lasted about twenty years. Spud Murray was a minor league pitcher the Yankees hired as a batting practice pitcher in the early 1950s. Stengel had moved over to the Yankees as their manager by then and wanted a steady batting practice pitcher.

Murray made all the team photos of those winning Yankee teams in the 1950s and 1960s until he was fired in an economy move by the Yankees in the late 1960s.

Ferrara's first season with the Yankees was 1969.

"I went to the University of Miami and played baseball there. I was a third baseman with a strong arm. Dick Howser was the assistant baseball coach at Florida State in those days during the winter. He was in the big leagues but he would come home to Florida and work with the team until he had to leave for spring training. Howser and Burt Reynolds were friends at Florida State. I knew both of them down there. I wasn't as good a player as Howser and I wasn't as good an actor as Reynolds," he says.

Ferrara, who was born and raised in Coral Gables, just outside Miami, was a noted local baseball player. He had professional ambitions and after college played some semi-professional baseball. His father, Joseph, was a tailor. Tony knew he didn't want to follow in his footsteps. He decided to come to New York and look for work.

A trim, good-looking fellow with gentle features, Ferrara got an agent after he arrived in Manhattan and began modeling clothes. He did some bit parts in movies but yearned to be around baseball.

"That's what I really loved. I wanted to be part of the game. I didn't care what I did. I just wanted to come to the ball park every day. I would help out any way I could. I just wanted to be part of the environment, suit up, throw batting practice, play catch. Just be around," he says.

He showed up one day early in the 1969 season. Howser, his Florida buddy, had just been named a Yankee coach.

"I just asked Dick if I could pitch some batting practice and he said he would ask the manager," says Ferrara.

Baseball is clearly one of the most traditional examples of the old boy network. It is nearly impossible to break into the game in an off-field capacity without close associates in the game. When a former player is hired as a manager, he most often will surround himself with old buddies as coaches. At this very moment two very old ball players are sitting at some bar in St. Louis or Boston or Detroit or Chicago promising each other faithfully that if either gets a job in baseball as a manager somewhere in the near or distant future, the other buddy will go along as a coach. In many cases, the word "coach" in baseball lexicon is a euphemism for drinking buddy. Owners and general managers do not frown upon that practice. It is the code of the road. They understand that the manager needs a buddy to talk to, a release from the pressure, an escape from the press and the unfriendly players on his team. That's what coaching buddies are for.

Billy Martin, for example, made a science of hiring Art Fowler as his pitching coach any time he managed the Yankees, or any other club for that matter. Fowler knew a little bit about pitching but he also knew a great deal about drinking beer. Many of Martin's barroom episodes occurred on nights when Fowler was absent from the scene for one reason or another. Yankee owner George Steinbrenner vowed that if he hires Martin again, this time he hires a bodyguard to go with him.

So Howser was a buddy of Ferrara and as the system

works, he recommended Ferrara highly to Ralph Houk. The veteran Yankee manager believed the team needed another batting practice pitcher after Spud Murray had been let go and convinced the Yankee management that this time the expense would be minimal.

"I think they gave me twenty or twenty-five dollars a game when I started," says Ferrara. "I was working in acting and modeling. I didn't care about the money. I just cared about being close to the game."

At Yankee Stadium Ferrara was given a locker, allowed to dress with the players and asked to pitch batting practice for half an hour. Unlike Spud Murray, he would not accompany the team regularly on the road.

"Once in a while Ralph would ask me to go on a trip to Boston or Baltimore, someplace near like that. They picked up the hotel tab and gave me meal money. That was always a lot of fun. I did get to go to the playoffs and World Series when the Yankees won in 1977 and 1978," he says.

By that time Ferrara had become friendly with Joe Torre, the third baseman of the Mets who was soon to become their manager.

"I started at Shea when Joe asked me to come in and throw some extra batting practice because a lot of their guys had sore arms," he says. "I don't get sore arms so I was ready when he asked."

The Yankees of 1969, the team Ferrara first joined, were not a successful baseball team. They did have some quality players in Bobby Murcer, Roy White and Mel Stottlemyre but the others were mostly second-division players. Not too many fans noticed much or could remember much about the Yankees of 1969 anyway. That was the year the New York Mets captured the heart of the Big Apple with their first pennant and first World Championship season.

"The Yankees didn't win but they had a great bunch of guys. I really liked all of them and they treated me like one of them," he says. "I spent a lot of time with Murcer and Stick Michael. The next year Curt Blefary joined the Yankees. He hit six huge home runs in a row off me. That was my finest hour. I almost cried when he dribbled the seventh one off the side of the cage. You can't imagine how depressing that was for me."

Two Hall of Famers in Ferrara's book are Ron Swoboda and Fran Healy. Both are now broadcasters. In their playing days, both were large fellows who just didn't seem to be able to hit big league pitching.

"Fran could hit me," says Ferarra with fierce pride. "He hit more balls out against me than any other Yankee player of his time, more than Reggie, more than [Graig] Nettles, more than any of them. I'll tell you another thing about Fran. He was an upper-deck guy. When he hit the ball it usually went into the third deck and way back. He didn't hit those soft fly balls that just drop over the fences."

Swoboda's name brought back memories of one of the heroes of the 1969 Miracle Mets. Swoboda starred on that team and made a memorable World Series catch off the bat of Brooks Robinson that saved a World Series win for Tom Seaver. That game will probably be remembered by Mets fans as long as the Mets play in the National League. It made Swoboda, always a fan favorite, a very special person around Shea.

Swoboda's talents didn't quite equal his enthusiasm and by 1971 he was gone from the Mets in a trade with Montreal. He would reappear in New York as a member of the Yankees in 1971, 1972 and 1973 before being released. His career was probably a disappointment for all concerned. It ended in the big leagues just as Swoboda turned twenty-nine years old.

"He was incredibly strong," says Ferrara. "I never figured out why he couldn't hit. He always hit me good. One of his problems was his lack of discipline at the plate. He tried to hit every pitch five hundred feet. He got some long ones off me, not that far, but certainly over four hundred or four fifty. I guess I wasn't curving them."

Ferrara says that a good part of his satisfaction comes from watching the game and seeing the guys have a big day at bat. Especially if the batter had a big day against him in batting practice.

"I can't say for sure that having a good day in batting practice and hitting a few against me is going to guarantee a guy a chance at a big day in the game but I think it helps," he says. "I can see the good hitters leaving the cage after batting practice when they hit me hard with all the confidence in the world. When a guy hits a few big ones off me he just feels good about his chances. He has confidence at the plate when he goes up there and he has confidence in his swing and stance."

In a sport where failure seven times out of ten at the plate is guaranteed, confidence tends to rise and fall like the stock market. It may vary with each at-bat, each pitcher the batter faces, sometimes as minutely as each swing.

"One of the things I'm trying to do is help a guy become a consistent hitter," says Ferrara. "If I can do that by throwing the ball at the same spot with the same speed and having the guy hit it hard all the time, I think that helps him become consistent. I'll throw a curve if the guy wants it but mostly they don't. They just like to take batting practice so they can get loose and develop that confidence they need. It's a little different facing me and then facing Roger Clemens but if they do it on a high from a good batting practice they have an edge."

Ferrara, who admits to being forty-seven years old though some players who have been around ten or fifteen years say he was about that age when they broke in, did double duty with the Yankees and Mets through the 1986 season. The Mets won the pennant and the World Championship that year. Ferrara felt he was part of the team.

"They took me up to Boston for the World Series. I threw

about half an hour of batting practice every day. I really got Darryl Strawberry in shape for the Series. He hit about a dozen over the screen off me," he says.

When the Series ended in an exciting New York Mets triumph, Ferrara was as thrilled as any of the players on the team. Then came a major disappointment.

"They gave out the World Series shares and I only got four hundred dollars. I thought that was a little cheap from guys making five, six or seven hundred thousand dollars a year. That wouldn't have been so terrible. But the real blow came when they gave out World Series rings to just about everybody in the organization from the scouts to the office people. I helped a lot of those players have big years and I didn't get a World Series ring. That was the appreciation I got from going there every day and pitching for hours to those guys," he says.

Besides his in-season performance, Ferrara spends a good part of the winter at Shea Stadium. Hitters begin coming in shortly after the World Series ends to begin working out for next season. The way hitters work out is by swinging at batting practice pitching. Ferrara doesn't look at the pitching machines, the so-called Iron Mikes, as any kind of threat to his batting practice work.

"Once in a while a pitcher will want to throw fifteen or twenty minutes. I'll catch him and turn on the pitching machine for the other guys. They just go through the motions with the machine. Nobody learns anything about the art of hitting by working with a machine. You gotta have that live pitching," he says.

When Ferrara's unhappiness about not getting a larger share of the World Series money and a World Series ring filtered back to the team authorities (there are spies everywhere in a baseball clubhouse) Ferrara was asked not to return.

"That really hurt me. I was real down for a long time after that. I just enjoyed going to the park every day during the season and throwing for both the Yankees and Mets. When I realized I was finished at Shea, my life was very empty," he says.

Just before he could get too far down the ladder, Ferrara got another big boost. He was invited to Florida as one of the instructors at the fantasy camp run each winter by Mickey Mantle and Whitey Ford.

Fantasy camps have sprung up all over the country and have become the perfect fix for middle-aged baseball junkies. For a goodly sum, in the neighborhood of three thousand dollars, successful businessmen, professional people or guys who have just saved the admission fee from a blue-collar job—and even a few women—journey to an unused spring training site in Florida or Arizona. For a week they work out with the same routine as big league players at the direction of some former well-known names. At Ferrara's first camp, where his seventy-five-mile-an-hour fastball was a little too quick for most of the campers, he was joined on the staff by Tom Tresh, Moose Skowron, Bobby Richardson, Joe Pepitone, Roy White and Clete Boyer. Mantle and Ford were also on hand but their chores were mostly confined to ceremonial roles, autograph signing, reminiscing about their brilliant careers or spending an evening in the hotel bar regaling the campers with heroic tales of days gone by.

"It was just a terrific thing to do and if Mickey and Whitey didn't allow me to come down as one of the instructors I would probably come down as one of the campers," says Ferrara.

Ferrara says he approaches the batting practice sessions at the fantasy camps—and the real games there—with the same attitude with which he approaches the hitters at Yankee Stadium in the pennant race.

"I just want everybody to hit me and have a good time. A guy pays three thousand bucks, he isn't going to have a lot of fun if he comes up to home plate and strikes out all the time. I recognize that these guys don't have a lot of skills so I'm very happy when one of them gets a line drive off me. It doesn't have the same ring as a line drive hit by Mattingly or Winfield but for the guy who hits it, the line drive has the same kind of pleasure. That's why so many people love baseball. There just aren't a lot of things you can do that are as much fun as hitting a baseball hard," he says.

When the fantasy camp weeks end, Ferrara returns to his Manhattan apartment and prepares for spring training. The Yankees have invited him down at their expense the last few years. They always need pitchers to throw batting practice, especially in the early days of the camp, because so few regular pitchers are ready.

"One year I must have thrown a half hour every day for a week because we had so much rain the regular guys all fell behind," he says.

Ferrara's modeling work and acting chores—he has been in many soap operas—led him to his biggest role. He played in *The Natural*. Robert Redford also was in the film.

"I taught him everything he knows," says Ferrara. "I'm only kidding. He is a great actor and he also knows a lot about baseball. They didn't have to work with him very much about his stance and his swing. He really looked like a guy who had been on the field a few times before he took that role."

In baseball circles more people know Ferrara was in the movie than can name the star. Ferrara had a lot to do with that. He would often walk up to a Yankee player or a visiting player and ask, "Did you see my movie?"

When most of them confessed they didn't know he was in a movie, he would say, "Oh, yeah, I'm in *The Natural* with Redford." According to Ferrara only Redford and Wonderboy, the lightning-producing bat Redford uses, earned more acclaim for the movie than he did.

"It was fun making the picture. The only problem was the filming was in Buffalo and who wants to be in Buffalo for six or seven weeks? I was actually glad when the filming was over and I could get back to the Stadium and back to throw-ing batting practice," he says.

Going on twenty years with the Yankees as a batting practice pitcher, Ferrara still recalls the first day he arrived in that locker room.

"I saw Phil Rizzuto and I introduced myself as the new batting practice pitcher. He said he was thrilled to meet me. He said he was tired of being the only Italian around the Yankees all these years," he says.

Ferrara said that he is as wrapped up in baseball today as he was the first day he put that famous Yankee uniform on.

"I could think of only one thing that could be better for me," he says. "When Bob Lemon was the manager of the Yankees he really liked the way I threw batting practice. He could also see that I knew a lot about the game. 'Did you ever think of coaching?' That's all I ever thought about. I would give anything for a chance at a big league coaching job. I think I could be a terrific coach. I've been in the game a long time, I've learned from some great managers like Houk and Howser and Billy and Lemon and all the rest and I could do a lot of things. I can pitch, I can catch, I can work out infielders, I have a great fungo bat and I know the game. I think that I would really be an asset to a ball club, espe-cially with younger players. It isn't just talent that makes a guy successful in this game, it's being smart, knowing the game, knowing what to do and when to do it. That takes some guys a long time to learn. I know all that. I've sat on the bench of some great teams and absorbed a lot in the years I've been around."

While Ferrara has never played any professional baseball, he does know a lot of professional baseball players. It is one of the reasons he is an important part of a new lower Manhattan restaurant called Legends. Ferrara is one of three owners along with Art Shamsky, a hero of the 1969 Mets team, and current Mets pitching star Ron Darling. The appeal of the restaurant may well be the possibility of sitting down to lunch next to any of the big stars of the game.

"A lot of the players come into our restaurant. It has a sports flavor and we show games on large-screen television. The players can come in and scout the opposition players in other games being shown on the screen. It's a comfortable place," he says.

Darling, of course, is busy with the Mets during the season and promoting for the Mets in the off-season. Shamsky has outside investment and television interests. Ferrara, a bachelor, would seem to have the most time to devote to the restaurant, especially in the off-season.

"I really enjoy it because you get to meet a lot of baseball fans in a place like that. Any time I am around baseball players or baseball fans I am happy. It is the greatest game in the world and I'm just thrilled to be part of it, even a small part."

Ferrara may work in his restaurant or do a bit part on a soap opera or stroll across the big screen for a blinking instant. All of that adds to his resume. What he really cares about, what he really loves, what is really the essence of his life is walking through the door of the Yankee clubhouse, suiting up in those famous pinstripes worn by Ruth and Gehrig and Mantle and DiMaggio and Mattingly and walking to the mound.

"When I get out there and turn around and see that famous Stadium outline behind me I still get a lump in my throat," he says. "I can't imagine anything more exciting than what I do. I just love it when I throw a good pitch and Winfield or Mattingly or Pags or one of those big Yankee sluggers just crushes it. That's heaven."

Ferrara may be on the edges but he is in The Game. He knows he is part of baseball. He knows that he walks the same paths as the big guys, sits in the same dugout, steps on that same hallowed Stadium grass.

"I love it," he says. "I love everything about it. Maybe

the only thing better would be to be a coach and help out even more. For now, this is plenty good enough for me."

Remember this. Tony Ferrara gets to spend part of every winter in Florida with number 7 and number 16 of the Yankees. He can call them Mickey and Whitey and they know his name. They really do.

19 Buddy Kerr

LOOKING FOR
THE BEST

▬▬▬ IN THE SUMMER OF 1945, THE NEW YORK GIANTS WERE boarding a train at Grand Central Station in New York for a weekend series against the Braves in Boston. The manager of the team, Mel Ott, who was also the team's right fielder, sat alone in a corner of the car as the players picked their seats. The conductor was on the platform looking at his watch.

"All aboard," the conductor bellowed, "all aboard."

Smoke billowed from the engine. The players settled down to their newspapers or their card games as the train lurched forward. Suddenly, it stopped as a conductor signaled an engineer.

A large man was moving through the station with his wife. A breathless porter trailed behind with a cart of suitcases.

"That was the first time I saw Babe Ruth in person," recalls New York Mets scout Buddy Kerr, the shortstop on that New York Giants baseball team of 1945. "He came into our car and sat down next to Ottie. For the rest of the way up to Boston he just talked to him about the team, talked to him about the Yankees and told a million stories. We all just sat around and listened to the Babe. I can't remember any details of his conversation. I do remember he kept repeating over and over again how anybody could hit a home run in

254

the Polo Grounds. 'That park is so small I could spit them over the wall,' Babe said. It was just exciting listening to the Babe."

As he completes fifty years in baseball in 1988, Kerr is still as excited about the game and the people he meets as he was that first day he showed up for a Polo Grounds tryout in 1938.

"I was still in George Washington High School in Manhattan then," he says, "and I was also a wild Giants fan. Just the idea of being in the ball park and seeing those New York Giants on the field with us was thrilling. I don't think kids today have that same sensation. They see all the players on television and they get to meet so many of them at the Little League dinners and public functions they attend now. For us, they were all figures of heroic proportions."

John Joseph Kerr was born in Astoria, New York, and soon moved with his family to Manhattan.

"My father was a crane operator and I was the second of his ten children. He had over forty grandchildren. I played on the streets of the Washington Heights area and I started following the New York Giants in the 1930s," he says.

Early on, Kerr was called Butch or Buddy by his family.

"John was too common a name and every kid on the street was named John. I think I was Butch for a little while and then it became Buddy. There are people who know me in baseball over fifty years who have no idea of my first name. I have all kinds of troubles in hotels. A guy calls the hotel operator and asks for Buddy Kerr. The operator says there is no Buddy Kerr listed but there is a John Kerr. The caller, if he is in baseball, will invariably say he doesn't know any John Kerr. All my documents, social security, driver's license, credit cards, all read John Kerr. Generally, it works out sooner or later."

Kerr was only sixteen years old when he had his Giants tryout.

"They didn't have the rules about signing free agents they have today. If a club liked a kid they signed him. That was all there was to it. I tried out in 1938 and I was signed when I graduated from high school the following year. Nick Shinkoff signed me for the Giants. He was an area scout but I don't think he was even paid by the ball club. I think he had a big job down in Wall Street, made a lot of money and did it because he loved the game," Kerr says.

Years later Shinkoff retired from Wall Street and did become a full-time scout in the New York area for the Giants, then already resettled in San Francisco.

"When he told me I had a chance to play professional baseball I just jumped at it. He gave me five hundred dollars as a bonus and sent me off to Fort Smith, Arkansas, in the spring of 1940. It was all I ever wanted to do," he says.

Minor league baseball proved rougher for the shy, youthful, skinny shortstop than he had imagined.

"I was sent to Clinton, Iowa, the next year and it was a rough time. I didn't do well, I had trouble with some older players and I lost my confidence. There were so many long bus trips and they would actually make me ill. We bounced around on those buses so much I felt like a bottle in a storm. I decided this was no life. I wanted to go home. I didn't consider what else I would do but I figured I could learn how to operate a crane and make a living the way my father did. His children never went hungry. I figured if it was good enough for him, it would be good enough for me," he says.

Kerr returned home to New York. He did nothing for two weeks. Then he received a telegram from the front office of the New York Giants. It ordered him to report to the Giants farm club in Orlando, Florida. He was going to play in a league the Giants thought he could handle.

"It was one of those tough telegrams that ball clubs used to send out in those days, kind of a take-it-or-leave-it tone to the telegram. If I wanted to play any more baseball I'd better get myself down to Florida in a hurry. It was signed by Bill

Terry, who was the boss of the Giants in those days. I took the next train out," he says.

In a few weeks the confidence returned, the hitting stroke was there and the desire was back.

"I realized I wanted to play ball. That's all I ever wanted to do. It was just that as a kid I was having trouble with the buses and the conditions and I didn't know if I could make the adjustment," he says.

Kerr regained his baseball legs that summer and was soon headed up the baseball ladder. There was one other event he remembers in that league in 1940.

"There was this kid pitcher in Daytona Beach by the name of Stan Musial. He pitched and played a little outfield. All of a sudden I heard that he wasn't going to pitch anymore. He had hurt his arm and after about a week or so they converted him into a full-time outfielder. I remember going against him a couple of times that year and you had to play him deep. He could hit the ball hard to any part of the field. I wasn't very surprised when he went up to the National League the next year and tore it up."

Kerr spent another season and a half in the minor leagues before joining the Giants in New York in 1943.

"I was still pretty nervous but I knew I could field well enough to play in the big leagues. I got a few base hits early after they brought me up and that made things easier," he says.

Many believe the talent in baseball was at its thinnest in 1944. The pool of young athletes had been severely depleted by World War II. It would be a year that saw youngsters such as Tommy Brown in Brooklyn and Joe Nuxhall in Cincinnati play in the big leagues. Brown, a handsome shortstop, was sixteen years old and Nuxhall, a lefthanded pitcher, got into a big league game while he was still fifteen, the youngest player ever to make a big league box score.

"I was still in high school when I signed with the Reds," Nuxhall recalls. "I would pitch only when the Reds were in

Cincinnati. I would be driven over to the park from my home in Hamilton by my dad. When the Reds went back on the road, I went back to school."

Nuxhall would pitch in only one game in 1944. He faced nine batters, gave up two hits, allowed five walks and seven runs. His 67.50 ERA for the season was a record. It would be eight years before Nuxhall returned again to the big leagues.

Brown would get into forty-six games as a sixteen-year-old Dodger shortstop in 1944. He hit .164 but claimed over fifty batting practice home runs. He managed to hang around the big leagues for nine years as a utility player. He batted .241 lifetime.

"I might have been helped a bit by the lack of talent around in those days," admits Kerr, "but my best big league season came in 1947. Everybody was back from service by then and I hit .287."

The 1947 season was most memorable for the arrival of Jackie Robinson in the big leagues. The Brooklyn Dodgers, under general manager Branch Rickey, broke the color line with the all-around athlete from California. Robinson was named the National League Rookie of the Year in his first big league season.

"We were all curious about Jackie but our club didn't do much to bother him. We were more concerned about beating the Brooklyn ball club than we were bothering Robinson. The only thing that mattered to us in those days was the rivalry with the Dodgers. If Robinson helped the Dodgers win, we didn't like him. It didn't have anything to do with his color."

Kerr became the regular shortstop on the 1944 Giants. He played in 150 games and batted .266.

"I was only twenty-one years old when I joined the Giants that season. I was a shy kid and I was still a little awestruck being in the big leagues with all those players I had read about for so many years. It was a tough adjustment but I was able to do it," he says.

The Giants finished fifth in the eight-team league but they did have no fewer than three future Hall of Famers on the ball club, outfielder Joe (Ducky) Medwick, catcher Ernie (Schnozz) Lombardi and right fielder/manager Mel Ott.

"Ottie was really a wonderful player, still effective that season and a great person. He was kind to me and very helpful and I admired him very much. It was really a tragedy when he was killed in that car accident years later. He was still a young man. Ottie could really play that wall in the Polo Grounds and he knew an awful lot about positioning infielders and outfielders," he says.

Ott's personality led to one of the most memorable baseball lines of all times. A couple of seasons after Kerr joined the club, Ott was leading his Giants team into Ebbets Field for a big series against the Brooklyn Dodgers. As usual, the flamboyant manager of the Brooklyn Dodgers, Leo Durocher, was sitting in the Brooklyn dugout entertaining sportswriters with his pugnacious personality and aggressive philosophy. He was extolling the virtues of toughness in the game, a trait he pushed hard on his players.

As he spoke the Giants began filtering into their dugout from the visitor's clubhouse. They were led by their gentle manager, Mel Ott.

"See Ott over there," Durocher screamed. "He's a nice guy. Where has it gotten him? Last place, that's where. He is a nice guy and he is in last place."

By the time the sportswriters got finished paraphrasing what Durocher had said his statement came out, "Nice guys finish last," something he never actually said. No matter, it is recorded in *Bartlett's Familiar Quotations* as "Nice guys finish last." It is no more accurate than Greta Garbo's supposed words, "I want to be alone" (actually "I want to be left alone") or the memorable "Play it again, Sam," from the film *Casablanca* (actually, "You played it for her, now play it for me, play it, Sam," is what Humphrey Bogart said).

"Ottie could be tough when he had to be," says Kerr. "He cared about discipline and he certainly cared about mistakes in the ball game. He was just not a guy who believed in bawling out a ball player in public or embarrassing him."

Kerr had another steady season in 1946 and then played shortstop on the 1947 team, one of the most awesome power-houses in baseball history. Another Hall of Fame slugger, Johnny Mize, hit fifty-one home runs for the 1947 Giants, with Willard Marshall collecting thirty-six homers, Walker Cooper hitting thirty-five and a youngster from Staten Island named Bobby Thomson hitting twenty-nine. Thomson, of course, would gain much fame four years later when he hit the most famous baseball home run of all time, the home run that defeated the Brooklyn Dodgers in the 1951 playoff game, a blast forever known as the Shot Heard Round the World.

"That 1947 team was really a very powerful outfit. There wasn't a weak hitter in the lineup. We were helped playing in the Polo Grounds, of course, where everybody had a chance to hit one out if he swung the bat. I think we might have had a few cheap homers that year but not many. They were all legitimate sluggers and our run producing was something to watch. With any kind of decent pitching and a little more team speed we might have won it all," he says.

Kerr had two more decent seasons with the Giants in 1948 and 1949 before being traded to the Boston Braves in the major deal of the time, with fiery Eddie Stanky and talented Alvin Dark coming over to New York from the Braves. It would prove to be the foundation for the exciting Giants team of 1951.

Kerr finished out his active big league career in Boston with a .227 mark in 1950 and a .186 mark as a utility player in 1951. The Braves released him at the end of that season and he played a couple more years of minor league baseball before hanging up his spikes.

"I wanted to remain in the game in some capacity but wasn't sure anything would work out," says Kerr. "I had been in the game since I was sixteen years old so I wasn't really prepared for anything else. While you are playing you don't think of the day when you won't be playing. Salaries weren't very big then—I never made more than twenty-one thousand —so we weren't playing for dollars. We just loved the game. I knew that I could probably find something else that would pay as well as baseball. I also knew that I could never find anything else that I would enjoy as much as baseball. I called a few people, asked around but nothing developed. I just figured my baseball days were over and I would have to make the best of it."

Then came the next big baseball break. Nick Shinkoff, the New York Giants scout who had signed him, called Kerr at his New York home:

"I was just talking to Horace [Stoneham] and he says we may have an opening for a managerial position in our organization. He asked me to find out if you might be interested."

Kerr never even asked Shinkoff where the job was or what the salary was. He just knew he was going. Giants owner Horace Stoneham would have himself a young manager.

For the next ten years he managed in the Giants system, in the Eastern League, the Midwest League, the Florida State League, bouncing from team to team, helping the Giants develop young players, teaching the fundamental skills he had learned under Mel Ott and Leo Durocher and Billy Southworth.

"It was a rough life. My wife, Kathleen, and I had a growing family [there would eventually be four Kerr children, all college graduates and on their own now] and the moving around and being away from home was difficult. Kathleen did a lot of the raising of the kids by herself during the season. I spent as much time as I could with them when the season was over. We never made much money in baseball," he says.

Kerr developed a second career as a liquor salesman to help support his family and was soon living in suburban New Jersey and traveling the state in the winter.

"It was all local travel so it was no burden. I enjoyed it because I always liked to be around people and being a salesman was like trying to sell a kid on changing some of his baseball habits," he says.

The Giants had moved, along with the Dodgers, to California in 1957. San Francisco was not quite the franchise Los Angeles was but Horace Stoneham, the Giants owner, was still loyal to his employees. Kerr had a job every season.

"Finally, in 1964 he asked me if I wanted to give up managing and become a scout for the organization. That seemed like a good idea. I wasn't advancing in my managerial career so I took a shot at it. I found that scouting was really what I enjoyed the most," he says.

Kerr was soon working as a special assignment scout for the Giants. He was located in the East near his New Jersey home and was on the road much less than he had been as a manager.

"I could see a lot of the ball players in Yankee Stadium or at Shea or in Philadelphia," he says. "Most of the time I slept in my own bed. That was a wonderful change after all those years in hotel rooms. I enjoyed working on reports and I enjoyed being with the other scouts. It is a very tight fraternity."

Baseball scouts may well be the most important, least understood and least appreciated people in the game. They explain what they do to others but can only be truly understood by one another.

"I watch a game differently than a fan, differently even than a member of the ball club. I have scouted mostly on the big league level so I don't concentrate on potential. I concentrate on what a guy can actually do," he says.

Kerr keeps complicated game forms on every player he sees and also a notebook with special information he passes on to the front office for use during the season against that opposing player or for evaluation after the season in trades.

"We have our meetings and we discuss different players. I am also excited when the organization decides to make a deal on my recommendation. That's something that really makes you follow a guy's progress," he says.

Kerr enjoyed his scouting chores and saw no reason to change his job. Then the Giants were sold.

"Horace owned the club when I joined the Giants in 1940 and he was still running it when I became a scout. He was getting older and I could see that he would step aside soon. I figured he would keep it in the family. It didn't work out that way," he says.

In 1976 the Giants were sold to a grocery magnate named Robert Lurie. Stoneham retained a small share of the club but no longer had any say in its daily operation. Stoneham was the last of the traditional baseball-family-owned operators. He had inherited the club from his father and he had run it like a small family business. He always surrounded himself with longtime Giants. His employees including Bill Terry, Mel Ott and Carl Hubbell, all Hall of Famers who retained their association with the Giants organization for many years after their playing days were over. Hubbell, the famed screwball-throwing lefthander of the New York Giants in the 1920s, 1930s and into the early 1940s, was still on the Giants payroll at the age of eighty-five in 1988. He was a frequent visitor to the Giants spring training headquarters in Arizona where he made his home after he left the playing fields. He once ran the Giants farm system under Stoneham.

"There had already been quite a few old Giants working for the team when I started," Kerr says. "I think Horace just felt a loyalty and a closeness to the players who had been with him. When he could, he brought them into the organization. He felt very strongly about that."

There had been some criticism of the Giants organization, first in New York and later in San Francisco, that there were incompetent people running the operation who owed their jobs to Horace. Outsiders felt that was no way to run an operation.

When Lurie took over the team, that was the first order of business. All of Horace's old cronies, from public relations men to batting practice pitchers, were let go.

"I wasn't actually fired," laughs Kerr. "I was just told that I wouldn't be rehired. They gave all the scouts time enough to find a job."

Kerr's expertise, dedication and success in his job made him a scout other organizations were interested in hiring. He got several offers and chose the one nearest home when the New York Mets hired him. It has been a successful marriage.

"The Mets have been wonderful to me," he says. "I was hired when the Joan Payson family still ran the team and I was kept on when the Mets were sold to the Doubleday people. My job has changed a few times through the years but mostly I am a special assignment scout and mostly I don't travel very far. Kathleen is happy about that."

In late September of 1988, Kerr was assigned to scout the American League East teams the Mets might meet in the World Series. He spent the last three weeks of the 1988 season watching Yankee games, Red Sox games or watching them play each other in Boston and New York.

"I'll compile a complete book on all the players before the season is over and get it to the front office. The team will then go over the material and use it in the Series."

The Mets never got past the Dodgers in the National League Championship Series so the material was never used for its orginal purpose.

"No material is wasted, no scouting effort is not put to use," he says. "Even though we don't win and don't face those teams, we have good reports on their players. It could help us in a deal or it could help us if one of their players comes over to our league."

Manager Davey Johnson of the Mets is a figure filbert. He was a mathematics major at Texas A&M. He enjoys looking at computer printouts of previous performance by opposing players. That information comes from the work done by Kerr and the other Mets scouts and is pumped into the computer for use in the pressure situations. Watch Johnson closely in tough games; he will often pull out a long piece of paper and study it in the dugout. It is one of his favorite printouts, with more information on it than most managers could imagine.

"Baseball has really become much more sophisticated than it was in my day," says Kerr. "We used to go over a hitter in the meetings by saying he was a pull hitter or he wasn't. That was about it. Now they get involved in whether he pulls the low pitch or the high one, how he hits the curve or the change or the slider and what part of the field he might use on a certain pitch. There never seems to be enough detail. It makes our job harder but it also makes it more rewarding."

Kerr rarely gets involved in amateur free agents. He is almost always working on the big league level. He did have some input on one free agent amateur player. It was a kid pitcher in Florida named Dwight Gooden.

"I was in Florida on some other scouting business and they asked me to run over and take a look at this kid Gooden in Tampa. Several other guys in the organization had seen him. Everybody liked him. I had also seen the kid shortstop in Brooklyn, Shawon Dunston, and I thought he was a tremendous prospect. I think the consensus was that the Mets needed an everyday position player more than they needed a pitcher. I am sure the idea was to take Dunston if he was still available. The Cubs picked Dunston and the Mets took Gooden when their turn came up. I was very happy. I just felt he was going to be exceptional. I have always felt that you build a team from the pitching staff on. If you could get a Gooden, that was the way to go," he says.

Kerr will celebrate his fiftieth anniversary in the game in 1989. He has not had one minute of doubt about his choice of careers.

"If you had your dreams answered you would play forever. That's the fun of baseball. Since that can't happen, you take the next best thing. That's watching it. I think I still love the game as much as I ever did and when a season ends I always feel a little sad. I just can't wait for the next one to start," he says.

At the age of sixty-six, still looking like Ichabod Crane with his lanky frame, Buddy Kerr wants nothing more than to continue in his job as long as he can:

"Sometimes we are all out there in the sun together on a nice afternoon, all the scouts behind the plate, and we're talking about some new kid and we're going over his skills and I just remember my own playing days. It's just wonderful being part of the game, even a very small part."

Kerr will be in those seats behind home plate with his notepads and his scouting charts and his scouting buddies for a lot more years.

"We kid around a lot, we share good times, we eat and talk and laugh together," he says. "One thing we never do is share information. The idea is to beat the other team."

He played the game that way half a century ago.

KEEPING THE GAME GOING

■■■ CONFETTI FLOATED DOWN FROM HIGH ATOP THE huge office buildings in Manhattan. Delirious members of the World Champion New York Mets smiled and waved and exchanged greetings with the huge crowd on that memorable October afternoon in 1969.

The Miracle Mets, under manager Gil Hodges, had just defeated the Baltimore Orioles and were now being lionized with this enormous outpouring of good will. All New York seemed anxious to share the excitement created by this talented group of young players.

In a Rockefeller Center office, as cars holding Tom Seaver and Art Shamsky and Jerry Koosman and Cleon Jones and Ed Charles and Hodges and his wife, Joan, rolled by, the secretaries at the Singer Sewing Machine Company headquarters opened their office windows.

"We had ticker tape confetti and old torn-up phone books. We began shredding all that paper and sailing it out of the windows to the cars below," remembers Phyllis Merhige.

She was a secretary then, a graduate of the famed Katharine Gibbs School, and now, twenty years later, she sits in her handsome Park Avenue office as the public relations director of the American League.

Baseball has a handful of female executives. There are a few female owners, including Marge Schott at Cincinnati and Jean Yawkey in Boston. Joan Payson owned those 1969 Mets. There are a small number of female sportswriters.

In this almost all-male world of baseball, Phyllis Merhige and Katy Feeney, the public relations director of the National League and daughter of Chub Feeney, a lifelong baseball executive, hold significant and distinct positions.

Much of the image of baseball as it is presented to the press and through them to the public comes from these women.

"Sometimes I sit here," Merhige says, "and I still can't believe I'm doing this."

If the designated hitter is the most significant rule change in baseball over the last two decades, the presence of women in baseball press boxes and the authority of women in the game may be the most significant off-field changes.

Merhige's path to this important baseball position took several twists and turns, all beginning with her interest in the game as a youngster growing up in the New York City borough of Queens.

"I was born in Brooklyn but we moved to Queens when I was very young," she says. "My father had always been a Dodger fan. The darkest day in our house was when the Dodgers moved west after the 1957 season. I was ten years old."

Phyllis's father, Mitchell, and her mother, Evelyn Aboumrad, were both born in New York but their parents had come from Lebanon.

"All four of my grandparents were born there and they all came to this country to find a better life. My father was in the carpet business. He just loved baseball and I remember him taking me as a small girl to Brooklyn games at Ebbets Field.

"I guess my first baseball memory was Johnny Podres beating the Yankees in the 1955 World Series for the first

Dodger Series win ever. Everybody in our house and around our neighborhood was excited at this great event," she says.

Two traumatic events had a strong bearing on Merhige's baseball identification. One was the premature death of her father in 1965 when Merhige was only seventeen years old and the other was the death of her young cousin Tina.

"I sort of lost interest in baseball when my father died," she says. "I spent a lot of time with my aunt Ginny after my father died because my mother worked. My aunt Ginny wasn't interested in baseball at all. Her daughter, Tina, who was about my age, was my best friend."

Shortly after her father died, her cousin Tina was killed in an automobile crash while on a vacation trip to Brazil.

"That was devastating to me," she says. "We were more like sisters than cousins. We looked alike, dressed alike, shared each other's clothes, spent a great deal of time together. Her death really left me feeling lonely."

Merhige soon graduated from William Cullen Bryant High School in Queens and entered Katharine Gibbs.

"I wasn't a great student in school so I wasn't interested in college. I thought I would learn secretarial skills and get a decent job. That was back in the early 1960s and there was not a great deal of business opportunity for women at that time," she says.

She graduated from Katharine Gibbs and soon had a fine position with Singer.

"I don't want to brag but I was a very good secretary. Katharine Gibbs was a wonderful training school for that. I graduated with all the necessary tools of typing and shorthand and stenography and the rest and I was certain I would get a good position," she says.

She was soon running the office of one of the Singer executives. It was a position that suited her well.

"I think the experience with Singer certainly helped me later on in baseball. One of the things I enjoyed most was the responsibility. I was sort of the power behind the throne in this office. That feeling of status and importance on the job was gratifying."

Merhige's skills were quickly noticed around the company. She was soon graduating from the routine chores of being a secretary to more responsible posts. She was soon moved up and named a dealer sales coordinator. She had authority over others for the first time.

"I probably never would have left Singer. I enjoyed the work, I enjoyed the people I worked with and I was making a decent salary," she says. "Then word came about the possible move."

Late in the 1960s, after about five years with the company, Merhige went to a Mets game at Shea Stadium at the urging of a friend. It was the first time she had been in the ball park and the first time she had indicated any interest in baseball since her father had died. After that event, there was simply no one to enjoy the game with.

"This friend kept suggesting we go to the game. She had followed the Mets from the beginning. I really wasn't interested. She simply kept working on me, suggesting it would give us another interest and also help me to forget the tragedy of the loss of my cousin. After the first time I went I realized one of the wonderful attractions of baseball. It is impossible to feel lonely at a ball park," she says.

The Mets won the title in 1973 in a furious finish in the Eastern Division. They went on to beat the Cincinnati Reds in one of the fiercest playoff battles for the division crown ever staged. That was the National League Championship Series made famous by a brawl between Pete Rose and Bud Harrelson. The chesty Cincinnati star had crashed into the Mets shortstop at second base. Peace could not be restored until several Mets stars, including Tom Seaver, Rusty Staub, Cleon Jones and Willie Mays, marched out to the left field stands to calm down marauding fans.

Merhige watched every game of the World Series on television and when it ended with a bitter Mets defeat in the seventh game at Oakland, she felt overwhelmed.

"I had really become a fanatic Mets fan by this time. I would go to quite a few games and always have a good time. I enjoyed kidding with the people around me and I enjoyed watching the game and looking at the grass and listening to the noise. I felt terribly depressed when the Mets lost that last game. I was very small when the Brooklyn Dodgers moved away. The Mets had clearly become my team," she says.

Merhige was twenty-six years old that summer and was becoming depressed.

"Singer was moving the headquarters to Elizabeth, New Jersey. I just didn't want to go. I wasn't about to give up my home and my friends and my community. I didn't like the idea of a big journey to New Jersey each morning. I had an important career decision to make," she says.

For several weeks, Merhige debated her choices. She considered staying on with Singer and making the New Jersey move. She knew her heart was not in that. She considered looking for a new corporate position in Manhattan. She was certain she could obtain a fine job with another large company after ten years with Singer. Then she thought about what she had come to enjoy the most.

"I realized that I was happiest when I was in the ball park. I enjoyed everything about the game. I knew that if I could somehow obtain a position in baseball that would be the ultimate for me. I decided to write the New York Mets and ask them for a secretarial job," she says.

Business manager Bill Murray received the letter, was impressed with Merhige's credentials and wrote her a pleasant note.

"He told me that there were no jobs in the New York Mets organization at that time. He said there might be something later on down the line. He said he would hold on to my resume and if anything came up in the future, he would get back to me. I didn't put much faith in that," she says.

Nearly six months went by. Singer set the date for their move. All employees had to make a decision within one month. The paperwork would soon begin. Merhige still had her life on hold. Then there was a move that would change her situation forever.

Early in January of 1973, the New York Yankees were sold to a Cleveland shipping industrialist by the name of George Steinbrenner. That would lead to several resignations at the end of the 1973 season, including manager Ralph Houk and New York Yankee publicity director Bob Fishel. The plot was beginning to come together.

"As I pondered my next move I got a call from Bill Murray," says Merhige. "He told me the situation had not changed with the Mets. He also said that baseball was making some changes in the commissioner's office and in the office of the American League. He asked if I would be willing to have my resume forwarded to the American League office."

Merhige agreed even though she actually had never been to a Yankee game. She was a Mets fan. Period. Her resume was forwarded to the American League office and she was interviewed by Henry Fitzgibbon, the league's director of personnel.

The American League office was changing with Lee MacPhail, former general manager of the Yankees and Baltimore Orioles and an assistant to the commissioner of baseball, taking over. His longtime friend, Fishel, would soon be moving in from the Yankees. Fishel's secretary would stay with the Yankees.

"The next thing that happened was a call from Don Marr. He was the business manager and he asked if I would come in for an interview," she says.

Looking neat and attractive as always, Merhige journeyed up to the offices of the American League. She was ushered into the office of Marr, a quiet, soft-spoken businessman.

"He was incredibly nervous. I could feel the sweat in his palms when we shook hands. I might have been the first person he ever interviewed for a job. He seemed much more uncomfortable in the interview than I did," she says.

Regardless of the circumstances, the interview went well. Merhige left the office with good vibes about the job. The next day she was called by Marr. He seemed in better control.

"We'd like to have you with us," he said.

"I'm thrilled to have the position," she said.

Phyllis Katherine Merhige of Brooklyn, New York, was in the baseball business. The Game.

She was hired as a secretary to MacPhail but when Fishel came into the office she quickly moved in as an assistant to the league's public relations director and assistant to the president.

"I was smart enough to attach myself to Bob," she says. "Almost everything I learned about working in baseball I learned from him. He was the smartest, kindest, most considerate man I ever knew."

Fishel, who died in 1988, was a legendary figure in the game. He was born and raised in Cleveland, entered the advertising business after military service in World War II, gained the account of the Cleveland Indians and was soon wooed and won by Cleveland owner Bill Veeck.

Veeck, the flamboyant operator of the Cleveland team, and Fishel, the low-key, conservative, dignified gentleman, made for an odd couple. Their styles were different but their closeness was unique.

Fishel was soon Veeck's public relations director in Cleveland. The Indians won the pennant in 1948 with Veeck's promotional genius—Veeck created the schemes and Fishel carried them out—getting as much attention as the team. Veeck had broken the American League color line a year earlier with the signing of Larry Doby, signed Negro League star Satchel Paige and built a team good enough to win the pennant in a playoff against the Boston Red Sox. His team went on to win the Series in six games against the Boston Braves.

Veeck later moved on to St. Louis with Fishel. The most notable accomplishment there was the presentation of Eddie Gaedel, the three-foot-seven-inch midget, who was inserted into a game as baseball's first, last and only midget player. Midgets were immediately banned by the league, causing the tongue-in-cheek Veeck, via Fishel, to issue a statement asking if Yankee shortstop Phil Rizzuto, who stood five-six in his stocking feet, was "a tall midget or a short man."

Veeck sold the team before it moved to Baltimore. Fishel would later emerge as the public relations director of the New York Yankees, a position he held for twenty illustrious years.

Few people were better liked or more highly regarded in baseball than Fishel. He was honest, hard-working, accurate, dedicated to the good of the game and dignified.

This was the mentor that Phyllis Merhige would have as she embarked on her baseball life. The success of Phyllis Merhige's career can certainly be credited to Fishel's willingness to work with this young woman, train her and deliver responsibilities to her. It is accurate to say Merhige might not have survived her first season under a different boss.

"I think Bob felt I could do the job," Merhige says. "One of the things I actually had in my favor, besides my skills, was a lack of aggressiveness. I did what I was told and I learned every day."

The jungle of baseball administration can be difficult and confusing. The hours can be brutally long with a full day in the office and a full night at the ball park. There are pressures in the league office from the individual clubs, from the fans, from the press, from the advertisers and from the executives. It is not a job for the weak.

Baseball, like all sports, has never really opened up its administration to a woman above the secretarial level. There were occasional advances but no one could consider it a career with attractive possibilities for women. The attitude seemed always to be to keep the women home or in the secretarial pool.

Fishel, a dapper, slight man with a 1920s haircut parted down the middle and an 1820s sense of chivalry, treated Merhige with the professionalism and respect with which he treated all others.

"He felt I could do the jobs assigned to me," she says. "If there was a chore to be done he let me do it. He never hovered over me. He respected my skills and he expected performance. If there was anything wrong he would simply explain that it could be done a better way. I was always learning, always growing in the job, always maturing. With each day I was gaining more confidence and assuming more responsibility."

Fishel had a master plan. He would keep it to himself. He would proceed as if it were a normal course of action.

"I knew that Phyllis could handle the job," he once said. "As Lee was using me more as his assistant I turned over more of the public relations responsibilities to Phyllis. She would simply become the PR director. The owners would look up and notice the job was filled by a woman. It wouldn't concern them because by then she had proven how capable she was."

By 1975, Merhige was assuming more of the chores of the job. One of the most important jobs was to handle the needs of the press in the American League Championship Series and in the World Series. She would make her national debut on television during the 1975 ALCS when she stood before a crowded room of reporters and before a national television audience asking questions of players posed by the press.

"I felt as if someone had just kicked me in the teeth," she says. "I was so nervous I couldn't breathe. I had been a secretary all my life and here I was standing in front of a microphone with all the baseball world paying attention to everything I said and did."

There were very few females around the World Series scene. Phyllis and Katy Feeney went almost everywhere together.

"I wasn't such an expert on the game that I could talk baseball with the guys. I knew the players. I knew the news information that we were releasing. I knew what I had to do. I didn't know how to make small talk with the newspapermen. I had been a Brooklyn Dodger fan as a kid. I had been a Mets fan later. Those were the only two teams I really knew anything about. To this day, I'm still short on baseball history. I have to get better on that. I want to be able to talk about a player today in relationship with the players of the past," she says.

Merhige did have one vital area of strength.

"Everywhere I went I carried Bob's aura with me. They knew I worked for him. He had so much credibility in the game, so much status that it was an enormous help. The attitude seemed to be if I was saying something it had been cleared with Bob. That way it had to be accurate and worth listening to," she says.

Merhige survived the playoffs and the World Series and was soon being accepted by the members of the press as a reliable spokesperson for the league. Many of the reporters began asking for Phyllis directly when calling into the American League office. If they wanted information on this year's players, if they wanted anything about current policy, Phyllis could do the job. If it was history they were after, they had to wait until Bob was off the phone.

"As the years went on I began developing closer relationships with the press and the players. I got to know people. It was easier to reach them. The players were all helpful and friendly and there never seemed to be a barrier. I don't know how much of that had to do with me working for Bob and how much had to do with my own relationship with the players. All I know is that there never seemed to be any friction," she says.

A good part of Merhige's success in the position can be accounted for by her skills. She is smart, articulate and helpful. Unlike many professional public relations people she does not see the press as an enemy.

"I understand we work for the clubs. I also appreciate how much help the media give to the game. I can't see making the job of the media any more difficult than it already is," she says.

By 1978 she had assumed most of the duties of public relations director. Fishel was involved in more significant league business. All this became official when she was named the assistant public relations director in 1979. She was now holding the title as well as the position.

"There were still some considerations I had to accept in the job. For example, I never entered a baseball clubhouse. I didn't do it then and I don't do it now. I know that would be embarrassing for the players. Whenever I have to talk to a player I can easily enough do it outside the clubhouse. If something is vital, we can always dispatch a young male assistant to the clubhouse," she says.

Through the years she has learned to appreciate the players and their incredible skills. She also has her favorites among the players, with Don Mattingly, Lance Parrish, Kirby Puckett, Dan Plesac, Frank Viola, Bruce Hurst and Tom Brunansky among them.

"I always get down to the field when a team comes to town and talk to the coaches, the trainers and the club public relations people. I feel it is part of my job to be seen and have them know me if there is anything I can help them with," she says.

As for baseball wives being concerned that the female public relations director of the league has so much opportunity to socialize with these players, Merhige laughs at the suggestion.

"That might have been a possibility when I took this job fifteen years ago. Now I'm too old for these kids," she says.

Her job calls for complete impartiality but Merhige admits once in a while she finds herself rooting for a favorite team.

"For some reason the 1987 Minnesota Twins became my favorite team. There were just so many wonderful guys on that club," she says.

Unlike many public relations people, Merhige does not force herself into the center of the action. There is a subtlety to the way she operates. She allows the club PR people to get the attention and keeps the league position far removed from the center of the action.

"Even when I go into the press box I never sit in the front row. Bob taught me that. I sit in the back where people can see me and say hello but where I am not being conspicuous about a league presence," she says.

Merhige admits that she has patterned much of her professional life after Fishel's. She often sees a problem, thinks about it and then asks herself, even now, "What would Bob do?"

Though Merhige loved Fishel as a friend, as most baseball people did, there could be no romance. Fishel once said he had a love affair while in the Army during World War II in Mississippi, saw it disintegrate for a variety of reasons and never became emotionally attached to anyone again.

"Toward the end of his life he seemed to get a little more nostalgic," says Merhige. "He had been ill for a long while and maybe he knew that he wouldn't be around much longer. He talked of the past a lot, about his old friends, about how much he missed Bill Veeck, of theater and music he had enjoyed. One day he just blurted out that he had only two regrets in his life. The first one was that he never married and had a family. He would have made such a wonderful father. He was so incredibly kind. The second regret had to do with work. He said he regretted so much that he had never learned to touch type."

Like Fishel, Merhige is taking advantage of her position. She can go to as many baseball games as she likes and is a frequent visitor to the press boxes in stadiums around the league. She enjoys a good restaurant, attends the theater regularly (Fishel was one of the city's most devoted theater-goers), attends New York Knicks basketball games in winter, visits zoos and loves art exhibits. She also has one hobby.

"If you won't laugh," she says, "I'll tell you."

Promised no laughter she announces, "I take tap dancing lessons at the West Side YMCA."

Smiles didn't count.

"I still keep an apartment in Queens and ride the subway to work," she says. "I know I should get an apartment in the city but I enjoy being in my old neighborhood and being near my family."

On January 1, 1984, Merhige was named the public relations director of the American League. This caused no waves.

"They named Bob the executive vice-president of the league at the same time. I got lost in the shuffle just the way I liked it," she says. "People seemed happy for me. The league PR directors were very supportive and many of the newspapermen called to congratulate me. One said I was now the yardstick by which the press would measure the league. That embarrassed me a bit."

In some strange way her most difficult chore was also her most splendid. When Fishel collapsed and died on a Manhattan street after returning from the American League office one summer afternoon, Merhige arranged for a eulogy in Yankee Stadium.

Speaker after speaker extolled the career and personality of Robert O. Fishel. League President Bobby Brown, the former Yankee third baseman, handled the introductions. There were a dozen male speakers.

"I never considered speaking," Merhige says. "I'm not that outgoing."

Like Fishel before her, Merhige almost always defers to others. She sees a public relations position as secondary to the people she serves. That's about the way Fishel created the position.

Her office walls are filled with baseball photographs, including a memorable All-Star home run by Kent Hrbek, a tobacco-chewing session by Don Zimmer, shots of Fred Lynn making a brilliant catch and Dave Stieb firing a fastball, a negotiation truce picture of Lee MacPhail and Don Fehr of the Players Association. There is a desk plaque reading, "A cluttered desk is a sign of a genius."

Merhige hardly claims to be that. Besides, her desk is not cluttered. What she does do is handle the public relations of the American League with poise, professionalism, dignity and class. She dresses smartly and appears properly coiffed and cool on the hottest summer days. If Fishel was recognized for his knowledge and style, he was also singled out for wearing suits and ties on blistering summer afternoons. The American League will never have to worry that Phyllis Merhige will show up in shorts and put her feet up on the seat in front of her. Not that her legs are all that bad.

Merhige says that the public relations job may not have the excitement a few years from now that it does at this time. She may move on to something else. If she does, she is hopeful it will be in the game.

"If nothing else I think I have proven that a woman can do this job. I hope I have opened up opportunities for women in baseball. We may not be able to hit and throw but there's no reason we can't do the administrative work. I don't think it is too farfetched to see a woman in baseball's future as an important executive. I would think women could be general managers of teams. I could see myself doing that in future years," she says.

For now, she is happily contributing to the game, handling the needs of the press in playoff and Series events, overseeing the logistics of the All-Star game, serving the clubs in the finest administrative way possible.

"I'm so fortunate to be part of it. I love baseball so much. I want to do what I can to help. Sometimes I think the game doesn't get the appreciation from the public it deserves as part of the American scene," she says.

There would be a game soon and Merhige would be at Yankee Stadium. She would sit unobtrusively in her back-row seat, lean forward to listen to the crack of the bat, study the richness of the grass and grow joyful at the noisy excitement of the fans.

Bob Fishel would have been very proud.

ALL IN THE FAMILY

███ WHEN ELEVEN-YEAR-OLD BOB QUINN PILED INTO HIS father's white Chrysler on the morning of October 6, 1948, he was almost breathless with anticipation.

He squeezed into the back seat next to his brother Jack while his three sisters, Joan, Margo and Susan, pushed together on the other side. His father, John Quinn, general manager of the Boston Braves, and his mother, Miriam, huddled together in the front seat as the car stopped in front of a Boston apartment.

John Mullen, farm director of the Braves, moved into the empty seat.

When young Quinn blurted out a few childish things, Miriam Quinn turned around slightly and warned the children to ride silently the rest of the way to Braves Field.

"Your father and Mr. Mullen are talking baseball," she sternly announced.

"No conversation could be more sacred," says Quinn, now the general manager of the Cincinnati Reds after a lifetime of baseball jobs as the third generation in his family to work in the front offices of the game.

The elder Quinn and Mullen, now the vice-president of the Atlanta Braves, talked about the upcoming game as they rode on to the ball park. There could hardly have been a more excited group of people in Boston that day of huge promise.

After all, the Boston Braves, under manager Billy Southworth, had won their first pennant in thirty-four years and only their second in the twentieth century. The other Boston winner was the famed 1914 Braves, a team that was in last place on July Fourth and won the pennant.

"That 1948 club had to be my father's favorite team. It had been such a long struggle to get there. That was the team of 'Spahn and Sain and Pray for Rain' and so many other fine players. We were very close to all of them, Tommy Holmes, Bob Elliott, Phil Masi, Vern Bickford, the entire team. My father was espècially close to Southworth. Billy liked to drink and sometimes he was unreliable. I think that entire summer he just about spent in our house. My father would bring him home after every game to watch over him. He was under house arrest," says Quinn.

The general manager drove on to Braves Field where a huge press party was being held before the first game of the 1948 World Series between the Braves and the Cleveland Indians. The Indians, under young manager Lou Boudreau, had won the pennant in a one-game playoff against the crosstown rival Boston Red Sox.

"The party was being held in an armory right across the street from Braves Field," remembers Quinn. "There were tanks and guns piled up outside the building. All of the Army equipment had to be emptied out of the armory to make room for the baseball people. It was thrilling to be involved in this event and see so many of these people close up I had only read about."

One of the people young Quinn was most interested in meeting was Bill Veeck, the flamboyant owner of the Indians. Veeck had led his team to the first Cleveland pennant in twenty-eight years. Excitement was as high in Cleveland as it was in Boston.

"Veeck had been a very colorful figure and was in the newspapers every day," says Quinn. "Even though I was more involved in my father's team, of course, I was still a baseball fan. I knew what the Indians had done and I was very anxious to meet this fabulous character."

From the opposite end of the armory, young Quinn could see Veeck across the floor. He asked his father if he could tag along as the two leading executives of this Series met.

"Come along, son," said John Quinn. "I'll introduce you to Mr. Veeck."

John and Bob Quinn strolled across the floor to where Veeck was holding court before a cluster of sportswriters. He loved the excitement and the attention of the Series but he immediately stopped what he was saying to turn his attention to his opposite number.

"He had a cigarette in his hand as we approached," Quinn recalls. "As we approached he shifted the cigarette from his right hand to his left hand. He shook my father's hand and then he turned his attention to me. As he did I could see him putting the cigarette out in his leg. I thought I would pass out."

What young Quinn did not know was that Veeck had lost a leg at Bougainville in the South Pacific during his service with the Marines in World War II when he was struck by the recoil of an artillery piece. He wore a wooden leg and near the bottom of the leg, he had inserted a metal ashtray.

"I think he did that as much for a conversation piece as anything else. All I know is that I never forgot that experience. I saw him do it many times when I got to know him as an adult but you can imagine what an impact that had on an eleven-year-old kid. Here it is more than forty years later and I'm still talking about it," Quinn says.

After the press party, the Quinn family moved across the street for the game. It was a thriller. The Braves won the opener 1–0 when Johnny Sain outpitched Bob Feller. The key play of the game came in the eighth inning. Phil Masi, a catcher with good speed, was a pinch runner for Boston catcher Bill Salkeld, who had walked and been sacrificed to second. Feller and Boudreau tried a pickoff at second base. The diving Masi was called safe by umpire Bill Stewart as Boudreau, the manager and shortstop, hotly disputed the call. Films in those days were primitive at best and inconclusive photographs only heated the argument.

"No question about it," says Quinn, as he sits now in his handsome Yankee Stadium office with the hindsight of forty-one years, "Masi was safe."

The Braves did win that game but they would capture only one more in the Series as the Indians went on to victory. It was still a momentous year for the Boston Braves and the Quinn family. They had taken a lot of heat from the press for many lackluster finishes in Boston. Now they finally had a pennant to gloat over.

"Winning a pennant is as elusive as catching a butterfly," says Quinn. "I have always told baseball people to enjoy it while they can."

When the Braves moved on to Milwaukee for the 1953 season, the team would become a serious contender most of that decade, with pennants in 1957 and 1958. It was never the same in Boston.

"In our home in the Boston area at 808 Commonwealth Avenue in Newton," says Quinn, "we still have the Braves field logo built into our basement floor. It's probably the last remembrance of the Boston Braves still in the Boston area. It is still a wonderful conversation piece."

Robert Edward Quinn was born February 1, 1937. His earliest memories are of baseball games and baseball players. His father's father, James Aloysius Quinn, called Bob or J.A., was the general manager of the Braves, St. Louis Browns, Boston Red Sox and even Brooklyn Dodgers for a short while. He died in 1953. His father, John, joined the Red Sox out of Boston College in 1929. He later became general manager of the Braves for twenty-three years and the Philadelphia Phillies for thirteen seasons.

"When I was small I remember him conducting business of the ball club on the kitchen telephone. My brother Jack [now the president of the St. Louis Blues of the National Hockey League] and I had our bedroom just above the kitchen. We would get down on the floor and listen to him make deals. I vividly remember him making the deal with the New York Giants for Sid Gordon and Willard Marshall in exchange for Alvin Dark and Eddie Stanky. He was burned over that one when they went on to help the Giants win the pennant in 1951. That's what a general manager's lot is like. Some deals work out, some don't. You have to be able to roll the dice. God hates a coward. If you think a deal will help your team you have to go after it full speed ahead."

Quinn has seen enough deals to know that the law of averages is probably fifty-fifty on any trade you make. It was that way with his grandfather, it was that way with his father and it probably was that way with him as he attempted to restore George Steinbrenner's Yankees to the top of the American League.

Regardless of how the Yankees do, Quinn has already made some sort of baseball history by taking over the general manager's chair. Only the MacPhails—Larry MacPhail, Lee MacPhail and Andy MacPhail—can rival the Quinns as third-generation baseball executives.

"I have children older than the MacPhails. If one of my boys, Michael or Bob, gets into baseball and becomes a general manager that will be quite a family record," he says.

Quinn often thinks back to the way his grandfather and his father did things in their days.

"I guess the biggest change is the relationship with the players. You don't have that family closeness my grandfather and father had with the players. The agents won't allow that. Now we negotiate contracts for millions of dollars; they did it for thousands. There also seemed to be more trust," he says.

Quinn is fond of telling a story about his father negotiating one year with Johnny Logan, the feisty shortstop of the Braves:

"My dad was at home in Boston just before spring training. Logan was at his home in upstate New York in a town called Endicott. This was late in February and there must have been a lot of snow on the ground. Logan wanted twelve thousand dollars and my father was offering ten thousand. Neither one would budge. Finally my father said he would toss Logan for the difference. He said if the coin came up heads he would give Logan his twelve thousand. If it came up tails he would cut it down the middle and give him eleven thousand. Logan agreed. This was over the phone, mind you. My father told him he was tossing the coin. I was sitting right there in the kitchen as he talked on the phone. He never tossed any coin. He just waited a few seconds and announced, 'John, it came up tails. You lose. You'll have to accept the eleven thousand.' Logan agreed meekly. My father hung up the phone and just started laughing. Then he said, 'He knows we'll give him the twelve thousand anyway.' That's the way things were done in those days."

Quinn was privy to many thrilling baseball moments in his own living room. Warren Spahn, Johnny Sain, Tommy Holmes, Bob Elliott were frequent visitors in his home. The baseball talk was constant and exciting.

"I remember once my father was discussing pitching with Sain. He had that great curveball. He said that he thought that was the best pitch in baseball. My father looked at him and said, 'Every club should have a spitballer.' I don't know if Sain took his advice later in his career," Quinn says.

"I was about sixteen or seventeen when the Braves signed Johnny Antonelli in my father's living room. Antonelli had been one of the most highly touted young pitchers of his time. All the clubs were after him. My father got his signature and the signature of his father on a contract because the pitcher was underage. Then he broke open the champagne and we all had a sip to celebrate," he remembers.

The Braves fell on bad times again after the 1948 victory. They finished fourth three times in a row and slipped to seventh in 1952. Fans became disenchanted. The Red Sox were more and more Boston's favorite with exciting teams led by Ted Williams. When Boston owner Lou Perini got an offer he couldn't refuse, the Braves moved to Milwaukee.

"That was quite a shock for the family to pick up and move from the Boston area to Milwaukee after all those years. It was the first franchise shift in modern baseball history and it caused quite a stir. The people in Milwaukee were just overwhelmed with the excitement of big league baseball," Quinn says.

Milwaukee citizens welcomed the Braves organization and the players with open arms. Many of those Boston-to-Milwaukee veterans tell some wondrous stories about the kindness of the local gentry.

"My wife used to go shopping in this local store," remembers Warren Spahn, "and she would come out of there with bags and bags of groceries. There would never be a bill. They just wouldn't let us pay because they were now Braves fans and they said we were helping make Milwaukee famous."

Quinn entered Marquette University in Milwaukee, ran on the track team and played a little baseball as a catcher.

"The desire was always there but never the talent," he says. "I did start to think about entering baseball as a profession around that time."

The elder Quinn put young Bob to work for the ball club during his school vacations, running errands, typing letters, working in the ticket office and learning the business from the bottom up.

"In 1958 I turned twenty-one and graduated from college. My father decided it was time I went out on my own. If I really wanted to work for a big league club I would have to learn the business in the minor leagues. He helped arrange for me to get a job as the business manager with the Braves' farm club in the Northern League at Eau Claire, Wisconsin. I really had a chance to do a lot of things there I never would have been able to do then on the big league level. I knew after one season there that baseball administration was what I wanted to do," he says.

The Braves had built a fine farm system by then. Two youngsters on that team would later move up to the Braves with a significant difference in results. One was Tommie Aaron, the husky brother of Hank Aaron, already making his mark in the National League as a future Hall of Famer.

"He was a decent player who might have made more of his career if he wasn't Henry's brother. That was a pretty heavy burden for a youngster to carry. No matter what he did people were always comparing him to Henry. Few players could ever be compared to Henry Aaron," Quinn says.

The other youngster, even younger than the twenty-one-year-old business manager, was also a brother of a Milwaukee player. This one was to outshine his older brother and become one of the National League's finest receivers. His name was Joe Torre, then a chubby, slugging younger brother of Milwaukee Braves first baseman Frank Torre. Joe had few burdens to carry as the younger brother. He was clearly the better ball player of the Torre brothers and his rise to the Braves was rapid.

"Besides those two the manager was also a recognized baseball name. This was Travis Jackson, the old New York Giants shortstop, who later went on to the Hall of Fame. I worked closely with him because in the minors any job not designated to someone else usually is passed on to the manager. He passed a lot of those chores on to me and I did them all willingly," he says.

Quinn spent the 1959 and 1960 seasons as the business manager of the Eau Claire club. As always in the minors, money became a problem for Quinn and his new bride, Kathryn Paulus of Milwaukee. He left the baseball business and went to work for the Northern States Power Company as their manager for advertising.

"It was a real good job and I enjoyed it very much. I also began to realize after a year or two how much I missed baseball. I wanted to get back into the game but I wasn't quite sure of exactly what I wanted to do," he says.

In 1965 he left the advertising job to take a business position with Fleer's Chewing Gum Company.

"I was involved in their baseball card division. I traveled around to all the camps and met with all the players. It got me back in the game and I began thinking more seriously of a full-time baseball job," he says.

He ran the idea by Kathryn and she said she would go along with any decision he made. If he thought he would be happier in a lower-paying job in baseball, she would cut corners and the family would get by somehow. Most baseball people, once the bug strikes, can get away for a while but they always seem to follow their hearts and get back into the game.

"I never would have left baseball if it wasn't for the money," he says. "I had a wife and two sons by now and I felt I could not afford to be in baseball. After I realized how much I missed it, I looked for a job in the game. Somehow I knew we would make it financially."

Quinn became the general manager of the Philadelphia Phillies farm club in Reading, Pennsylvania. His father was now general manger of the Phillies.

"I was so happy I could cry," he says. "I was back in baseball where I knew I wanted to be. When I was out I missed everything about it, the games, the fans, the noise, the excitement. I also knew that if I worked hard and did a good job I would be promoted to the big league club. Conditions would be better, the money would be better and I could plan more carefully for the future."

Quinn was so successful in Reading that he was hired away by the independent Omaha club to run that team in

1969 and 1970. His manager was Jack McKeon, now the manager of the San Diego Padres.

"We had a real good ball club and Jack was a terrific fellow to work with. I know that there were hard years in the minor leagues and we had to sacrifice some things but I loved every minute of it. I also made a lot of baseball contacts and I know that those things pay off years later. I can pick up the phone and make a deal with Jack or any other person in baseball I have met along the trail. That's a big part of my job."

Quinn remembers Gabe Paul's old definition of a great general manager. "A great GM," the veteran baseball executive used to say, "is a guy who can call up another GM at three in the morning, wake him up and have the guy say, 'Do you need a shortstop? I have one who can help you.'"

After two more successful seasons in Omaha, Quinn was ready for his big league opportunity. It came calling in the person of Frank Lane, the flamboyant general manager of the Braves. Lane was one of the most colorful characters the game has ever seen. He loved to talk baseball in hotel lobbies for hours on end with anybody around, he loved to trade players just to get the sportswriters excited and he loved to enjoy himself with good meals and fine wine.

"With all the show business noise he made," says Quinn, "Frank Lane was a very capable baseball executive. He knew everybody in the game, he was fearless and he could make some quick decisions. They may not have always been the right ones, but he could make them."

Lane helped Quinn learn a lot about the baseball business. It may well have been from Lane that Quinn learned to deal courageously. The New York Yankees of 1989 were a far different team in personality and performance from the 1988 team largely because of Quinn's moves. He traded away such Yankee stalwarts as Jack Clark and Rick Rhoden, allowed Willie Randolph to become a free agent and move to the Dodgers, pushed for the signing of Steve Sax, allowed Claudell

Washington to move away and brought in some untried pitchers.

Quinn saw Lane take a lot of heat for some of the deals he made. He knows it goes with the territory.

"God hates a coward," says Quinn. "It is my responsibility to do what in my best judgment will help the ball club. Any criticisms leveled if the deals don't work out, I'll accept."

Frank Lane could not have said it any better.

In 1973 Quinn moved to Cleveland under general manager Phil Seghi, who took over from Gabe Paul. Paul had moved on to New York with a Cleveland shipping industrialist named George Steinbrenner. Quinn and Steinbrenner would cross paths again with the Yankees.

"When you work for George you know you will be fired. That doesn't bother me. I've been fired before. I might be fired again. In the meantime I will do what I think is right and work as hard as I can improving the ball club," Quinn says.

Quinn had a pleasant, quiet time in Cleveland under Seghi. The Indians didn't win anything but Seghi was a low-key, soft-spoken, pipe-smoking baseball gentleman. The gentlemanly Quinn got along famously with his Cleveland boss.

"Phil was one of those fellows who just believed that if you had a job you were supposed to do it. He didn't interfere in your work. His idea was to get the best people he could get and give them authority over their departments. I had a good time in Cleveland and I really enjoyed working with him," he says.

The Indians last won a pennant in 1954. The Cleveland fans were probably the most understanding in the game because they continued to come out to Municipal Stadium despite the ineptness of the Tribe. Every so often the Indians would come up with a promising player or two. It never was enough for a real run. Quinn handled the farm department, developed some young talent but lost out when free agency changed the balance of power in baseball.

"We never had the kind of money to compete with the Yankees or the Angels or the Rangers in the spending department," he says. "We knew that we would have to develop our own stars to be competitive. We did the best we could under the circumstances."

In 1985 the Indians were sold again. Peter Bavasi, son of former Dodger, San Diego and California general manager Buzzie Bavasi, became the new operating head. Bavasi fired Quinn.

"I remember the date. It was February 17, 1985, right before spring training. He decided he wanted to rebuild the organization with his own people. I understood that. I was terribly disappointed but there wasn't much I could do. If you love baseball as much as I do, you have to take some of the blows and hang in there. I figured something else would come up. I had been around the game a long time by then. People knew where to find me," Quinn says.

Baseball people did know where to find Quinn. They just didn't bother looking. After taking a couple of months off without any job leads, Quinn made another career move.

"All I really knew was baseball but nothing seemed available. I had to do something. I got into real estate and sold shopping centers in the Westlake area of Cleveland. It wasn't much fun. Nothing is as much fun as baseball. I had to support my family so sometimes you make compromises and do what you have to do," he says.

As a third-generation baseball executive, Quinn remained close to the game. He watched on television, he visited the ball park once in a while to renew old acquaintances, he talked on the phone with friends.

"I knew real estate was only a temporary situation. I was a baseball man. That was where I wanted to be. I just sat back and waited for something to develop. That's all you can do in baseball when you are out of work," he says.

What developed was a phone call from Woody Woodward, the general manager of the Yankees. Steinbrenner had run through managers and general managers. His 1985 cast included Woodward as the general manager and Yogi Berra as manager. Berra was fired less than a month into the season and Billy Martin came back for his fourth tour of duty. One of the other people in the Yankee administration and a man with Steinbrenner's ear was Clyde King. Quinn had known King as far back as the former pitcher's days with the old Brooklyn Dodgers.

"One day I got this call from Woody Woodward. He told me that the Yankees were looking for somebody to do some work for them in the area of scouting and player development. He said they didn't have a definite position but he thought they could use my services on some special projects. I told them I would be happy to discuss the situation with them. Woody called back to make an appointment," Quinn says.

Woodward, now the Seattle general manager, and King, still one of Steinbrenner's most trusted aides, came to Quinn's Westlake home for a meeting.

"It was the Fourth of July in 1986. I think I fed them hamburgers and hot dogs and we talked about the Yankees," he says. "I agreed to look into a few things for them."

Putting his real estate work on hold, Quinn plunged into baseball scouting. He not only looked at every team, he looked at every park in the league. Steinbrenner was interested in learning what other teams did in certain areas of the baseball business. He wanted to learn how to sell more hot dogs in the park, how to make the rest rooms more accessible, how to move the fans into and out of the ball park in a more comfortable manner.

"I typed up these reports a short time after I finished scouting the players and the parks. George must have been impressed. A few weeks later I got a call from Woody asking me to come to New York. He said the Yankees might have a position for me. I was thrilled. I jumped on the next plane, met with Woody, Clyde and George and was offered the position of vice-president of baseball administration. I was incredibly happy to be back in baseball," he says.

Lou Piniella became the Yankee manager and would be named general manager of the club after the 1987 season. Billy Martin was back for his fifth tour of duty. Martin would last into June this time, Piniella would go back onto the field in 1988 and Quinn would assume the duties of general manager of the New York Yankees on June 23, 1988.

"My grandfather had been the GM of the Brooklyn Dodgers and my father had worked for George Weiss when he ran the Yankees. I did have that New York connection. I also knew that this was the most prestigious executive position in sports. It was terribly exciting just to sit in this office, look out the window at that Stadium field and appreciate all that Yankee history," he says.

No Steinbrenner employee can ever truly enjoy the fruits of his labor. There is an axe constantly hanging over his head. Only the brave can survive even for a little while. Quinn was remarkably moving into his fourth Yankee season in 1989, an example of exceptional longevity around the Yankees of George Steinbrenner. He will enjoy it while it lasts. Each day that he survives in that Yankee GM's chair he considers a victory.

As he sat in his office chair one afternoon, the phone rang constantly. Agents were calling asking for more money for their players. Players were calling asking for more money for themselves. Club executives were calling about deals. George was calling about everything.

"Sure, things are different now than they were with my father and grandfather but it is still a wonderful way to make a living. George is tough but he is fair. He asks that you work hard but he works hard. He wants everybody to pull together for the common good of the team. All he wants is a complete victory. You can't criticize the man for that," Quinn says.

As he talked it was clear Quinn enjoyed what he did, was

emotional about the game but still had a part of him in the past.

"Maybe there was more camaraderie then between the players and the club officials. I remember days sitting around the piano in our home with three or four of the players, with my mom and dad and sister, with the friends coming to the house and all of us joining in to sing, 'Who Threw the Overalls in Mrs. Murphy's Chowder?' I guess I couldn't imagine anything like that today," he says.

He suddenly began talking of those wonderful days in Boston more than forty years ago when his father and his players were truly one big happy family.

"My bedroom was a good listening post and even when Billy Southworth and my father sat together and talked baseball, I could listen in. My brother and I were learning how to deal with managers. I always thought we were sort of a secret service picking up that wonderful inside baseball information," Quinn says.

Quinn was asked if he would ever consider any other career now that he can look back from a significant baseball position.

"Never," he says. "This is exactly where I want to be. Maybe if the Boston Braves were still out there I would think about that. Who knows? To be the general manager of the New York Yankees is more than I could ever have expected."

Quinn is hopeful his Yankee team is on its way to another title. The Yankees have not won anything since 1981 and have not won a World Series since 1978. The natives are getting restless.

"We feel we have improved the club. We are certain the team will be different and we think we are good enough to win. That's our goal. Winning pennants is a difficult chore. Still it is just thrilling and satisfying to be in this position and have the opportunity," he says.

It was time for Quinn to get back to his trades and his salaries and his agents. He remembered one last moment from his Boston past.

"There was this lady in Braves Field, an elderly lady by the name of Lolly Hopkins. She sat behind the Boston dugout in every game. She was a marvelous fan, always pulling for the Braves and cheering them on as loudly as she could. She would come to the ball park with a bagful of small Tootsie Rolls. Every time a Braves player did something good, made a great catch, got a big hit, struck out a key batter, she would stand up from her seat and heave a few Tootsie Rolls into the Boston dugout. The players would scramble after the candy," he says. "Maybe we can get our own Lolly Hopkins in New York."

Yankee fans are enthusiastic but not that forgiving. Players are concerned more dangerous things will wind up in the dugout if they don't start winning soon.

"The real fun in baseball," says Quinn, "is winning."

Index